American Catholic Lay Groups

and Transatlantic Social Reform

in the Progressive Era

American Catholic Lay Groups
and Transatlantic Social Reform
in the Progressive Era

• • • • •

Deirdre M. Moloney

THE UNIVERSITY OF NORTH CAROLINA PRESS

CHAPEL HILL & LONDON

© 2002

The University of North Carolina Press

All rights reserved

Designed by Eric M. Brooks

Set in Bodoni by Keystone Typesetting, Inc.

Manufactured in the United States of America

The paper in this book meets the guidelines
for permanence and durability of the Committee
on Production Guidelines for Book Longevity
of the Council on Library Resources.

Library of Congress Cataloging-in-Publication Data

Moloney, Deirdre M.

American Catholic lay groups and transatlantic social

·reform in the progressive era / Deirdre M. Moloney.

p. cm.   Includes bibliographical references and index.

ISBN 0-8078-2660-x (alk. paper)

ISBN 0-8078-4986-3 (pbk.: alk. paper)

1. Catholics—United States—History—19th century.

2. Catholics—United States—History—20th century.

3. Laity—Catholic Church—History—19th century.

4. Laity—Catholic Church—History—20th century.

5. United States—Social conditions—1865–1918.

6. Sociology, Christian (Catholic)—United States—History

of doctrines—19th century. 7. Sociology, Christian

(Catholic)—United States—History of doctrines—20th

century. 8. Progressivism (United States politics) I. Title.

E184.C3 M65   2002   305.6'2073—dc21

2001049161

Cloth   06 05 04 03 02   5 4 3 2 1
Paper   06 05 04 03 02   5 4 3 2 1

TO MY MOTHER

Marion Shea Moloney

Contents

Illustrations

Acknowledgments

I have been extremely fortunate to have had the abiding support of my professors, colleagues, friends, and family while researching and writing this book. At the University of Wisconsin–Madison, Diane Lindstrom, Stanley Schultz, and David Zonderman provided invaluable advice and suggestions from the early stages of designing this project to the process of revising it for publication. They helped me to make the transition from graduate student to historian. James Donnelly and R. Booth Fowler also asked helpful questions about my research that shaped my thinking on this topic. I owe a significant debt to Thomas Archdeacon, my graduate advisor, who has instilled in me an even greater appreciation for the history of immigration and ethnicity as well as of American Catholicism. He carefully reviewed countless drafts, provided excellent advice at several crucial points, and challenged me to clarify my arguments. I also thank the University of Wisconsin History Department for awarding me travel grants to enable me to visit archives vital to my research. Christopher Kauffman's evaluation of the manuscript led to significant improvements, and I greatly appreciate his continued interest in my work. A second, anonymous, reader for the University of North Carolina Press also proved quite helpful. As I presented my research at conferences and in article form, I received particularly helpful comments and encouragement from Ronald Bayor; Corrie van Eijl; Grace Donovan, S.U.S.C.; and Dolores Liptak, R.S.M.; as well as from audience members and anonymous reviewers. Philip Gleason graciously agreed to read an early draft of the manuscript, and his suggestions helped me to refine aspects of my approach.

Thanks to many friends from graduate school, whose support continues to be vital: Maureen Conklin, Regan Rhea, and Landon Storrs, whom I met soon after arriving in Madison, as well as Andrea Bailey, Sue Giaimo, and Tim Longman. Fellow history graduate students, many from my dissertation group, provided research advice as well as perceptive comments on my work. They include Maureen Fitzgerald, Jennifer Frost, Lian Partlow, Beth Rose, Ayesha Shariff, Nancy Taylor, and Susan Traverso. At Saint Francis University, several colleagues and friends offered encouragement as well as advice on writing and publishing. Sara King, Rebecca Kingston, the late Gorjana Litvinovic, Joseph Melusky, and Timothy Whisler were particularly helpful in that regard. I also thank Snezana Litvinovic and Kata Lukic for their support.

This project was helped immeasurably by several archivists and librarians who gave generously of their time and expertise. My home base was at the library of the State Historical Society of Wisconsin, and I benefited from its wonderful collection and expert staff. Thanks to Michael Edwards, Ellen Burke, and the many other people there who made the library such a rewarding environment for undertaking research. At Saint Francis University, the library staff, especially Peg Hanlon, worked hard to fulfill my steady stream of interlibrary loan requests and provided me with access to other research materials.

Robert Johnson-Lally, his predecessor, Ron Patkus, and the entire staff of the Archives of the Archdiocese of Boston went far beyond the call of duty, and my many trips there were always pleasant as well as productive. Kevin Cawley and others at the University of Notre Dame Archives helped make my extended trip there very rewarding and graciously handled my many follow-up requests. Reverend John H. Miller, archivist at the Central Bureau, Catholic Central Union of America, where the Central Verein Archives are housed, made my research trip to St. Louis a great success. I further appreciate the assistance of William Fowler and Virginia Smith at the Massachusetts Historical Society, Nancy Sandleback at the Archdiocese of Chicago Archives, Phil Runkel of the Marquette University Archives, Steven Granger of the Archives of the Archdiocese of St. Paul and Minneapolis, and Valerie Miller at the Print Department of The Library Company of Philadelphia. I also thank Reverend George Lane for permission to use photographs originally appearing in books published by Loyola University Press in Chicago. Heather Bird and Michael Martin of Cobh, and Gráinne MacLochlainn of the National Photographic Archive in Dublin, also helped me to locate appropriate photographs.

At the University of North Carolina Press, my editor, Elaine Maisner, took an interest in my manuscript and brought it through the editorial process with incredible skill and sensitivity. She, Pamela Upton, Mary Reid, and others at the Press have been everything an author could hope for.

My family, living across three continents and constituting an excellent case study of an ongoing transatlantic migration, provided a great deal of encouragement as well as hospitality throughout this project. My brother, David, generously accommodated me during my frequent Boston stays. Both the Moloney and Shea families have consistently demonstrated their enthusiasm for this project. The entire Kinnaman family has also been an important source of support. Jackie Kinnaman and her husband, Henry Bayer, hosted me while in Chicago, and Ken and Kelly Kinnaman welcomed me to St. Louis. My husband, Ted Kinnaman, has known me for almost as long as I've been involved in this project. He has helped me to complete this book in a myriad of ways, both tangible and intangible, from keeping my spirits high and serving as a sounding board on our walks to proofreading and providing sustenance. I can't thank him enough for his love and support. My father, David, encouraged so many of my interests, and I regret that he did not live to see me write this book. My mother, Marion, to whom this book is dedicated, has nurtured my academic goals, provided me with encouragement at every stage, and offered me a strong model of achievement.

Abbreviations

APA
American Protective Association

CCB
Catholic Charitable Bureau

CIS
Charitable Irish Society

COS
Charity Organization Society

CTAU
Catholic Total Abstinence Union

CWU
Catholic Women's Union of the Central Verein

ICCA
Irish Catholic Colonization Association

KDF
Katholischer deutscher Frauenbund

LCW
League of Catholic Women

NCCC
National Council of Catholic Charities

NCCW
National Council of Catholic Women

NCWC
National Catholic Welfare Council

PTAL
Priests' Total Abstinence League

WCTU
Woman's Christian Temperance Union

YMCA
Young Men's Christian Association

YWCA
Young Women's Christian Association

American Catholic Lay Groups

and Transatlantic Social Reform

in the Progressive Era

Introduction

This study examines the social reform activities of Catholic lay groups in the United States from 1880 to 1925. The emergence in the late nineteenth century of a significant Catholic urban middle class led to tensions over the goals of Catholic reform. The growth of the Catholic middle class helped Catholics to gain greater respectability in the eyes of the Protestant majority. But for many in the church, that growth also signaled a shift away from traditional ethnic identities, a muting of the distinctiveness of Catholic institutions and goals, and an embrace of modern values, particularly those related to gender roles. As middle- and upper-class laywomen carved out greater roles for themselves in Catholic social reform, their actions precipitated fierce debates over women's roles and responsibilities in the home and in public, especially among those in the church hierarchy. Social reform efforts in this era illustrate how Catholics struggled to reconcile the advantages that upward mobility brought for their minority position in American society with a desire to preserve their distinctive ethnic and religious traditions. The dual focus of Catholic efforts distinguished them from Protestant ones, even when their activities shared common characteristics.

The international scope of the Catholic Church provided its American members with preexisting models for social reform. Those models were often, although not exclusively, appropriated from the reformers' own countries of origin. Contemporary political events and social reform initiatives in Europe influenced American Catholic efforts, even among those whose families had immigrated from Europe one or two generations before. Irish American reformers, for example, drew extensively from Father Theobold Mathew's mid-nineteenth-century Irish temperance campaign in forming an American Catholic movement, while women's groups affiliated with the German-based Catholic Women's Union based their efforts on those launched by middle-class Catholic women in Germany, and the Society of St. Vincent de Paul was a direct import from France.

Ethnic nationalism was another crucial aspect of the international influence on American Catholic lay reform. Irish nationalism, particularly the brand associated with the Land League of the early 1880s, influenced several of those reform efforts—including Catholic temperance organizations, rural colonization efforts, and immigration assistance programs at urban ports. Irish American Catholics appropriated Irish nationalist rhetoric in order to bolster support for reform movements and emphasized economic self-sufficiency, thrift, sobriety, landownership, and democracy as critical to the improvement of the Irish community in the United States. Moreover, while some Irish Catholics supported Catholic temperance on the basis of ethnic interests, German Catholics opposed temperance on the grounds that it was detrimental to the expression of their cultural traditions.

Therefore not only did Catholic reforms in the United States appropriate established models of reform from Europe, but concurrent European social and political movements also shaped the activities undertaken by the American Catholic laity in the late nineteenth and early twentieth centuries. As Daniel T. Rodgers has argued, Progressive-era reform in the United States, far from exemplifying American exceptionalism, owed much to related developments in Europe.[1]

Lay leaders involved in the Catholic temperance movement, immigration protection and rural settlement programs, urban welfare and settlement house work, and women's voluntary associations created transatlantic reform networks that transcended national boundaries. Moreover, because reformers often viewed each of these initiatives as vital to strengthening the Catholic community, many became active in more than one movement. Activists such as William Onahan, Charlotte O'Brien, and Leonora Barry Lake viewed these movements as mutually reinforcing. Thus members of the St. Vincent de Paul Society in the United States were required to be temperate, and women's groups compared themselves to the St. Vincent de Paul Society. Dependency was a theme common to discussions of the Land League, rural colonization, programs addressing poverty, and alcohol abuse.

The following chapters delineate the evolution of lay activities from those that were predominantly male in the 1880s toward those allowing greater roles for women in reform by the early twentieth century. They demonstrate the ways in which European aspects of reform were adapted to American circumstances, as well as the range of efforts, from those based on self-help, and those that assisted immigrants upon their arrival, to those that focused on the urban neighborhoods in which Catholics resided. This study focuses on several lay groups at the national level by analyzing the ways in which class formation, gender ideology, and ethnic identities intersected in social reform efforts and illustrates the ways in which Catholic efforts compared with Protestant-oriented ones.

Catholic reformers sometimes portrayed the social problems they sought to address as particular to their ethnic group and as imported directly from Europe. Some temperance activists, for example, asserted that the Irish had a unique proclivity toward alcohol abuse, while others suggested that their excessive drinking could be traced to the impact of British colonial rule. Those Irish Catholics who supported rural colonization programs in the late nineteenth century attributed the lack of Irish economic mobility vis à vis other immigrant groups to the sociability of the Irish and to their tendency to gather in urban enclaves rather than pursue more promising opportunities. Both reforms stressed self-help as the major route to economic and social improvement. Concurrently, Catholics increasingly invoked stereotypes of Protestants themselves, such as the social-climbing female charity provider and the "Puritan" temperance advocate. Such stereotypes were also applied to Catholic reformers straying too far from Catholic values.

In highlighting the European roots of their reform efforts, Catholics often argued that their initiatives both preceded and surpassed those espoused by American Protestants. Pope Leo XIII's 1891 encyclical, *Rerum Novarum*, inspired many Catholic laity to enter the area of reform. That encyclical called for a more equitable relationship between capital and labor in industrializing countries, while it denounced socialism. In emphasizing their connections to Europe and to Rome itself, however, Catholic lay groups drew attention to the very associations that tainted them in the eyes of many Protestant Americans.

Although Catholic lay reform had distinct international origins, many Catholics active in those movements sought to demonstrate to American society in general that their religion was compatible with American traditions and values. Archbishop John Ireland of Minnesota was the major proponent of that goal in the American church. As a leading advocate for increased lay participation in the church, he was influential in many lay reforms of the era. In fact, lay group activities reflected the tension between the goals of Ameri-

canization and ethnic retention that served as the source of a major controversy among the members of the American hierarchy in the 1890s. The
emphasis on Americanization within the church also arose in response to the
resurgence of late nineteenth-century anti-Catholicism, particularly during
the early 1890s.

The Americanization issue for Catholic lay reformers was closely linked to
the emergence of a significant Catholic middle class. Middle-class Catholics
active in social reform employed a defensive strategy of reform by seeking respectability and approval for themselves and their religion from other Americans. Through their involvement, they sought to prove that not all Catholics
were poor, foreign, or intemperate. Those goals were articulated during the
1893 Columbian Catholic Congress in Chicago, which served as a forum for
those laity who, like Archbishop Ireland, were Americanists.

The process and timing of Catholic middle-class development in the late
nineteenth century differed from that of American Protestants and influenced
Catholic reform efforts. Protestants on the East Coast had begun to form a
distinct middle-class culture by the mid-nineteenth century, while a Catholic
middle-class culture slowly emerged only in the last three decades of the
nineteenth century.[2] Although many Progressive-era Catholic reformers were
middle class, and some were even wealthy, most reformers had not attained
the social and economic status of their counterparts in Protestant-oriented
movements. For example, the officers of the Catholic Women's Union tended
to belong to families of small business owners, and several were employed in
those companies. In stark contrast to the majority of Protestant-oriented
settlement house reformers, Mary Agnes Amberg, the daughter of a wealthy
Catholic businessman, did not attend college, nor did her fellow workers at
Chicago's Madonna Center settlement.[3] Other reformers, such as William
Onahan, had achieved success but had been born into modest circumstances.
Some advocates of reform, especially those involved in the temperance movement, were working class, although they espoused values such as thrift and
sobriety that are commonly associated with the middle class. They too sought
respectability but strove primarily for greater economic independence rather
than for upward mobility.

Those who chose to become involved in Catholic lay reform efforts, and
the people who inspired them, were a diverse group. Some of those integral to
Catholic reform are well-known figures: Terence Powderly, Archbishop John
Ireland, and Charles Parnell. Other activists, such as William Onahan, Charlotte O'Brien, Leonora Barry Lake, Peter Cahensly, Father James Nugent, and

Frederic Ozanam, are less familiar but left written accounts of their accomplishments. Yet we still know very little about the lives of Sophia Wavering, Julia Hayes, and several others involved in important initiatives in American Catholic lay reform, and even less about most of the people who benefited from their efforts.

The emergence of middle- and upper-class Catholic lay leadership did not occur easily, nor did increasing wealth among Catholics lead to a natural sense of noblesse oblige. American members of the St. Vincent de Paul Society, for example, frequently bemoaned the difficulty of attracting wealthy Catholics, especially those with college educations, to their organization. That difficulty contrasted starkly with the situation in France, where elites routinely supported the Society. Therefore reformers such as William Onahan and Thomas Mulry actively promoted among their fellow Catholic laity a greater sense of responsibility for the poor.

In light of the relatively modest socioeconomic status of Catholic activists, Catholic converts, especially those from established Protestant New England families, took a more prominent public role at forums such as the Columbian Catholic Congress at the 1893 Chicago World's Fair. Their high profiles underscored the achievements of American Catholicism by demonstrating the religion's appeal to members of established American families. Yet their prominence in Catholic public life proved somewhat paradoxical in light of widespread Catholic denouncement of Protestant proselytizing.

Middle-class Catholic reformers vacillated between seeking approval from the society at large and criticizing those from whom they desired acceptance. They sought approval from the larger society for their efforts, and their publications documented praise for Catholic efforts from Protestant elites. Yet they also viewed Protestant-oriented groups as dangerous because of their proselytizing of Catholic immigrants and portrayed some of their charitable efforts as alternately harsh or superficial. They promoted stereotypes of Protestant-oriented reformers in order to gain support for Catholic efforts and stressed the long and distinct history of Catholic reform.

Despite the apparent incongruity of the two goals—maintaining international and ethnic ties and demonstrating the compatibility of American values and Catholicism—elements of both often coexisted in various reform efforts. Because of that dynamic, Catholic social reforms were different in important respects from those of Protestants.

In contrast to many reforms discussed in this study, Catholic settlement house workers generally patterned their efforts on American rather than on

European models. Catholic settlements provided programs and services that were very similar to those of the Protestant ones. Settlement work offered opportunities for unmarried middle- and upper-class Catholic women whose career choices remained limited, just as for Protestant women. Yet Catholics came into the field belatedly and as a defensive measure, because of their fears that Protestants were proselytizing Catholic immigrants. They argued that as Catholics, they were uniquely equipped to care for their poor immigrant coreligionists, in part because of the religion's international nature. Mary Agnes Amberg, for example, stressed the fact that the parish priest associated with the Madonna Center settlement had been trained in Italy, spoke Italian, and understood the culture. Her remarks about a shared community, however, sometimes were as romanticized as Jane Addams's view of Greek immigrants' affinity for classical culture.[4]

Although scholars of reform have often emphasized a social control model in describing the charitable efforts of the Charity Organization Society and similar organizations comprised largely of elite, urban Protestants, that conception does not adequately explain the reasons that Catholic groups engaged in reform. For many Catholics, as for Protestants, charitable action toward the poor was a concomitant obligation of their own improved economic status. On the other hand, because the social status of Catholics in the United States remained tenuous, Catholics involved in charity recognized that continued poverty among their coreligionists reflected negatively on their religion as a whole. Moreover, Catholics operated from a proprietary notion of charity—the idea that each religion should take care of "its own." By undertaking programs for the poor, the church gave evidence of its own solidity. While modest when measured against better-funded Protestant efforts, middle-class and upper-class lay Catholics slowly developed a greater sense of obligation toward the poor as they entered the field of charity and reform in increasing numbers.

Despite the emphasis placed on reform as a means to respectability, Catholics worried about the consequences of increasing economic prosperity for the religious and ethnic identities of the church's members. Catholics in the laity, clergy, and hierarchy criticized married women in the middle and upper classes who did not direct sufficient amounts of energy into motherhood and housekeeping. Those "idle" women were seen as emulating Protestants too closely. They were often viewed as less virtuous than the hardworking single Catholic women whom they hired as servants. For Catholic women in the late nineteenth and early twentieth centuries, charity work increasingly served as an appropriate focus for their activities. Yet their actions became controversial when they patterned their efforts on those of Protestants. Their loyalty to their faith, and often to their ethnicity, came into question.

The years between 1880 and 1925 brought significant changes for the Catholic Church in the United States. The last two decades of the nineteenth century saw the growth of a significant Catholic middle class and a distinct domestic ideology in the United States, accompanied by an increase in lay activity. During the 1890s the pope issued *Rerum Novarum*, and the Columbian Catholic Congress in Chicago demonstrated an increasing public role for Catholic laity, while organized anti-Catholic activity also underwent a resurgence.

At the same time, the new wave of Catholic immigration posed additional challenges to the church and demands on its resources. The new Catholic immigrants did not form lay groups beyond the parish level to the same degree that the Irish and Germans did. Their efforts tended to be more localized and more focused on achieving economic stability within their own communities, particularly through creating fraternal societies. As a result, Italians and Eastern European Catholics in this period were more often the recipients of the church's charitable endeavors than its providers. At the same time, Irish and German Catholics, whose communities had matured, began directing more of their efforts toward incoming immigrants, a process that revealed ethnic and class tensions. All of those developments gave rise to the emergence of Catholic lay reform efforts in the United States.

The years following World War I signaled a distinct shift in the nature of Catholic lay activities. First, localized efforts became more professionalized as the disciplines of sociology and social work became more widely accepted among Catholics. Second, lay efforts came increasingly under the control of centralized authority at the national level, and members of the clergy and hierarchy expanded efforts that had been undertaken by lay groups in various cities. Many members of the hierarchy created diocesan social service bureaus to coordinate myriad charitable activities, to prevent overlap, and to make charity provisions more efficient. Such oversight by the hierarchy often eclipsed prior lay efforts in those areas and, in some cases, hampered new lay initiatives. For example, following World War I, professionals increasingly replaced lay volunteers in leadership positions within the National Council of Catholic Charities (NCCC), formed in 1910.

Most historians view the Progressive movement as ending with America's entry into World War I, or with the passage of the Nineteenth Amendment.

But World War I, and the creation of the National Catholic War Council, proved to be a watershed for American Catholics because of that body's importance in shaping national initiatives in social reform and charity following the war. Supervised by the American hierarchy, the council emerged after the war as the National Catholic Welfare Council (NCWC). Formation of the NCWC, along with the trend toward creating diocesan bureaus, led to significant changes in charity structure and provision mechanisms—changes that had already occurred for many Protestant-oriented and government-funded charities. Therefore a fuller understanding of the Progressive movement requires that historians expand the chronological boundaries of that era.[5]

· · · · ·

Catholics currently constitute the largest religious denomination in the United States. Yet, despite the religion's strength in American society, there are few general historical journals in which issues pertaining to Catholicism are addressed. Almost two decades ago, Timothy Walch lamented that there had not been "a single study of Catholicism in the American Historical Association's recent assessment of contemporary historical scholarship."[6] Despite some gains in the past decade, the study of Catholicism has yet to emerge from the margins of U.S. historical research. Social historians writing about the United States have rarely looked to Catholic scholarship to inform their debates on the nature of social reform, the creation of domestic ideologies, middle-class formation, national identity, or urban growth. We can gain a much fuller understanding of those developments by analyzing them within the context of the American Catholic experience.

    Several earlier studies have examined social reform efforts in the Catholic Church. Aaron Abell and David O'Brien have written monographs on American social reform. O'Brien's study focuses on a later period than mine, the 1930s, while Abell does not discuss lay goals and programs in great detail. Dorothy Brown and Elizabeth McKeown's book, *The Poor Belong to Us*, is a more recent analysis of the development of charitable activities among Catholics, although it does not focus specifically on lay groups. William Halsey's intellectual history of American Catholicism in the early to mid-twentieth century demonstrates the maturation of the Catholic middle class and the ensuing development of a set of Catholic cultural organizations among its members that paralleled those of Protestants. While my work concentrates on an earlier era, it also discusses the formation of groups arising from the emergence of a significant Catholic middle class, and how their efforts reflected distinctly Catholic concerns and points of view that sometimes ran counter to prevailing trends in American society.[7]

Monographs such as Paula Kane's *Separation and Subculture: Boston Catholicism, 1900–1920*, Philip Gleason's *The Conservative Reformers: German-American Catholics and the Social Order*, and Christopher Kauffman's *Faith and Fraternalism* examine themes of Americanization and ethnicity among the laity. Kane's cultural history focuses exclusively on Boston, however, while Gleason's and Kauffman's books each concentrate on single lay groups. By examining several groups at the national level, one can discern the many common threads unifying various reform efforts, as well as the ways in which such initiatives responded to local, ethnic, or regional concerns.[8]

Although my study has a national scope, it focuses primarily on two regions—the Northeast and the Midwest. That cities such as Milwaukee, Minneapolis, Chicago, and St. Louis played increasing roles in the church suggests the expansion of Catholic influence beyond Boston and New York at the turn of the century. Those last two cities, not surprisingly, are the subjects of a significant percentage of all historical research on the Catholic Church in the United States. By expanding the analysis of reform groups to the growing Catholic populations of the Midwest, one can detect distinct ethnic and class patterns that were not always apparent in eastern cities. Southerners did not belong to the Catholic Church in large numbers in this era, and therefore their lay organizations were, for the most part, limited and localized. Moreover, while there were important settlement houses and other lay groups elsewhere—in California, for example—German and Irish Catholics were not heavily concentrated in the West. Likewise, Hispanic Catholics did not develop nationally based lay groups directed toward social reform until later in the twentieth century.

Because of the hierarchical structure of the Catholic Church, it is important to understand lay activity in the context of actions of clergy, women religious, bishops, and the pope. While some members of the hierarchy and clergy supported and encouraged lay activity, lay initiatives often lacked such support. Indeed, reform activities among the laity resulted in public and private controversies on many occasions during the period from 1880 to 1925, particularly surrounding the issue of total abstinence and over the nature and extent of laywomen's participation in public activities in conjunction with the church. In contrast to Protestant women, Catholic laywomen's full participa-

tion in charity and social reform was delayed by the significant achievements
of American women religious in those endeavors.

Lay groups involved in social reform nevertheless pursued their own interests by initiating efforts in new and influential areas—such as by developing
immigrant assistance and port programs, establishing settlement houses, and
creating the largely male St. Vincent de Paul Society. They also transformed
existing reform initiatives into successful lay-based organizations. For example, lay leaders in the United States organized a more permanent structure to
institutionalize Father Mathew's original temperance movement. Some organizations, such as the Irish Catholic Colonization Association, served as lay
counterparts to existing diocesan programs. In each case, lay participation
expanded the scope of social reform efforts within the church, enlarged their
base, and gave further legitimacy to the church as an American institution
concerned with the needs of its poorest and newest members. Despite the fact
that some lay initiatives encountered opposition and others were ultimately
subsumed by diocesan bureaus and national initiatives of the hierarchy, the
laity profoundly shaped many of the programs emerging from the church in
the late nineteenth and early twentieth century. Viewing Catholic reform
from the lay perspective provides greater insight into how social change affected the church in this era and demonstrates how lay efforts broadened the
role of the church in the United States. The history of lay involvement in the
church has become an increasingly relevant issue today, as the role of American lay Catholics continues to increase in response to the current shortage of
clergy and women religious.

This examination of the Catholic social reform movement analyzes lay
groups working on behalf of several shared goals and values. It demonstrates
the ways that women's roles, and concepts of masculinity, shaped reform efforts among the Catholic laity. The study emphasizes the ways in which
European traditions were embraced and adapted to American circumstances,
and the reasons why other groups modeled their efforts closely on American
Protestant-oriented efforts. It examines issues of ethnic character, ethnic
nationalism, and the prevalence of a Catholic critique of Protestant reformers. Further, it shows how the debate over Americanization in this era mani-
fested itself in lay group activities. Despite the hierarchical nature of authority
in the Catholic Church, lay groups often initiated their own activities and
challenged the opposition or indifference of church leadership. By placing
Catholic efforts in the broader framework of American reform during the

Progressive era, we can better understand the ways in which increasing centralization and bureaucratization among organizations in the United States affected the localized, voluntary nature of lay programs in the post–World War I period, as well as recognize the diverse origins of the American social reform tradition.

Celebrating
an American
Catholic Legacy

The 1893 Chicago World's Fair marked the four-hundredth anniversary of Columbus's voyage to North America by celebrating the achievements of American culture and industrial capitalism. Situated on the Lake Michigan shore, the fair attracted over 27 million visitors after opening in May. The fairgrounds, in which imposing neoclassical structures surrounded a lagoon, sat on 664 acres and featured replicas of the *Niña, Pinta,* and *Santa Maria.* Antonín Dvorák composed a symphony commemorating the event. A statue of Columbia, torch in hand, sculpted by Daniel Chester French and Edward Potter, presided over the fair. Diverse luminaries such as President Grover Cleveland, Swami Vivekananda, Frederick Douglass, Elizabeth Cady Stanton, and Herbert Spencer congregated in Chicago, reflecting its new status as a major city and its full recovery from the devastating 1871 fire.[1]

That year William J. Onahan, a Catholic layman from Chicago, organized the Columbian Catholic Congress, held in conjunction with the World's Fair, to highlight the legacy of American Catholics. Catholics also arranged an educational exhibit and participated in the World's Parliament of Religions. Although many members of the hierarchy and clergy attended the congress, it arose from a lay initiative and many of the presentations centered on the roles of the laity. The issues debated at the Columbian Catholic Congress would challenge lay Catholics for the next thirty years, particularly the reformers examined in this study. Those issues having particular relevance to lay reformers included the impact of the Americanist controversy, which fueled the debate over the extent to which European traditions and languages should be preserved in the United States; the greater role of laywomen, African Americans and converts in the church; and the extent to which lay opposition to hierarchical positions would be tolerated. The changing ethnic composition of the church was another significant issue encountered by Catholics convened at the 1893 congress, as new, predominantly Catholic, immigrants from countries other than Ireland and Germany were arriving in steadily larger numbers, precipitating yet another stage of growth for the church. Despite the focus on unity at the congress, Catholics faced the challenge of reconciling the diverse traditions and experiences within their ranks. The issues addressed at 1893 lay congress reveal the context in which Catholic lay reform efforts occurred and demonstrate the growing confidence among Catholics in claiming their place in America's past as well as in contemporary society.

A similar congress had been held in Baltimore in 1889, days prior to the dedication ceremony for the Catholic University of America in Washington, D.C. The organizing committee members had voted to hold their subsequent congress during the 1893 World's Fair. The linking of the 1893 Catholic Congress to the World's Fair signified the emergence of Catholicism in the United States as a major religion, but it also highlighted the difficulty Catholics faced in gaining acceptance among their fellow Americans, as well as the internal divisions the religion faced in the 1890s.

Architect Daniel Burnham's creation of the White City fairgrounds sought to evoke elements of a past that could reconcile the new industrial order and concepts of progress with the values of an earlier era.[2] Catholics, to some degree, shared with others that optimism about the United States and its future. The chairman of the Columbian Catholic Congress and well-known Knights of Columbus leader, Judge Morgan O'Brien, stated: "Naturally our minds go back to that event through the vista of years; we see the march of progress, the development of material and mechanical triumphs, and above all the struggle for emancipation and freedom."[3]

Catholics had an additional goal at the fair: to prove the compatibility of their minority religion with the ideals that were articulated in the other forums and exhibitions. Yet their participation was marked by internal divisions over ethnicity and points of view to be expressed at the fair. Catholics still needed to reach a consensus about their own identity, even while seeking to change perceptions held by others. The controversies surrounding the nature of lay group participation both reflected and anticipated the changing roles of those organizations.

The timing of the 1893 lay congress was also significant because just two years earlier Pope Leo XIII had delivered his encyclical letter on the condition of labor, *Rerum Novarum*, which precipitated a greater emphasis on social issues among the laity, clergy, and hierarchy. *Rerum Novarum* would serve as the catalyst for the advancement of Catholic lay reform initiatives just as the Social Gospel movement inspired a greater commitment to social reform among Protestants in the United States.

The Catholic use of the symbol of Columbus arose primarily as a defensive tactic in an era in which anti-Catholic prejudice remained strong. The era, however, was also one in which the Catholic Church was better equipped to address prejudice than it had been in the past. As historian Christopher Kauffman has argued, while Italians in the United States were adapting Columbus into a symbol particular to their ethnic group, the founding of the Knights of Columbus in 1882 marked a simultaneous effort by Catholics to transform him into a universal symbol of their faith.[4] As part of their effort to demonstrate the compatibility of their religion with American institutions and traditions, the 1893 Catholic Congress attendees sought to establish a Catholic American historical memory based on Columbus and his voyage. Catholics appropriated the symbol of Columbus and his benefactors— Ferdinand and Isabella, the king and queen of Spain—as their own. They thus promoted their claims as authentic Americans and challenged the prevailing view that English Protestantism constituted the United States's only valid religious legacy.[5]

Daniel Dougherty, a layman from New York and speaker at the 1889 congress, marked the impending Columbus quadricentennial by asserting that "without Catholic Columbus, America would not have been discovered." He further argued that "the finding of the new world, and the vast results that have flowed to humanity, can be traced directly to the Roman Catholic Church and the Roman Catholic church alone." Dougherty thus rewrote the history of the settling of America as a Catholic rather than as a Protestant event.[6]

The Americanist Controversy of the 1890s

In his speech inaugurating the 1889 lay congress, Archbishop John Ireland proclaimed his optimism about the new century and the role of Catholics in it. "Despite its defects and its mistakes, I love my age. I love its aspirations and its resolves. I revel in its feats of valor, its industries, and its discoveries. I thank it for its many benefactions to my fellow-men, to the people rather than to princes and rulers. I seek no backward voyage across the sea of time. I will ever press forward. I believe that God intends the future to be better than the present."[7]

As leading members of the liberal contingent of the hierarchy, Ireland and his allies attempted to increase the power and action of the laity to address social issues and to become fuller participants in the church and in American life. He exclaimed: "Let there be individual action. Layman need not wait for priest, nor priest for Bishop, nor Bishop for Pope." Alluding to tensions that would soon culminate in the Americanist crisis, Ireland asserted: "The Church of America must be, of course, as Catholic as ever in Jerusalem or Rome; but so far as her garments assume color from the local atmosphere she must be American. Let no one dare paint her brow with foreign tint, or pin to her mantle foreign linings."[8] Ireland and his Americanist allies soon clashed with conservatives in the hierarchy, who maintained close ties to Rome and stressed the unique role of the Catholic Church in American life.

Four years later, the opportunity to present the merits of Catholicism and its compatibility with American institutions in conjunction with the commemoration of Columbus's voyage heightened the significance of the Catholic Congress in a decade of intense controversy within the American church. Internal tensions arose during a period of external conflict, as anti-Catholicism underwent a resurgence. The American Protective Association (APA), an anti-Catholic, anti-immigrant group, had formed in 1887 and experienced sharp growth in 1893. Some Catholic newspapers split their front-page coverage of the 1893 congress with news of APA activities.[9]

The Americanist controversy of the 1890s, which divided the liberals, or Americanists, within the American hierarchy against the conservatives, also had ramifications for Catholic lay groups. Along with Ireland, the leaders in the former camp included Bishop John Keane of Richmond and Reverend Denis O'Connoll, rector of the American College of Rome, a good friend of Ireland, who would later succeed Keane as bishop. Archbishop Michael Corrigan of New York and Bishop Bernard McQuaid of Rochester led the conservatives and gained the support of German Catholics. Cardinal James Gibbons of Baltimore generally sided with the liberals, while Bishop John Lancaster Spalding of Peoria refrained from aligning with either group. The split reflected a fundamental tension between the church's emphasis on ethnic issues and the view that Catholics must demonstrate the compatibility of their religion with American life. Americanists sought to gain legitimacy within society as a whole and to promote the acculturation of Catholics. The tension between these two points of view permeated many lay activities until after World War I.

Yet the dichotomy between the liberal and conservative views, as traditionally presented, often misses the complexity and contradictions inherent in the two sides' positions, and in the labels assigned to those views. For example, McQuaid differed from Ireland on several points—he held a more pessimistic view of American society, vigorously supported parochial schools, and eschewed participation in party politics. But McQuaid also strongly supported *Rerum Novarum*, the separation of church and state, and an emphasis on English language instruction in parochial schools. He sought to train and educate American priests "who were prepared for the world as it is today" and rejected proposals to appoint bishops for each immigrant group. Conservatives such as McQuaid argued that because acculturation of immigrant Catholics would occur over time, it need not be actively promoted. Similarly, Ireland's Americanist perspective, which lauded America's achievements over those of Europe, revealed nationalist sentiments that meshed well with American foreign expansionist views and was in some ways too eager to embrace Anglo-American culture. Personality clashes and representation of the issues in the press accentuated actual differences between the two perspectives.[10]

The Americanist controversy reached its pinnacle in 1899, when Pope Leo XIII issued an apostolic letter, *Testem Benevolentiae*, declaring unorthodox some of the views often attributed to Americanists. These included the idea that in order to attract followers, the Catholic Church needed to change its doctrines in accordance with modern circumstances in the United States. That view gave rise to the fear among the hierarchy that doctrine would vary and change, rather than rest with tradition and papal authority. The pope's objection to the Americanist view emphasized that the individual needed external direction for his or her spiritual life. The letter further declared that there could be no distinction between passive and active virtues; all virtues required action and therefore humility, obedience, and abstinence remained necessary to modern life.[11]

The immediate controversy, and the subsequent apostolic letter, had emanated from a translation from English into French of a biography of Isaac Hecker in which Hecker's views were interpreted by some conservatives as constituting Americanism. Hecker, a well-known Catholic convert born in New York in 1819, was a former Lutheran, Methodist, and transcendentalist who founded the Paulist Congregation in 1858. Hecker was known for his emphasis on the importance of the indwelling Holy Spirit to the internal guidance of Catholic spiritual life. The translation of his biography, however, went farther than that. It suggested to some that Hecker believed that natural virtues were superior to the supernatural and that the Holy Spirit's presence in the individual soul was more important than the sacraments and institutional aspects of Catholicism.[12] For many in the hierarchy, these ideas attributed to Hecker strayed dangerously toward Protestantism and the heterodoxy of illuminism. That latter concept emphasized a direct relationship between God and the individual, implying that the priest's role as liturgical mediator was not essential to religious practice. Although no one was actually accused of heresy during the controversy, the liberal members of the hierarchy felt they had been placed on the defensive and denied that they had ever espoused the views said to be Americanist. Recently, however, several historians have suggested that Americanists did in fact advocate views that were later denounced in *Testem Benevolentiae*.[13]

The Americanist controversy of the late 1890s has been the subject of several studies by historians of American Catholicism.[14] While acknowledging the Americanists' emphasis on a more active role for the laity, few historians have discussed in depth the implications of the controversy for the development of lay groups in this era. In fact, this tension between acculturation and accommodation into American society, on the one hand, and the ethnically based traditions of Catholicism, on the other, permeated organized lay activities, from Catholic temperance to the German Catholic Central Verein, from efforts to assist immigrants to the views inherent in the Catholic settlement house movement.

Ethnic tensions within the American church escalated further following a call for increased numbers of Germans in the hierarchy of the American church and increased attention to immigration issues. In 1871 Peter Cahensly, a German businessman and Reichstag member, had founded the St. Raphael Society as an immigrant aid organization for German Catholics emigrating to the United States. He was especially critical of the American Catholic hierarchy's role in immigration; in 1891 he maintained that because of their inaction, a large number of Catholics left the faith upon their arrival. In addition, he advocated the continued use of the German language among the immigrants and the appointment of German and other foreign bishops to the United States. Cahensly belonged to a lay group from a Catholic congress in Lucerne, Switzerland, which voiced those concerns to the pope. Members of the liberal American faction in the United States, especially Archbishop John

Ireland, condemned Cahensly's actions as highly inappropriate, and others characterized "Cahenslyism" as foreign interference.[15]

The Americanist controversy was intensified by the fact that in the United States the church allowed ethnic groups to establish their own parishes within their communities rather than join existing ones. While that issue might have faded in importance as subsequent generations of German Catholics gained a preference for English, the infusion of other non-English-speaking Catholic immigrants beginning in the 1880s again brought the issue to the foreground. Once considered a temporary measure by the hierarchy, national parishes were now viewed by many Catholics as integral to their religious life. This system allowed German, Italian, Polish, and other Catholic immigrants to hear sermons, give confessions, and educate their children in their native languages, although mass was universally conducted in Latin. As we will see, the creation of these new parishes fueled controversies between immigrant laity and the American-born hierarchy, and amongst immigrants themselves.

Another issue that concerned Americanists was the fate of labor organizations to which large numbers of Catholics belonged. The church had condemned Catholic involvement in secret societies. Cardinal Gibbons, however, interceded on behalf of the Knights of Labor, which had enjoyed strong support among Catholic workers, so that the pope would not prohibit Catholic involvement in that group. Terence Powderly, an Irish Catholic who strongly advocated total abstinence, headed the Knights of Labor. Powderly attended the World's Fair but did not speak at the Catholic Congress.[16]

While language as a component of ethnic identity was not an issue among Irish Catholic groups, the continuity between their brand of Catholicism and nationalist issues was heavily emphasized by many Irish Catholics in the American church in the late nineteenth century. The Land League, an Irish nationalist group formed by Charles Parnell and Michael Davitt to achieve Irish home rule and to secure greater land tenancy rights, became especially popular among Irish American Catholics in the 1880s. The Land League agitation of that decade received widespread support from many Irish Catholic clergy members as well as laity and permeated much of the lay activism in the late nineteenth century and later, while nationalist sentiment laced the rhetoric and agendas of other lay groups active in this era.

Another dispute that illustrates the coexistence of Americanist and ethnic tendencies is the McGlynn affair. Dr. Edward McGlynn, a well-known New York priest and pastor of St. Stephen's Church, served as one of the earliest supporters of the Land League movement among the American clergy and spoke at the 1893 Columbian Catholic Congress. McGlynn served as an important figure in the period of Americanist controversy because of his liberal political stances, including his staunch belief in the separation of church and state, his opposition to government funding of private or parochial education, and, most important, his support for Henry George's single tax plan. In the 1860s McGlynn and other liberal New York priests had been involved in a group known as the Accademia, which expressed views similar to those later expressed by Americanists, particularly those concerning the reconciliation of American democratic values with the church and the parochial school issue. Despite widespread support for McGlynn among the laity, especially women, the conservative archbishop of New York, Michael Corrigan, suspended him twice and then prohibited Catholics from attending his lectures. After McGlynn was summoned to Rome and refused to go, he was excommunicated. The pope later overturned McGlynn's 1887 excommunication, and Corrigan reassigned him to a parish north of New York City.[17]

Just as many individuals held both ethnic and Americanist views, the actual demarcation between Americanist and conservative approaches toward issues was far from absolute. For example, while stressing that their movement would help the Catholic position in the United States and increase individuals' upward mobility, temperance advocates also emphasized their ties to Father Theobold Mathew's midcentury campaign in Ireland and their support for Irish nationalism. And Archbishop Ireland, a major advocate of the Americanist position on behalf of the laity—especially in the areas of temperance and Catholic colonization—had views that reflected elements of acculturation as well as a strong identification with specific ethnic issues.

The labels characterizing the two views prove somewhat misleading in describing the groups' goals. Certainly the conservatives sought to preserve many European Catholic traditions. Yet while that stance has been described as conservative, it was the liberals who often advocated an accommodationist rather than a cultural pluralist solution to the conflict between American and European values and traditions. Some elements of the Americanist stance, therefore, might better be characterized as conservative.

Anti-Catholicism served as yet another factor in the debate between the Americanists and the conservatives because the former group feared that cultural retention would serve to exacerbate growing charges that Catholics were disloyal to the United States. The decade of the 1890s, when these internal conflicts emerged, was also characterized by an upsurge in anti-Catholicism. Anti-Catholicism had subsided for a few decades but arose again in part because of increased Catholic immigration from southern and eastern Europe, and also because of the growing fear of Catholic political control in cities with substantial Catholic populations, including Boston, New York, and Chicago.[18] Prejudice and organized activity were strong in Massachusetts as well as in the Midwest, where Catholics had established significant roles in urban politics. Anti-Catholicism was also reconstituted as a result of the increasing profile of the Catholic Church outside the Northeast. Therefore, by suggesting their growing presence in American society, participation by Catholics in a highly visible forum such as the World's Fair had the potential to heighten, as well as to dispel, antagonism toward them.

The American Protective Association gained a substantial increase in members beginning in 1893, following William Traynor's rise to leadership in the group and the occurrence of the severe economic depression that year. In 1893 Traynor's Detroit newspaper, the *Patriotic American*, published a fabricated papal encyclical supposedly issued by Leo XIII. The fake encyclical was said to release Catholics from their loyalty to the United States and to order them to "exterminate all heretics" in September of that year, a date that roughly coincided with the one on which "the Roman Catholic Congress shall convene at Chicago, Ill." Anti-Catholicism also flourished in many Protestant churches. But other Protestants, such as Washington Gladden, an influential minister closely identified with the Social Gospel movement, strongly condemned anti-Catholicism. Gladden began an article in *Century* magazine by noting the irony in the fact that anti-Catholicism had undergone a resurgence during the same year that the Parliament of Religions at the World's Fair sought to promote religious toleration. Citing *Rerum Novarum*, Gladden asserted that Leo XIII had proved to be "perhaps the most enlightened and most progressive pontiff who has ever occupied that throne: the whole policy of the Church under his administration has been tending toward a reconciliation with modern civilization."[19]

It is not surprising then, in such a hostile climate, directed both against Catholics and toward the 1893 congress in particular, that Catholics at the congress felt compelled to highlight their loyalty to American values and institutions, to emphasize that Catholics had been integral to the nation's founding, and to discourage those who sought to emphasize Catholics' European heritage from participating freely at the fair.

• • • • •

The Laity at the Congress

Both the 1893 congress and the earlier one that took place in Baltimore in 1889 stressed themes of Catholic unity. Henry Brownson, a layman from Detroit and the son of Orestes Brownson, the famous convert, had conceived of the 1889 congress and gained Archbishop Ireland's support for it. Though Bishop John Henry Newman and Cardinal Henry Edward Manning of England had earlier proposed hosting a congress for English-speaking Catholics patterned on those in continental Europe, their plans never came to fruition.

William Onahan was the most prominent layman at both the first and second congresses. An energetic man and inveterate organizer, Onahan was involved in a number of lay activities at the local and national levels. In addition to organizing the 1889 and 1893 congresses, he served as an officer of the Irish Catholic Colonization Association, became president of the Holy Name Conference of the St. Vincent de Paul Society when it formed in 1857, and joined the Catholic Institute, a lay group that sponsored public lectures. As a young man in Chicago, he had attended lectures by such Catholic luminaries as Orestes Brownson, Thomas D'Arcy McGee, and Bishop John Lancaster Spalding. Those speakers seem to have influenced his activities in later years, since both McGee and Spalding were major proponents of rural colonization efforts. Later he hosted both Charlotte Grace O'Brien, an Irish reformer, and Father James Nugent of Liverpool when each toured the United States promoting immigration assistance programs.[20]

Onahan served as an impressive example of upward mobility among the Catholic laity and as a spokesman for an emerging sense of noblesse oblige. The son of a carpenter, Onahan was born in Leighlin Bridge, County Carlow, Ireland, in 1836. His older siblings had all died in infancy. He came to the United States as a teenager with his family, which had initially immigrated to Liverpool, hoping to improve their economic opportunities. His mother died there of cholera. After a brief time in New York, Onahan arrived in Chicago in 1854 with his father and his two younger sisters, both of whom later joined the Religious of the Sacred Heart. He worked as a shipping clerk at the Rock Island Railroad, using his income to support both his father and sisters. Soon he became a city booster, serving on the Chicago Board of Trade and the Board of Education, and helping to organize the Hibernian Savings Bank in 1867. He also served as president of the Illinois Catholic Historical Society. He benefited from political patronage by becoming first the city's collector and

William J. Onahan.
(From Gallery, Life of
William J. Onahan;
reprinted with permission)

then its appointed comptroller. In addition to his political and civic career, Onahan owned a real estate and insurance firm and became a bank president. In 1890 the University of Notre Dame awarded him the Laetare Medal, presented to an outstanding layman, largely in recognition of his efforts in organizing the first congress. In his later years, he donated his private library, rich in Irish history and literature, to the Quigley Preparatory Seminary. For Onahan, the 1893 Catholic Congress, convened in his adopted city, represented a culmination of his efforts to champion Catholic lay activities.[21]

Katherine Conway, a Boston journalist and novelist, was another layperson involved in planning the 1893 congress. She complained that New England delegates felt "crowded out" of the congress, in part because it was hosted by Chicago Catholics. The fact that the congress was held in Chicago instead of a more established eastern city further highlighted the growing influence of midwestern members of the hierarchy, as well as the burgeoning numbers of Catholics outside of major East Coast cities and the increasingly national character of the church.

The participation of women in the 1893 congress signaled a significant departure from previous gatherings, from which women had been excluded. In fact, the 1893 congress featured several women speakers, most of whom emphasized topics of a historical or artistic nature rather than contemporary issues. The decision to include women's speeches at the 1893 congress, in contrast to the 1889 gathering of laity, gained impetus from the fact that women had organized a Congress of Representative Women at the 1893 World's Fair. That gathering had the potential to appeal to Catholic women, had they been excluded from the Catholic Congress altogether.[22] During the planning stages, the position of women at the Catholic Congress became sharply contested. The inclusion of Catholic laywomen thus reflected both their emergence in the public sphere and the continued controversies surrounding their roles.

Katherine Conway objected strenuously to the concept of a "Woman's Day" that would separate women presenters from the rest of the program. Conway, the acting editor of the Boston *Pilot*, was a contradictory figure. An active, assertive, and unmarried career woman, she extolled the importance of marriage for women and strenuously opposed women's suffrage initiatives in Massachusetts.[23] She repeated her objections to the forum in several letters to William Onahan, in every instance providing a different argument against, or an alternative plan to, Woman's Day. Later she asserted that men would not attend the program, because it would seem a "dreary bore" to them. She told Onahan to withdraw her name from the program, contending that "that 'woman' business is overdone in non-Catholic circles." She also appealed to Onahan's primary goal of improving the image of Catholics among the public in general. "Let us show to the observant non-Catholic public that clever women are not a brand-new thing, not a nine-day's wonder in the Catholic church." Conway implied that women should not raise issues of particular interest to their sex but should instead demonstrate their intelligence only on general topics in forums alongside men.[24]

In objecting to what she viewed as a pale imitation of Protestant and secular groups, Conway sought to keep American Catholicism free from critical discussions of women's roles and rights. She complained about the segregation of women: "I have always had a horror of the exploiting of women *as* women in any public gathering," adding that she opposed "the raising of 'the woman question' among Catholics."[25] These comments suggest that it was not simply the fear that women's segregation would marginalize them that displeased her, but also the idea that such a forum could lend itself to the expression of prosuffrage or feminist viewpoints. To bolster her view, she listed the names of those who agreed with her position, including the husband of Rose Hawthorne Lathrop, a Woman's Day speaker. She mentioned having dined with Cardinal Gibbons, implying that he, too, supported her position. Conway's opposition to the Woman's Day forum extended beyond her private correspondence. As editor of the *Pilot*, she ran articles questioning its appropriateness.[26]

The relationship of women to the Catholic community as a whole became a point of contention between Katherine Conway and Onahan (and others), who sought to emphasize women's issues by having a separate program for them in the congress. Conway denounced Alice Toomy, who helped to promote Woman's Day. Toomy supported feminist causes to a greater degree than did most Catholic women. Conway threatened to withdraw her participation from the congress if Toomy spoke.[27] Apparently, Toomy did not become involved in the Catholic forum on women, speaking instead on dress reform and marriage at the Congress of Representative Women.

Conway eventually proved unsuccessful in her efforts to eliminate the Woman's Day program from the congress; the organizers devoted one day to women speakers. Yet Conway may have won a battle over semantics. The official proceedings indicate that the organizers ultimately skirted the issue of an official Woman's Day program. They recorded that "Thursday, the fourth day of the Congress, *might well be* called Woman's Day, the claims and glories of the gentler sex being eloquently presented by some famous Catholic ladies."[28]

In contrast to many of the papers given by Catholic laymen, and by many women in the Congress of Representative Women, the women's topics presented at the Columbian Catholic Congress focused on historical subjects rather than on contemporary Catholic women's issues. Isabella, the Catholic queen of Spain, became a popular historical symbol for modern-day Catholics discussing the role of women in the church. Mary Onahan's speech on "Isabella the Catholic" asserted that "the age of woman dates not from the 19th century, but from the 1st; is due not to modern civilization, not to modern progress, but to something grander than either—the mainspring of both—the religion of Christ and his Church." Onahan lauded Isabella as an exemplary Catholic woman, because "this inner spirit of religion, of law, permeated [her] whole life and character."[29] By using a fifteenth-century example, Onahan challenged the notion that modern values were responsible for the improved status of women and drew upon a Catholic legacy of female influence. Archbishop Ireland also commended Isabella, noting that Columbus "could not have succeeded without the practical patronage of Isabella. Be

Isabella honored by America's generous recognition of women's sphere." He also applauded women's enlarged role at the 1893 congress.[30]

Rose Hawthorne Lathrop's paper, "Women and Mammon," served as an exception to the dearth of discussions on contemporary women's issues. She described diametrically opposed archetypes of women and warned of wealthy and vain women who concerned themselves with material matters at the expense of their spiritual lives. She contrasted this dichotomy, essentially that of Eve and Mary, with the more universal representation of man as "courage, energy, [and] constructive force." Lathrop then called for women to "arise and defend your rights, your abilities for competition with men, intellect, and professional endurance. The hour [has arrived] when you are to prove that purity and generosity are for the nation as well as for the home. If it is well for you to imitate the profoundest students, the keenest business minds, the sublimest patriots, is it not well for you to imitate the noblest and tenderest of your sex?" While Lathrop did not reject public and professional roles for women, she highlighted the importance of domestic virtues of purity and tenderness, as opposed to those of "idle" and material women. That theme permeated contemporary discussions of Catholic domesticity and the views of Catholic women's groups.[31]

By providing a voice for women in the Catholic Congress, organizers could regulate the content of women's issues and provide a more traditional forum for women than existed in the secular and more feminist-oriented setting of the Congress of Representative Women. The inclusion of women occurred partially in response to external forces, particularly the increasing prominence of Protestant-oriented feminists and reformers in the public sphere. But the development also coincided with an increasing recognition in the 1890s of American laywomen's roles within the church, which expanded as they became involved in new activities. Yet, despite women's progress, their responsibilities and roles in the church remained subordinate to men's.

African American Catholics:
A Minority within a Minority

African American Catholics held their fourth annual congress in Chicago in conjunction with the 1893 Columbian Catholic Congress, having held separate congresses in 1889, 1890, and 1892. To some extent, the gathering of black Catholics at those earlier congresses reflected the primary motive of the participants in the 1889 and 1893 general Catholic lay congresses—to achieve wider respectability in the majority society. But African Americans within the Catholic Church, a minority within a minority, sought to gain acceptance among their coreligionists as well. Therefore their meeting at the general gathering of lay Catholics was an important development in their status both as African Americans and as Catholics.

The black lay congress in 1889 marked the first time that members of the African American Catholic laity met as a group at the national level. That congress was organized by Daniel Rudd, an African American journalist raised in Bardstown, Kentucky. The son of former slaves who had brought up their twelve children as Catholics, Rudd hoped to encourage black Catholics in the United States, whom he estimated to number around 200,000, to join together to promote their interests within the Catholic Church as a whole. Early in 1889, eleven months prior to the general lay congress, African American Catholics gathered in Washington, D.C., and met with President Grover Cleveland at the White House.[32]

Daniel Rudd also served on the organizing committee of the 1889 general lay congress and encouraged the committee members to include blacks in their forums. He came under criticism for his stance, however. Despite Archbishop Ireland's strong support for African Americans in the church, his secretary, Father Byrne, complained about Rudd's seeking a greater role for blacks at the general congress. Byrne closed a letter to Father John Slattery, one of the foremost advocates of African Americans in the church, with a racial slur against Rudd, a remark that reflected the continued racial intolerance among many Catholics.[33]

Byrne's reaction was not surprising, in light of the uneasy, often hostile, and sometimes violent relationship of African Americans with immigrant German and, especially, Irish Catholics in the United States during the nineteenth century. Immigrant Catholics had overwhelmingly supported the Democratic Party, in part as a result of anti-Catholic sentiment in the other parties—Whig, Republican, and Know-Nothings—during the antebellum era. Irish American racism emanated to a large degree from the fear of economic competition with free African Americans and the threat of intensified competition and northern migration after emancipation. In urban areas in the North, both groups were heavily concentrated in manual labor and domestic service positions. The Democratic Party in the North was far more receptive to the needs of immigrants and other poor urban whites than was the Republican Party, while few Democrats supported abolitionism. This uneasy relationship between urban Catholics, African Americans, and Republicans erupted in violence during the 1863 New York City draft riots, in which members of the urban working class, many of whom were Irish, protested the class bias of a Union conscription law allowing military exemptions for $300. The mainly Irish protesters assaulted and killed, or looted the property of, free blacks, elite abolitionists, and others associated with the war.[34]

But, as historian David Roediger argues, job competition and other economic circumstances cannot entirely explain the animosity that Irish Americans held toward African Americans. In fact, their major competitors for jobs were other white workers. Roediger also rejects the notion that Irish Americans felt animosity toward African Americans because they associated abolitionist sentiment with the British. He argues that Irish Americans expressed animosity toward African Americans openly because such racial violence was widely acceptable in America. Many white Americans had, during the mid-nineteenth century especially, cast Irish Americans in a separate racial category from themselves—as similar to, and sometimes inferior to, African Americans. Indeed, political cartoonists in both England and the United States in that era portrayed both groups as simian. Irish Americans gradually became defined as white, and they used their increasing political power to maintain their status.[35]

Roediger also discusses instances of successful intergroup coexistence and notes that the animosity between the two groups was not inevitable. In nineteenth-century Ireland, prejudice against blacks was not fixed, and several popular Irish leaders, most notably Daniel O'Connell and Father Mathew, strenuously supported abolition. But O'Connell's position against slavery did not receive support among Irish Americans. It was in the American context that Irish racism solidified.[36]

Given the history of Irish American racism during the nineteenth century, it is not surprising that the relationship between the African American participants in the Columbian Catholic Congress and other Catholic attendees proved strained. William Onahan asked Father Slattery, an advocate for African American Catholics who had helped organize one of the earlier black congresses, for suggestions on an African American speaker. Without elaborating, Slattery responded that few African American Catholics would prove appropriate. It is probable that Slattery had objected to Daniel Rudd's call for black Catholics to be integrated into the general program of the 1889 lay congress rather than being placed in a self-contained forum on black Catholic issues.[37]

On the surface, Rudd's objection to a self-contained forum for African

Americans at the 1889 Catholic Congress paralleled Katherine Conway's objection to a separate Woman's Day four years later. Yet there were significant differences in the two situations. In 1889 African Americans had already held their own conference to discuss issues particular to their community. Further, the view that African Americans should remain exclusively within their own forum during a general congress must be seen in the context of legal and cultural segregation, an ideology and practice that had been crystallizing in the South in the late nineteenth century and had solidified into a uniform social system by around 1900.[38]

Despite this tension, African Americans did participate in the Columbian Catholic Congress in 1893. In June of 1893, William Lofton, a black Catholic dentist from St. Augustine's Parish in Washington, D.C., wrote to Onahan requesting that he consider having a black Catholic representative read a paper at the congress. He suggested Joseph Spencer, president of the executive committee of the Colored Catholic Congress. Spencer asked whether there would be many black representatives at the Columbian Congress and suggested that when the black Catholic congress adjourned it might then join the Columbian Congress.[39]

In a letter to Onahan, Slattery noted that Lofton's idea for merging the Colored Catholic Congress into the Columbian Congress "would prove a good stroke in the eyes of the public."[40] Ultimately, however, Onahan passed over Spencer and selected Charles H. Butler, a Treasury Department clerk, to address the congress on the subject, "The Condition and Future of the Negro Race in the United States." Although Butler's speech avoided major controversy, he did criticize the Catholic Church for having failed to engage in missionary efforts among newly freed slaves in the South, noting that many Protestant denominations had done so.[41] Father Slattery reiterated Butler's view, adding that Protestants had allocated $35 million dollars into such efforts in the South, including the establishment of southern black colleges. During the 1893 congress, African American delegates approved the constitution of a new group, St. Peter Claver's Catholic Union, elected its officers, and arranged for a fifth black congress in 1894. The union, to be based in Washington, would support institutions to assist African American Catholics. The fifth conference occurred in 1894, but it had significantly fewer participants than the 1893 congress. Ultimately, however, the organizers of St. Peter Claver's Catholic Union lost momentum, in part due to conflicts over leadership, how strongly to oppose discrimination, and the Americanist controversy. A few decades later, the Federated Colored Catholics, a group that arose during World War I, revived national African American Catholic organizational efforts.[42]

According to historian Cyprian Davis, African American Catholics, at their late-nineteenth-century congresses and elsewhere, "appropriated for themselves a Catholic history. Where other ethnic groups looked to their European ancestors for their Catholic roots, the black Catholics in America looked to the early church in North Africa for theirs." Davis adds that African American Catholics often alluded to African historical references and to African Catholic saints, such as St. Benedict the Moor and St. Martin de Porres, a Latin American saint with African roots. In emphasizing such historical ties to Catholicism, African Americans strengthened their claims as equal participants in the American church. Indeed, by highlighting the international context of their religion, black Catholics showed distinct parallels with Catholics of recent European heritage.[43] Despite long-standing racial tensions, then, African American lay leaders were able to gain greater recognition from their coreligionists through a fuller involvement in public forums. The participation of African Americans at the Columbian Catholic Congress symbolized an important advancement in their relationship with other American Catholics and improved their status within the church.

Catholic Converts and Lay Viewpoints

Catholics at the 1893 congress also stressed the number of prominent Anglo-American converts to the faith. That group signaled the strengths of Catholicism and its compatibility with American institutions. Converts, especially those who were active in Catholic issues, tended to come from wealthier, better-educated backgrounds than the vast majority of Catholics. The fact that one participant, Rose Hawthorne Lathrop, was the daughter of Nathaniel Hawthorne, the well-known novelist, and that she was descended from some of New England's elite Protestant families was heavily emphasized at the 1893 congress.[44] Lathrop and her husband had converted to Catholicism in 1891, having previously baptized their only child as a Catholic.[45] Others at the conference highlighted the fact that General William Tecumseh Sherman's wife was a Catholic. This strategy of emphasizing the illustriousness of converts was evident to many participants at the conference. When Katherine Conway suggested some possible Boston delegates to Onahan, she remarked, "They are born Catholic, and between ourselves there is a little sensitiveness sometimes as to the seemingly less consideration for that element."[46]

The congress's emphasis on converts may also suggest that Catholicism had not produced sufficient numbers of successful individuals indigenous to its own community, or that Catholics remained less than confident about the ability of those born into the faith to serve as emissaries or symbols to American society at large. As subsequent chapters reveal, the tension between criticizing Protestants and simultaneously seeking their approval permeated Catholic reform. Any critique of Protestant reforms and approaches to religion could be subtly undermined as Catholics welcomed Protestants into the church and encouraged them to pursue leadership positions among the laity and hierarchy. The congress's emphasis on well-known converts from Protestantism, moreover, proved somewhat difficult to reconcile with their simultaneous condemnation of Protestant proselytizing efforts directed at new immigrants.

Although the congress was organized to demonstrate that the Catholic laity supported the principles articulated by the hierarchy, this issue also led to some controversy. The requirement that lay speakers and clergy submit a copy of their proposed papers to the congress's organizers for approval by the bishop came under fire from several participants. John Rozan, slated to discuss Polish Catholics, wrote to Onahan, "I must express my astonishment to hear that . . . I shall encounter any objections and be obliged to send my paper in advance for the approval of the Committee, a rule I suppose, which by the way I was unable to find in the programme." He then withdrew from the congress in protest.[47] Another layman complained that the policy would reinforce the notion among Americans that Catholics were "priest-ridden." Reverend Walter Elliott, Isaac Hecker's Paulist biographer, and conference speaker, stated: "I know, or think I know[,] why so odious a quarantine regulation has been made, but I wish some other means could have been found to secure the same good end."[48]

M. E. Elder, a niece of Archbishop William Elder of Cincinnati, also questioned whether the laity could freely express their views at the congress. Writing to Onahan regarding her paper on rural migration, Elder mused, "I fear that utmost freedom is not permissible in this case. Is it ever proper for the laity to discuss questions which imply blame to the bishops and clergy? . . . What does surprise me is the way we have of eulogizing ourselves." Elder thus criticized the congress for celebrating American Catholics' achievements at the expense of addressing their challenges.[49]

Onahan had discussed the issue of lay expression at the 1889 congress in a letter to John Lee Carroll of Ellicott City, Maryland, a conference participant, stating: "It will not do to allow the impression to go abroad that the Congress is in 'leading strings,' and that the members are not free to speak their minds."[50] John Hyde, a Detroit member of the organizing committee for the 1889 congress, objected to the policy of submitting conference papers to bishops on the grounds that it implied "a doubt of the layman's all-rightness." Hyde informed Onahan that both Henry Brownson, the originator of the 1889 lay congress, and M. J. Harson had criticized the policy. The policy had come in response to concerns expressed by Cardinal James Gibbons, who, in the wake of the McGlynn affair, feared that such papers would stir controversy in America and result in Vatican disapproval. Archbishop Ireland concurred with Gibbons, despite his public call for greater lay initiative.[51]

The freedom of expression issue was further complicated by the fact that the sessions were not open to all. Instead, both conferences required that attendees receive a letter from their bishops. The Organization Committee stated that while the congress "should be free and open to all Catholics, at the same time some necessary restrictions and limitations were obviously required to guard against the intrusion of persons who might claim to be Catholics and yet be possessed by a disloyal spirit and under the influence of false or pernicious principles." The statement implied that without restrictions, anti-Catholic groups might disrupt the congress's sessions. Therefore proponents of the approval policy prevented those Catholics who were known to hold significantly dissenting views from voicing their opinions at the public forum. Yet, despite those restrictions, controversies among the laity nevertheless emerged regarding the direction in which the church was moving.[52]

Organizers discouraged the discussion of ethnically based issues, despite their popularity among some attendees. One audience member brought to the floor an additional resolution condemning the British government's rejection of home rule for Ireland, which was rejected by the Committee on Resolutions. Some supporters of the resolution protested that action. But despite significant support for the Land League by the U.S. clergy and laity, the congress's organizers sought to avoid addressing any political issues that interfered with its goals of demonstrating the loyalty of Catholics to the United States and its government.[53]

New Immigrants and the Church

Although the participants at the 1893 congress sought to stress the compatibility of Catholicism and American values, neither they nor other Catholics could ignore the fact that ethnic issues would remain a major focus of the church in the ensuing decades. Debates over those issues would no longer be confined to the children and grandchildren of German and Irish immigrants. Instead, diverse groups of new, largely Catholic immigrants from Italy and eastern Europe, as well as French Canadians, reinvigorated long-standing debates over ethnic assimilation and identity among the laity, at a time when those more established groups had not resolved those issues among themselves. While the new immigrants had not yet organized significant social reform efforts by this era, the influx of those new immigrants made it more difficult for German and Irish Catholics at the 1893 congress to demonstrate the strong links between Catholic and American traditions.

Reverend Joseph Andreis of Baltimore presented a paper at the 1893 congress on the topic of immigrants, in which he called for greater toleration toward Italian Catholics. In particular, Andreis emphasized the need for better religious instruction of Italian immigrants. He stressed that while many Italians had never received appropriate religious instruction in Italy, they should nevertheless be considered Catholic. Appealing for greater tolerance among American Catholics for Italian immigrants, he argued: "If it is a crime to be Catholic, poor, ignorant of the language of this country, and possessed with customs at variance with the American-Born, they are certainly guilty; but, Thank God, this America repudiates even the thought of raising a tribunal to take cognizance of it."[54]

Concerns that rural Italian immigrants neglected to attend mass or participate fully in parish institutions, or questions about eastern European immigrant attitudes toward ecclesiastical authority, echoed earlier debates in the Catholic Church. In fact, Irish devotional practices had changed substantially since the "devotional revolution" of the 1840s, when Irish Catholics first began attending mass and participating in other religious rites on a regular basis. Moreover, among German Catholics in the nineteenth century, controversies had arisen over lay trusteeship and, more generally, the relationship between the laity, clergy, and hierarchy in cities such as New York. Thus, as members of those groups rose to positions of leadership in the hierarchy and gained middle-class status, they had to contend with such issues among new groups of Catholics whose religious practices seemed inimical to their own.[55]

New immigrants, the large group of predominantly Catholic people who arrived in the United States from southern and eastern Europe in the period from 1890 to 1930, were less likely than Irish or German Catholics to create regional or nationally based lay groups committed to social reform or charity in the Progressive era.[56] Through natural increase combined with heavy immigration, the American Catholic population grew rapidly, from 6.3 million to 16.4 million between 1880 and 1910. Italians comprised about 17 percent of the total permanent immigrants to the United States from 1899 to 1924, Poles over 7 percent, and other eastern Europeans combined, 9 percent.[57]

As recent arrivals in precarious economic circumstances, new immigrants often worked as low-skilled industrial laborers in steel, brass, and textile mills, in meatpacking and assembly plants, and in mining and construction. Women often found employment as domestic servants or as home-based workers. Immigrants tended first to establish institutions, such as union locals, building and loan organizations, immigrant banks, and mutual aid or fraternal societies, that would provide them with greater economic stability. Issues of economic opportunity, national identification, tensions over church leadership, and intra-group conflict also impeded the involvement of new immigrants in comprehensive social reform efforts in the early twentieth century. They tended to be the targets of such efforts more than the initiators. Along with addressing an increased diversity of religious traditions, the church was also faced with the enormous fiscal challenge of building and staffing churches, schools, orphanages, and other institutions to minister to its burgeoning membership. Many middle-class lay Catholics, including Columbian congress participants, were eager to prove the compatibility of their religion with American society. But new Catholic immigrants seemed to reinforce rather than minimize the impression that significant cultural differences separated Catholics and other Americans.

New immigrant Catholics often clashed with members of the Irish-dominated hierarchy, whom they often characterized as indifferent or hostile to their ethnic and religious traditions, and viewed themselves as second-class citizens within their church. Indeed, the fact that new immigrant groups often attended mass in the basements of existing churches (an arrangement known as a duplex parish) seemed to symbolize their unequal status. The uneasy relationship between new immigrants and ecclesiastical leaders had roots in Europe. Rural Italians arrived in the United States with a tradition of anticlericalism arising from the Italian clergy's alignment with Italian landholders.[58] The attitude of the American hierarchy and clergy toward the new immigrants was far from uniform, however. Many sought to accommodate the needs of the newest members of the church while facing financial constraints and shortages of priests of particular ethnic or linguistic backgrounds. Victor Greene has argued that tensions within the Slavic church emanated largely from intra-group conflict over nationalism or other issues rather than from tensions between the church's old and new ethnic groups. Similarly, Richard Juliani has suggested that in Philadelphia, conflict more often occurred among Italian priests concerned that new parishes would attract their parishioners than between the Italian laity and Irish hierarchy.[59]

To address the needs of its increasingly heterogeneous laity in the late nineteenth century, and to prevent major controversies from erupting, the American hierarchy allowed national (or ethnic) parishes to continue to exist, although some within the church argued instead for an Americanizing approach. The first national parish had been created in 1808, and the practice became common in midcentury during the period of heavy Irish and German immigration.[60] The system allowed for the establishment of new parishes based on a shared native language of a particular locality's Catholic residents, rather than the creation of new territorial parishes based on traditional geographical boundaries. Usually linguistic groups and ethnic groups were coextensive, but there were exceptions. For example, while many Lithuanians could speak Polish, they became increasingly opposed to joining Polish parishes, seeking to establish parishes based on shared ethnicity instead. The influx of new immigrants with diverse ethnic and religious traditions, languages, and economic issues thus posed new challenges for the American church, which had not fully resolved ethnic questions arising from the previous wave of immigration.[61]

Within the church, new immigrants tended to join parish-based organizations, including religiously affiliated fraternal organizations, devotional societies, and musical groups. One of the most widespread fraternal organizations was the Polish Falcons, a group still active today, which arose from the Polish National Alliance in 1886. Some parishes joined conferences of the St. Vincent de Paul Society, and many others provided financial support to ethnically based religious congregations, educational funds, or institutions such as orphanages.

A priest shortage further impeded the development of social reform efforts among the new immigrants by inhibiting the formation of ethnic parishes. For example, in Connecticut during the 1890s and early 1900s, Father Joseph Žebris of Waterbury also ministered to several other Lithuanian Catholic communities around the state. Often he visited each settlement just once a year in order to offer Easter confession. Among Czech Catholics, the shortage was also extreme. By 1880 the Czech American population had reached 100,000, but there were just 44 Czech-speaking clergy ministering to them.[62]

Similar circumstances existed among Poles. In the Italian community, as well, few Italian priests were available to serve as parish priests. In fact, many criticized Italian priests as negligent for failing to follow the immigrant laity to the United States. As late as 1899, the ratio of Italian Catholics to priests in the United States was estimated at 750,000 to 60. Even after that shortage was addressed, in 1918 just 718 Italian priests were available in the United States. As a result, non-Italian priests headed many Italian parishes.[63]

In response to the shortage of priests, many small Lithuanian communities ultimately joined Polish parishes in their towns. A major controversy erupted in 1907 when a group of Lithuanian Catholics in Ansonia, Connecticut, impatient with having no national parish of their own, formed a parish committee, incorporated themselves, raised money on their own, and then erected a church without Bishop John Nilan's permission. During the dispute, unpaid contractors placed a lien on the building, and the Lithuanian pastor of the territorial parish was reassigned, leaving Lithuanians with neither a separate parish nor a Lithuanian priest for a year and a half. Nilan ultimately authorized the incorporation of the Lithuanian church and appointed a Lithuanian parish priest. But neither event was reported in the diocesan newspaper, as was customary.[64]

Among eastern Europeans, especially, many Catholics became involved in controversies over parish administration. Some highly fractious disputes arose over the issue of lay trusteeship and influence. Clergy in eastern Europe, unlike their counterparts in the United States, did not have full responsibility for a parish's budget. Polish and Lithuanian laity, in particular, often initiated new parishes and later had a major voice in their administration. Those traditions continued among these immigrant groups in the United States. Although such lay initiatives were contrary to church law, reactions of clergy and members of the hierarchy varied. But the laity's belief in greater parish autonomy sometimes led to disputes.[65] Indeed, such controversies echoed earlier disputes among German Catholics, who also exercised a strong tradition of lay initiative and trusteeship at the parish level.[66]

In Detroit and other communities, parishioners and the hierarchy clashed over the appointment or dismissal of parish priests. Ultimately, several schisms arose as parishioners left to establish autonomous churches. The most significant schism occurred in 1901, when a group of Poles established a separate institution, the Polish National Catholic Church. Other permanent schisms occurred among Lithuanian Catholics in Lawrence, Massachusetts, and Scranton, Pennsylvania.[67]

Some priests within these new ethnic communities argued that the hierarchy was not sufficiently addressing the problem of "leakage," claiming that the lack of national parishes led Catholics to fall away from the church or join Protestant denominations who recruited members from the Italian, Lithuanian, and other urban communities with some success. Catholics expressed their greatest concern over the potential for Italian leakage. In part because their religious devotion was not as closely tied to the parish as it was for other Catholics, Italian Catholics were generally less likely than others to seek separate national parishes and often joined existing territorial parishes.[68]

In the early twentieth century, Italian Catholics did not view their religiosity as based in the institution or practices of the parish, but rather as an extension of the *domus*, or family-centered community; moreover, their identity was more closely aligned with their regional rather than national origins. Mutual aid societies outside the church, for example, often required church membership and were heavily associated with one's regional background, which in turn became important in establishing ethnic neighborhoods and parishes in the urban United States. Such societies, often named for a patron saint, served as social centers and insured that no matter how poor, their members would receive a proper burial. Over time, these Italian mutual aid societies would frequently became associated with the parish itself.[69]

Increasingly, local mutual aid societies became part of a national fraternal organization. The largest Italian society, Figli d'Italia, or Sons of Italy, had 100,000 members by the early 1920s but was not officially affiliated with the church. One observer suggested that a shortage of Italian clergy and the modest number of Italian national parishes, relative to the population, accounted for Italians' disinclination toward establishing lay organizations and supporting educational institutions.[70]

Nationalism among eastern Europeans became both a spur to organizing lay efforts within the church and a source of friction. Catholics sought to support political independence for Lithuania, long dominated by Russia, and for Poland, ruled by Russia, Prussia, and Austria. But they eschewed movements embracing socialist ideals. In fact, Catholic groups' initiatives often came as a response to the organized activities of socialists and "freethinkers" with anticlerical views among those of their nationality in much the same way that other Catholic groups of the time reacted to Protestant proselytizing efforts in their communities.

In the late nineteenth and early twentieth centuries, many new immigrant Catholics created benevolent or fraternal organizations whose primary goal

was to offer their members insurance and, in some cases, disability benefits, although the preservation of national and religious identity was often a
concurrent goal. In fact, insurance benefits were a major component of the
Knights of Columbus and the Catholic Order of Foresters. Immigrants had
less access to financial institutions and often had high-risk jobs. Because the
government system of providing survivor's benefits would not become standard until the passage of the Social Security Act, such efforts were, in many
cases, a critical aspect of upward mobility. Insuring the household's bread-
winner would, in the event of injury or death, allow a family's children to continue their education rather than leave school early to replace those earnings.

One such major benevolent group arose among Bohemian Catholics in St.
Louis in 1879, initiated by Father Joseph Hessoun, pastor of the St. John
Nepomuk Parish from 1865 to 1906. Responding to an article in *Hlas* (Voice),
a Bohemian newspaper based in St. Louis, ten parish societies formed a
national society, wrote by-laws, named themselves the "Bohemian Roman
Catholic First Central Union," and agreed to a $300 death benefit. Most of its
members lived in the Midwest. Professor Joseph Cada has stated that "such a
movement was truly pioneering. The Bohemian immigrant had nothing like
it in the country from which he came." In addition to calling for the creation of a nationally based Central Union, Bohemian Catholics in St. John
Nepomuk Parish established both a St. Vincent de Paul Society conference
and then, in 1905, an orphanage, which they named after Father Hessoun.[71]

As their numbers grew, Lithuanian Catholics also began establishing
Catholic-based organizations by the end of the nineteenth century. Lithuanians, who were most numerous in Pennsylvania, New England, and Illinois,
had formed over 30 parishes by 1900 and 100 by 1920. About 80 percent of
Lithuanians who arrived in the United States in that period were Catholic.
Many came in the late nineteenth and early twentieth centuries to avoid being
drafted into the Russian army. Once they arrived, they supported Lithuanian
independence efforts. Often they shared a parish with Polish Catholics, but in
many cases those arrangements led to disputes as one or the other ethnic
group ultimately prevailed in establishing control of the parish. After 1890,
when Lithuanian immigration levels rose significantly, Lithuanians increasingly defined their cultural, religious, and social institutions separately from
those of Poles. Two Lithuanians, John Šliupas and Father Alexander Burba,
were particularly influential in that development. Although Šliupas initially
worked within the Catholic Church, the two men gradually became ideologi-
cal opponents in the debate over nationalism and the role of the clergy.[72]

One group, the American Lithuanian Roman Catholic Federation, arose in 1906 as a national organization comprised of many local and regional affiliates. Following what many Lithuanian priests saw as a growing socialist nationalist movement, the federation emerged in 1906 as a Catholic organization whose leaders came from both the clergy and the laity. It drew members from its local affiliates, including local lodges, Workers' Alliances, the Knights of Lithuania, the Catholic Alliance (a large mutual benefit organization), and a student organization. Yet the federation's growth, budget, and agenda soon stagnated. Some attributed the decline in lay interest to Lithuanians' diverting their efforts to purely national causes rather than focusing on religious issues; others blamed clerical indifference or the lack of interest among the laity in promoting the ideals of the federation. By World War II, Lithuanian Catholics mobilized in order to provide war relief to Lithuania.[73]

Polish Catholics established two major Catholic fraternal organizations at the national level—the Polish Roman Catholic Union (PRCU) and the Polish National Union (PNA). These two groups were rivals and identified themselves distinctly in relationship to Polish nationalism. Complex and protracted controversies arose between the two groups and their adherents, especially in Chicago. Leaders of the PRCU defined themselves as Catholic first and Poles second, while the PNA believed that ethnicity should be paramount. Each group criticized the other—in the first case, for being priest-ridden, and in the second, for being aligned too closely with socialist and anticlerical ideals. The PNA admitted priests into its ranks, but on equal footing with lay members. The PRCU was founded in 1873 by John Barzynski, along with Reverend Theodore Gieryk of Detroit. The organization, which emphasized the preservation of Catholicism among Poles and the development of a parochial school system among them, left little room for lay initiative or leadership. It also drew a sharp distinction between its goals and those of nationalist-oriented Polish Catholics.[74]

These intra-ethnic tensions, as well as the need to obtain economic stability for the community, the priest shortage, a distrust of the hierarchy, and competing conceptions of the communicant-clergy relationship within the parish, all mitigated against lay social reform efforts among new immigrant Catholics. But beginning in the late nineteenth century, and especially by the early twentieth century, lay reformers, mainly from Irish and German backgrounds, having gained greater confidence in their economic position, began to address the needs of these new immigrants, who were still focused on achieving greater economic stability. As subsequent chapters reveal, they did so by founding settlement houses, engaging in charity, and establishing port assistance programs, though those efforts also were often directed at new arrivals from the reformers' countries of origin. Despite class differences and tensions arising from disparate cultural traditions, Catholics from more established ethnic groups sought to forge bonds with new immigrant groups, based on their religious ties. Those efforts had decidedly mixed results. In a rapidly diversifying religion, many reformers understood that their Catholicism reflected European traditions and values. But they further recognized that such traditions would have to be reinterpreted in an American context that was often hostile to, or suspicious of, such differences.

· · · · ·

The Columbian Catholic Congress set a precedent for American Catholicism and for the development of lay activism in particular. In the face of several major controversies, the organizers of the congress sought to foster a consensus among Catholics, to demonstrate to fellow Americans the basic compatibility of their religion with American life and institutions, and to illustrate the fact that the church had a significant core of its members engaged in social and intellectual efforts. The issues debated at the congress, including those pertaining to ethnic retention and assimilation, gender, and the relationship of the laity to the clergy and hierarchy permeated much of social reform in the ensuing decades.

To some extent, these reform efforts were successful. Participants highlighted the Catholic roots of Columbus and promoted the concept of a Catholic legacy of America as an alternative to the Protestant English model. By including women, the congress organizers sought to forestall criticism that the church was outdated in its attitudes and practices. Yet public efforts to widen the role of laywomen did not occur without controversy. The narrowly defined arena for women reflected the Catholic hierarchy's general opposition to suffrage and its ambivalence toward women's involvement in lay reform.

Congress organizers encountered additional challenges from participants as well as from those outside the church. The congress itself served as evidence to members of the American Protective Association that Catholics were planning to subvert American institutions and the government. In response, and also because Americanists had organized it, the congress eschewed any mention of ethnic issues, including those pertaining to the Land League or the Central Verein, despite their saliency for many Catholics. Indeed, some German Catholics refused to participate. While congress organizers sought to emphasize the connections between Catholicism and American traditions, they could not ignore the growing ethnic diversity within the church that was evident by the 1890s. The subject was raised by Andreis's lectures and by those speaking on Irish colonization, charity, and poverty. M. E. Elder criticized the attempt to celebrate Catholicism's achievements at the expense of true dialogue about the church's efforts. Others questioned the prominent role of converts at the congress, or the attempt to prevent lay criticism during the forum. Moreover, the congress led Cardinal Satolli and Pope Leo to conclude that the lay congress was a dangerous event. Indeed, the pope criticized Catholic participation in the World's Parliament of Religions. In 1895 he issued the apostolic letter *Longingue Oceani,* which praised the progress of the church in America but stated that the separation of church and state should not be a universal goal and that most secret societies would continue to be viewed as dangerous. He then dealt an even more severe blow to the Americanists with the 1899 *Testem Benevolentiae.*[75]

To a large extent, the 1893 Catholic Congress defined the parameters of lay involvement in social reform in the late nineteenth and twentieth centuries. It had important ramifications for lay activists, including William Onahan and others active in the St. Vincent de Paul Society and in temperance, colonization, and women's groups. Despite the restrictions placed on the laity, many continued to launch or support their own groups to address the needs and issues of contemporary Catholic life. Sometimes they did so over the objections of the clergy or hierarchy. During the 1893 congress, the role of laywomen was the subject of especially intense controversy, and in the ensuing decades, women's reform efforts would also become a major issue of contention. Likewise, the inclusion of African Americans in the congress suggested a more enlightened attitude toward race relations than had been associated with Catholics in the past, despite the fact that public effort to expand the role of black Catholics did not occur without tensions.

The Americanist controversy was also apparent in the activities and attitudes of the Catholic laity. By celebrating America's Catholic legacy in a time of renewed anti-Catholicism, Catholics displayed a confidence that was important to gaining new members and adherents to their reform activities. The church's growth outside the Northeast allowed for new focuses in the activities undertaken by the laity, including efforts in rural colonization and the development of German Catholic women's groups in the Midwest. Archbishop John Ireland, Bishop John Lancaster Spalding, and other midwesterners were the most supportive of lay actions, whereas Archbishop Corrigan and others tended to restrict the types of lay activities that were possible in their regions.

The catalysts for greater involvement by Catholics in lay social reform efforts were similar to those influencing their participation in the World's Fair of 1893, an event that highlighted the church's economic and moral successes while reflecting idealized notions of the past. Countering the idea that they were newcomers to the United States, Catholics at the fair traced their American origins to Columbus and linked their religion to the nation's democratic institutions and initiatives. "Old" Catholics legitimized their position by developing social reform efforts that demonstrated they were agents for improving society and not simply the objects of such efforts.

By engaging in reform, Catholics proved that they could devote time and resources to the needs of their less fortunate coreligionists and thus influence the future of their urban communities. *Rerum Novarum* served as a major impetus for Catholics to address social issues arising from industrial capitalism, such as poverty and immigration, and further illustrated the compatibility of church doctrine with its members' participation in American political and social institutions. Such reform efforts improved the reputation of Catholics and demonstrated to other Americans the international roots and Catholic dimensions of the reform tradition, as well as the long-standing history of social reform within the Catholic Church.

Combating "Whisky's Work"

• • • • •

Masculinity, Ethnicity, and Catholic Temperance Reform

Temperance has been a very significant topic to historians. Many studies on the subject in the United States have focused on the early nineteenth century, and much of that scholarship has stressed issues such as the role of temperance in the workplace and in working-class culture, its importance among women, and its ties to antebellum Protestantism. Paul Faler, for example, has emphasized the ways in which employers used temperance as an instrument of social control, as well as the ways in which some workers themselves embraced the issue. Others have stressed the relationship of temperance reform among women in the late nineteenth century to the development of the women's rights movement, women's political activism, and domestic ideologies.[1]

Historians who have discussed the temperance and prohibition movement in the United States have largely ignored or made only cursory mention of Catholic efforts in this arena. Readers of these works are often left with the impression that Catholics were opposed or indifferent to temperance.[2] Yet, during the late nineteenth and early twentieth centuries, a group of Catholics in the United States embraced this reform at the local as well as the national level. Their efforts did not merely reflect the influences of the Protestant-oriented movement. Instead, American Catholics drew extensively from an earlier movement launched by Father Theobold Mathew, a Catholic friar in Ireland. While Joan Bland's 1951 study, *The Hibernian Crusade*, provides an important institutional history of the Catholic Total Abstinence Union, her monograph predates recent historical debates over issues of the nature of social reform, gender, ethnicity, and class formation. While Irish historians have recently written on Catholic temperance organizations in Ireland, they do not discuss the impact those organizations had on Catholics in the United States.[3]

This chapter analyzes the ways in which Catholics adapted temperance reform to their particular circumstances in the United States. Members of total abstinence groups sought to challenge stereotypes of Irish immigrants as intemperate and to achieve a reputation of respectability for themselves among Americans as a whole. For some Catholics these concerns reflected a growing identification with the values of the American middle class, and sometimes membership in it. Rather than simply appropriating the strategies, arguments, and traditions of Protestant-oriented efforts in this arena, Irish American advocates stressed the connections between temperance, Irish nationalism, and the American labor movement. They further sought to demonstrate that these three issues were complementary and had similar constituencies. In fact, many temperance reformers were also active in at least one of those other movements, such as rural colonization, the Knights of Labor, or the Land League, thereby creating a transatlantic network of Catholic social reformers. Catholic advocates also differentiated themselves from Protestants in their approach to abstinence by stressing suasion and sociability as opposed to compulsion and denial. Finally, during an era in which women had moved to the forefront of the Protestant-oriented temperance movement, Catholics in late-nineteenth-century America considered abstinence a male movement. Although Catholic women eventually gained a place in the movement by the 1890s, their influence as a whole remained limited. This situation resulted from their status as religious and ethnic minorities and from skepticism about the reform among their coreligionists.

Father Mathew's American Tour

Father Theobold Mathew, a Capuchin friar from Cork, came to the United States in 1849, a decade after launching the popular temperance movement in Ireland. As he had traveled around Ireland, people from throughout the countryside gathered in cities and towns to hear him speak. He administered to those crowds a pledge to abstain from alcohol.[4] Father Mathew's leadership of the Catholic temperance movement had originated at the suggestion of an Irish Quaker, William Martin, and he was also encouraged by Unitarian and Protestant clergymen. Although the movement resulted from a Protestant initiative, it soon took on particular significance for Catholics, first in Ireland and then in the United States.

Father Theobold Mathew.
(From Maguire, Father
Mathew*)*

Father Mathew received such enthusiastic support from the poor in Ireland that, while some English leaders welcomed his movement, others worried that it would ignite a popular revolt against English rule.[5] Despite Mathew's reluctance to enter the political sphere, the mass movement gained momentum in the 1840s, when it coincided and sometimes overlapped with Daniel O'Connell's unsuccessful movement to repeal the Act of Union that had deprived Ireland of a separate parliament. In fact, as Emmet Larkin has argued, these two revival movements contributed to a devotional revolution in Irish religious practice. During a period of less than fifty years, the percentage of the Irish Catholic population who regularly attended mass increased from a prefamine level of about 33 percent to 90 percent, where it remained into the 1970s.[6]

During his two-year visit to the United States, the "Apostle of Temperance" toured the country, spending a great deal of time in Boston and New York. Mathew sought to promote his campaign among American Catholics and to encourage large numbers of them to "take the pledge." Toward the end of his tour, he ventured into the South, where Catholics remained a small minority, and lectured in cities such as Mobile, New Orleans, and Hot Springs.

Throughout his journey, he appeared at public forums that included politicians and Protestant ministers. He spoke before large and enthusiastic crowds, many of whose members had come to take the pledge from him. A White House dinner with President Fillmore highlighted Mathew's influence.[7]

The Making of an American Movement

Father Mathew and the Catholic total abstinence movement eventually became synonymous. Yet the movement did not gain widespread appeal in the United States until the 1870s, two decades after his tour. Despite the large audiences he drew, support for Father Mathew did not immediately translate into the establishment of a temperance campaign among Catholics in mid-century America. In the United States, the popularity of the reform effort coincided with the emergence of a large Catholic population with middle-class aspirations, which did not yet exist at midcentury.

The temperance movement failed to take hold among Catholics until the 1870s both because of the prejudice that existed toward Catholics and immigrants and also as a result of Catholic uneasiness with existing temperance groups. In the United States, temperance had roots in the Protestant Second Great Awakening of the early nineteenth century and, later, in "separate spheres" ideology, whereby women initially fought alcohol abuse in the name of home protection. Those involved in temperance efforts and other social reforms were often also responding to significant changes and growth in society, including immigration. Many American temperance organizations were clearly antagonistic to Catholicism and, despite the alarming rate of alcohol use among Americans prior to the mid-nineteenth century, sometimes treated "rum" as if it were a byproduct of "Romanism." Likewise, many within the Woman's Christian Temperance Union (WCTU) openly expressed their anti-immigrant views. Even Frances Willard of the WCTU, who initiated overtures toward the Catholic Total Abstinence Union (CTAU) in the wake of criticism by others in her organization, departed from her relatively tolerant view of immigrants at the 1892 WCTU convention. There she called for Congress to "enact a stringent immigration law prohibiting the influx into our land of more of the scum of the Old World, until we have educated those who are here." Such comments did nothing to assuage Catholic apprehensions about the WCTU.[8]

Catholics were absent from secular and Protestant-based temperance groups for other reasons as well. Their reluctance to join some early temperance societies stemmed in part from secret society prohibitions by the Catholic Church, which conflicted with requirements of some fraternally based groups, including the Sons of Temperance.[9] Moreover, the very names of popular temperance groups, such as the Sons of Temperance and the Washingtonian societies, harkened back to a native-born, Revolutionary-era tradition with limited appeal to those whose forebears had arrived far more recently.

Moreover, the Catholic total abstinence movement often encountered unenthusiastic responses from priests at the local level and from some bishops as well. Members of the Priests' Total Abstinence League (PTAL), a small national temperance group begun in 1900, expressed frustration that their colleagues not only were unenthusiastic about the issue but also occasionally expressed hostility toward its proponents. They articulated their concern that alcohol abuse among priests created a scandal. They also sought greater support for this often neglected issue among bishops and within the Vatican.

While temperance groups had priests as their spiritual directors, many directors were routinely absent from the regular meetings, and many did not abstain from alcohol themselves.[10] Reverend Ferdinand Kittel, a Pennsylvania priest active in the movement, described his frustration when Bishop Eugene Garvey of Altoona, whom he had invited to speak on the subject of total abstinence, "launched out into a bitter tirade against 'zealots' [and] 'Holier than thou' people, 'Pharisees who thank God that they are not like the rest of men,' . . . 'Hard Shell Baptists,' etc., etc." Kittel further bemoaned the fact that there were heavy drinkers in the audience, and others "who are on their feet after many falls," who took refuge in the bishop's remarks. He concluded that his attempt to organize a branch of the PTAL in the diocese would fail.[11] This reaction was especially ironic given the popularity of Catholic temperance societies in Pennsylvania, including Philadelphia and Scranton.

Despite these obstacles, the Catholic temperance movement did grow in the final decades of the nineteenth century. The movement never rivaled Protestant-based groups in popularity, but by the early twentieth century almost 90,000 members and over 1,000 societies were affiliated with the national Catholic Total Abstinence Union. The CTAU, formed in 1872, had affiliates throughout the country, especially in the Northeast and Midwest. In 1895 Philadelphia alone had 164 Catholic total abstinence societies, with 15,196 members in good standing. Participation in public parades and celebrations supporting the movement numbered in the thousands, and by some estimates, even in the tens of thousands. In the last decades of the century, some Catholic newspapers published more articles on total abstinence than on any other organized lay activity. In addition to covering temperance activity at the local and national levels, the Milwaukee *Catholic Citizen* published a column, "Whisky's Work," detailing crimes and misfortunes arising from excess drink. In the 1890s the *Pilot* ran a weekly column by a total abstainer, Edmund Phelan, who reported on Catholic temperance activities in the Boston area.[12]

In the United States, Catholic total abstinence advocates promoted efforts that would prove acceptable to the larger society by stressing the values of self-control and, to a lesser extent, thrift. Total abstinence represented a self-help movement in which the individual, who was nearly always male, could attain economic self-sufficiency and improve his family life by abstaining from alcohol. The movement's major goal was not to reform or redeem the "drunkard" but to prevent the individual's descent into alcohol abuse in the first place. In this way, it differed from the early-nineteenth-century Washingtonian society, which included many reformed alcoholics.

Catholic temperance reform efforts also contrasted with those of Protestant-oriented groups in terms of strategies. While Protestant groups eventually embraced legislative means toward attaining a sober nation, including the prohibition of alcohol's manufacture and sale, their Catholic counterparts generally avoided that approach. With the exception of high license laws and local restrictions on saloons, Catholics favored moral suasion over legislative coercion. That strategy included prohibiting men who earned their living through the production or sale of liquor from joining the Society of St. Vincent de Paul, the most important lay charitable society in the church.[13]

A minority of Catholic abstainers, however, eschewed or reinterpreted the official church position against prohibition. Archbishop Patrick J. Ryan of Philadelphia favored a Pennsylvania prohibition measure. He subsequently stressed that this opinion was a personal one and reiterated the official position that alcohol abuse, but not its mere use, was incompatible with Catholic doctrine. In 1883 a writer in the *Catholic Citizen* answered the rhetorical headline "Can a Catholic Be a Prohibitionist" in the affirmative. "We would much rather see a Catholic prohibitionist than a Catholic drunkard or a Catholic free whisky advocate. . . . Is it not known that Father Mathew, the world renowned founder of the total abstinence movement pronounced himself in favor of prohibition[?]"[14] Skeptical of the overzealousness in the temperance movement as a whole, Catholics in the United States distanced themselves from existing prohibitionist groups, including those of Protestants. Depictions of temperance advocates as humorless or disapproving worked to dissuade large numbers of Catholics from joining their cause, and the total abstinence societies were keenly aware of this danger. As one writer, attributing a recent drop in CTAU membership in 1880 to the prohibition sentiments of temperance advocates as a whole, put it: "Zealots are an injury to any cause: they are a destructive species under any circumstances, but the intemperate temperance man is the most intolerable fanatic of them all." This writer also concluded that many opposed to temperance did not comprehend the crucial distinction between prohibition and moral suasion.[15]

To counter the stereotypes of temperance advocates as "fanatics" and "Puritans,"[16] Catholics active in the movement portrayed themselves as fun-loving and social people who, while forsaking alcohol, were nevertheless the first to enjoy themselves in late-night revelry and were far from self-righteous in their mission. St. Stephen's total abstinence society, for example, held a party until the "wee small hours" with an orchestra and a catered supper. Coverage of temperance society events also emphasized the support of the "ladies," who were not formally involved in the movement but whose support was often symbolized by the presentation of a silk banner to a male society by "their lady friends." Those casual references suggested that young women found temperate men as attractive as men who drank. To counter "the oft-repeated charge that total abstinence makes men selfish and uncharitable," temperance advocates extolled Father Mathew's legendary reputation as a kind and compassionate man, especially toward the poor.[17]

Temperance as an Ethnic Issue

German Catholics were especially critical of the temperance movement. They generally felt that temperance, if carried too far, would impinge upon their right to continue certain cultural traditions in the United States, including Sunday beer gardens. In 1910 *Central-Blatt and Social Justice*, a publication sponsored by the Central Verein, a national federation of German Catholic parish mutual aid societies that became increasingly involved in larger social reform and religious issues, reprinted an article that criticized the Catholic Total Abstinence Union: "[T]he delegates conducted themselves as Protestant fanatics rather than Catholic Temperance advocates. . . . Many of the speeches given by Catholic priests would have been a credit to Carrie Nation."

The article went on to assert that temperance advocates should refrain from "fanatical onslaughts [against those] who happen to differ from them quite legitimately."[18]

An earlier controversy between Bishop Michael O'Connor of Pittsburgh and Father Boniface Wimmer in the 1850s prefigured the tension that would emerge between lay German and Irish Catholics over the temperance movement. Father Wimmer, founder of the American Benedictines, had established a brewery in Indiana, Pennsylvania, in the tradition of the Benedictine Abbey in Metten, Bavaria, which had been brewing beer since 1322. O'Connor, a temperance advocate, objected to the brewery and, at the same time, opposed Wimmer's plans to establish St. Vincent's Abbey in Westmoreland County, Pennsylvania, as an independent abbot. When Wimmer wrote to his patron, Ludwig of Bavaria, to request that he intervene on his behalf, O'Connor expressed his concern to Abbot Bernard Smith at the Vatican.[19]

German Americans could easily reconcile the image of a good Catholic with that of a drinker, even if a woman. In Boston, *Monatsbote*, a German parish publication, reported on the death of Christine Berresheim, "one of the most faithful and devoted members" of the church, who was, with her husband, the proprietor of a saloon. The article referred to her extensive knowledge of the bar trade, and her belief that "a woman needs a drink just as a man does." She was said to have conceded, though, that most women should limit themselves to four glasses of beer, even if a few women could drink "a glass of whiskey and six or seven glasses of beer without being foolish." Germans argued that drinking was an integral aspect of German culture. German Catholics had established many breweries in Milwaukee, St. Louis, and other cities. They staunchly maintained that they should not have to abide by restrictions on alcohol merely because Irish Catholics in the United States had a reputation for abusing it. Moreover, while the German reputation for drinking was widely recognized, because of their greater economic success they suffered less from drinking-related stereotypes than their less prosperous coreligionists.[20]

Among Catholics in late-nineteenth-century America, then, temperance became an Irish issue. For a population of Irish immigrants and their children, temperance represented an important point of continuity with Ireland. Many leaders and members of the movement had immigrated to the United States from Ireland. Bishop John Ireland of St. Paul, Minnesota, who served as a major figure in the promotion of American temperance efforts in the late nineteenth century, had emigrated to the United States from Kilkenny. Reverend Thomas Conaty had moved to Massachusetts from outside Dublin as a small boy, while Reverend Peter Cooney had been born in County Roscommon. Leonora Barry Lake, a leader in the both the Catholic temperance and American labor movements, emigrated from County Cork, the heart of the Irish temperance movement. Another native Irishman, Jeremiah Crowley, was in 1889 the president of the Father Mathew Society of Sacred Heart Parish of East Cambridge, the oldest continually organized temperance society in the archdiocese of Boston. Crowley also served as president of the Catholic Total Abstinence Union in the archdiocese and as grand marshal of at least one Boston total abstinence parade.[21]

More than a half century after Father Mathew launched the movement, total abstinence supporters still boasted that they, or their fathers, had taken the pledge from Mathew, either during his American tour or as youngsters in Ireland during the 1840s. James Carbery from Dayton, Ohio, wrote to the Boston *Pilot* in 1902: "I took the pledge from him at Dunshaughlin, County Meath, Ireland, January 16, 1841, when I was not quite eight years old." Patrick Spillane from Lowell, Massachusetts, writing in 1890, recalled taking the pledge in Skibbereen in February 1841 and joining the "band of the society which escorted him on his missions in West Cork," adding "[I] am now turned sixty years of age, and never drank a glass of intoxicating drink in my life." Other men, who had reached their eighties by the end of the nineteenth century or later, remembered having taken the pledge as adults. The appeal extended to an American-born generation as well, as parents who took the pledge brought up their children to honor total abstinence goals. Many of these "original Father Mathew men" rode in open carriages during temperance parades and celebrations. The veneration of these elderly veterans of Father Mathew's movement paralleled the honors given to veterans of the American Revolution and the Civil War in urban parades.[22]

While the temperance movement reflected Irish Catholics' links with their homeland, it also demonstrated their efforts to redeem themselves within the United States. In the late nineteenth century, as more Irish Americans entered the middle class, they sought to distance themselves from pervasive American stereotypes about the Irish propensity toward heavy drinking and alcoholism. Catholic total abstainers believed that all American Catholics suffered the ill effects of intemperate behavior by their coreligionists. Associated with urban squalor, violence, and poverty, Irish Catholics remained second-class citizens in the United States. Therefore, while some aspects of Catholic temperance reform, such as its emphasis on ameliorating poverty and improving family life, mirrored the efforts of Protestants, other dimensions reflected the need to improve the position of Irish Catholics in American society.[23]

While all temperance advocates viewed abstinence as a means to improve the status of Catholics in American society, they disagreed sharply over whether or not there was truth to the prevailing view that the Irish had a comparatively greater proclivity toward excessive alcohol use than did other groups. Some temperance advocates defended their compatriots by claiming that drinking among the Irish was no more prevalent than among other Europeans and, in fact, that rates of alcohol consumption were lower among the Irish than among Scottish and English populations.[24] Reverend William Dollard, speaking in New Brunswick, Canada, declared, "Great pains have been taken by our enemies to make [drinking and brawling] our national characteristics. . . . The normal condition of any Irish community, at home or abroad, in spite of all slander, is sober, pious and industrious." Peter Cooney, a midwestern priest, held that intemperance was not confined to a "particular nation or race."[25]

Other temperance advocates took the opposite position, asserting that drunkenness, or alcoholism, was in fact a particular weakness among the Irish, for which complete avoidance of alcohol was the most prudent remedy. Bishop Ireland, for example, claimed that "alcohol does them more harm, because their warm nature yields more readily to its flames."[26] In the same speech, Ireland also attributed crime in Dublin to alcohol consumption. John Francis Maguire, Father Mathew's biographer and a lay temperance advocate, reached a similar conclusion after a visit to the United States. Maguire maintained, according to Peter Cooney, that "the source of weakness and of failure amongst a large proportion of Irish people in that country was their love of intoxicating drink, and their unwillingness to turn their backs upon the insidious tempter and *tyrant.*"[27] In 1898 the *Pilot*, reporting on the CTAU convention, concurred with this view, noting that drunkenness still occurred in New England among immigrants and their children, although heavy drinking had been common among native-stock Americans in the mid-nineteenth century. Cooney's comment suggested that what separated Irish Americans from other groups was not a particular proclivity to drunkenness, but a lack of sufficient organized effort to eradicate the problem.[28]

Some proponents of temperance condemned drinking customs, including the practice of "treating," or buying rounds for one's companions. They viewed this practice as a particularly Irish phenomenon, and one that originated from good intentions rather than from moral weakness. As a writer in one temperance column stated, "The Irish spirit of hospitality reinforced by a false notion of good fellowship, no doubt originated the fashion, which soon became a grievous abuse of both instincts." Yet the practice of treating occurred throughout England and Scotland as well.[29]

Temperance advocates appealed to nationalists by linking the two causes and thereby broadening support for abstinence. In a lecture in Elizabeth, New Jersey, Father Thomas Burke, a major temperance organizer there, argued that drunkenness served as an Achilles heel for the Irish. As an example, he asserted that the English proved victorious in the infamous 1798 battle on Vinegar Hill in Wicklow because English soldiers had remained sober on the eve of the battle, while the Irish participated in revelry to such a degree that they were unprepared for warfare. He concluded that it was not the English who defeated the Irish, but "the demon of drunkenness." For his part, Bishop Ireland declared that temperance was "the work of true patriotism."[30]

Parallels between colonialism and alcoholism, or conversely, between freedom and total abstinence, were especially prevalent in the 1880s among Catholic temperance advocates in the United States.[31] In this period, Charles Parnell and the Land League sparked renewed hopes among Irish Americans for increased Irish autonomy. In fact, temperance reform and the Land League vied for attention among Irish Catholics in the United States to such an extent that the CTAU's "Bulletin" pleaded with members to remember the temperance cause amidst their involvement in the Land League. Alexander Sullivan, president of the Irish National League in the United States, a later incarnation of the Land League, spoke before the CTAU convention held in Brooklyn in 1885: "The cause of Ireland had no hope of success unless Irishmen were temperate. . . . It was only necessary to spread temperance among the Irish and God Almighty might do the rest. God had made the Irish naturally temperate, and if he kept from rum he would be successful."[32] Sullivan implied that sobriety was a prerequisite for independence, and that both colonial rule and alcoholism led to impoverishment and dependence in the individual and society.[33]

Although the CTAU proclaimed itself a religious, nonpolitical organization, it never completely avoided politics. Instead, it proclaimed support for various political efforts in Ireland. Among its 1883 resolutions was a proclamation that "the Irish people are our people. That as in past conventions as also now, we proclaim our heartfelt sympathy with the demand for their rights; and we rejoice exceedingly in the success which is attending their efforts and to the great organizations devoted to the Ireland's welfare, we extend our cordial greeting."[34] Numerous local temperance societies in Wisconsin sent donations to Ireland in support of relief of a second famine in the 1880s, further demonstrating the persistence of close ties between Ireland and United States. Yet Land League support was not universal. Bishop Richard Gilmour of Cleveland ignited a major controversy when he denounced the Ladies' Land League chapter there and threatened to excommunicate its members.[35]

In addition to supporting a self-help philosophy, those who advanced the position that the Irish had a weakness for alcohol implicitly suggested that colonialism was not singularly responsible for the political problems of Irish life. They insinuated that these problems emerged, in part, from a more fundamental weakness in Irish character and behavior. That many Americans viewed heavy drinking as a characteristic of Irish Catholics served as a stumbling block to gaining new members for the church and perpetuated anti-Catholicism. Father Morgan Sheedy quoted Bishop Ireland at the 1892 CTAU convention as arguing that intemperance "paralyzes our forces, awakens in the minds of our non-Catholic fellow-citizens violent prejudices."[36] Others supported temperance as one of many reforms and acknowledged that colonialism was indeed a major factor in the economic problems that the Irish had encountered. These advocates did not view alcohol abuse as an inherent character flaw among the Irish but as a problem that had been exaggerated by stereotype and exacerbated by circumstances, both in Ireland and in the United States.

The most common arguments on behalf of temperance were those that promoted it as a solution to various social ills and as a way to improve the family economy, domestic life, and health. Other temperance advocates likened the consumption of alcohol, with its relatively high price tag, to a tax on the working class. In Boston, for example, Father William Byrne noted that many workingmen objected to a $2 poll tax but voluntarily spent $100 a year in saloons. He observed that an individual could rent ten to twelve acres of land in Ireland for the amount he spent on liquor. While advocates hastened to add that the wealthy also succumbed to alcohol abuse, they nevertheless maintained that the poor suffered more because of their precarious economic position.[37]

In his diary entries in 1898, James A. Walsh, a Catholic priest in a Roxbury, Massachusetts, parish, chronicled several cases where a family member's excessive drinking resulted in physical abuse, destitution, heartache, or other problems. Often one family member would request that Walsh intervene in a domestic dispute involving alcohol. In the Murphy family, for example, the husband and father had disappeared. After Walsh helped Mrs. Murphy and one of her sons obtain jobs, the "father returned and was foolishly admitted. Then came a succession of troubles—man arrested for drink—returned—drunk again—promised confession, never came—blackened wife's eye—wife in drink—child ill—sent to Carney [Hospital]. . . . Finally induced the mother to take out warrant for father's arrest—which has kept him away for the past month." Walsh added that Mrs. Murphy also drank to excess but "keeps to her work."[38]

In order to increase the appeal of total abstinence, proponents emphasized the positive effects engendered by an individual commitment to temperance. They commonly argued that abstaining from alcohol allowed Catholics to become upwardly mobile and economically secure. In fact, Catholic temperance appealed to laborers and labor leaders in a way that other Catholic reform activities did not. Of the members of the Father Mathew Society at Sacred Heart Parish in East Cambridge who could be located in the city directory of 1889, most were skilled workers or day laborers, along with a few small-scale proprietors. Other historians studying the socioeconomic profile of Catholic temperance groups in late-nineteenth- and early-twentieth-century Massachusetts have described members as having some attributes associated with the middle class, such as residential stability, but not occupational mobility. In general, local members did not hold white-collar positions.[39]

In Pennsylvania especially, labor leaders realized that they could broaden their appeal among Catholics by supporting temperance efforts, and therefore the two issues of labor and temperance were used by proponents to reinforce one another, as was the case with temperance and political freedom. Reverend James Cleary of Wisconsin said: "The worst foes of the laborers are heartless, avaricious labor capital on the one hand, and the tempting, alluring saloon on the other. Those who help him to avoid the latter are at the same time helping him to secure his rights from the former."[40]

Terence Powderly, general master workman of the Knights of Labor, and later U.S. commissioner for immigration, served as a potent symbol for the Catholic total abstinence movement. He espoused many of the economic and domestic arguments regularly used by total abstainers. In 1887 he stated that he had taken the pledge and had kept it for nineteen years. Powderly was born in the anthracite coal district of Pennsylvania, one of the strongholds of the Catholic temperance movement. His parents had emigrated from Ireland to

New York State and then moved to Pennsylvania. Powderly, who sported a pince-nez and a neatly groomed handlebar moustache, had served as mayor of Scranton in his twenties before ascending to leadership of the Knights of Labor.[41]

Unlike many advocates of total abstinence, Powderly viewed the cause as a universal one for workers, rather than as a primarily ethnic issue. Powderly disagreed with Bishop Ireland's assertion that the Irish were exceptionally prone to alcohol abuse. He stated, "I have been among all nationalities, and have seen that the one withering curse, the demon that shatters every home, is drink." In addition to appearing at CTAU functions, Powderly spoke out at labor meetings on the importance of temperance. He told a labor audience of 4,000 in Boston, called in support of shoemakers who had been locked out of work for twenty weeks: "I know that the most damning curse to the laborer is that which gurgles from the neck of the bottle." And he urged his listeners to refrain from alcohol consumption.[42]

Powderly's position clearly favored moral suasion and opposed employers' efforts to control their workers through temperance. He claimed that his own views on total abstinence derived from his experiences visiting workers in their homes and argued that drunkenness should be avoided "for the sake of their families and to maintain positions of respectability in society."[43] He therefore promoted total abstinence as a self-help movement that would allow laborers to improve their economic and social positions in the United States. Like many supporters of Catholic total abstinence, Powderly sought to distance the issue from the existing Protestant-oriented movement. In his autobiography, he criticized prohibition as ineffectual and accused some pro-hibitionists of embracing the cause not to better the condition of working-men, but so they could pay less to laborers who did not drink.[44]

John Mitchell, an early leader of the United Mine Workers Union, was neither a total abstainer nor a Catholic. In fact, after years of abstinence and moderate drinking, he developed a severe drinking problem by 1906. Nevertheless, Mitchell recognized total abstinence as an issue that he needed to address in order to win the allegiance of Catholic workers in the anthracite coal fields; Catholics had organized 143 temperance societies in the Scranton diocese alone. To obtain the support of Irish and other immigrant workers, Mitchell solicited the support of Bishop Michael Hoban and Father John J. Curran for his efforts to organize labor. In 1905 he even appeared at a CTAU convention in Wilkes-Barre, Pennsylvania.[45]

Reconciling temperance with other social reform issues such as labor reform, land reform for Ireland, or discrimination against Catholics in the United States was not always easy. Total abstinence arguments tended to stress the role of an individual's behavior or a group's cultural practices. In contrast, those concerned with other issues, such as labor and Irish political reform, viewed the problems they identified as emerging from larger economic and political systems.

Activists who sought to associate temperance issues with other reforms had to tread a fine line to avoid claiming that intemperance alone explained the causes underlying poor conditions of laborers and Irish poverty, for example. Because Catholic temperance emphasized the creation of a cultural and moral atmosphere that would eradicate excessive drinking, political solutions such as prohibition were less important than they were to other groups. But temperance groups did not ignore the fact that conditions such as poverty, poor job opportunities, urban crowding, and the dearth of recreational alternatives all contributed to alcohol use and abuse. Therefore, while intemperance could result in poverty, many temperance advocates also acknowledged the reverse—that the conditions surrounding poverty often led to intemperance.

A Men's Movement: Temperance Activity at the Local Level

Alcohol use and efforts to limit it were predominantly male issues among Catholics in the United States. At the local level, total abstinence societies remained segregated by sex, despite the fact that women and children had comprised an important base of Father Mathew's efforts and support in Ireland.[46] In part, this occurred because the creation of an extensive network of local organizations was an American Catholic development. Father Mathew never emphasized the formation of locally based societies once his followers took the pledge from him, and this lack of sustained organization had contributed to the dissipation of the temperance movement in Ireland during the famine. Some historians have noted Mathew's desire to maintain control over all aspects of his movement and his reluctance to delegate responsibility to others. That situation, in turn, meant that the movement in Ireland was based on his leadership alone, rather than on institutions he helped to create.[47] During the transition to a formal organization of Catholic temperance societies in the United States, however, women were effectively excluded from participation in the movement.

Because Catholic total abstinence groups sought to avoid being portrayed either as "unmanly" or "Puritan" by other Catholics, they emphasized male-oriented social activities in their organizations. Temperance advocates were concerned that the issue would be perceived by the Catholic population at large as unmanly because it challenged the prevalent tradition of heavy social drinking that existed among male friends in Ireland, a tradition that immigrants brought with them to the United States.[48] Including women in their movement would further fuel charges of unmanliness, and therefore total abstainers initially defined temperance as a masculine movement.

The emphasis on bands and military drills suggests the extent to which masculinity became important. Bands served as a point of continuity with the Father Mathew tradition in Ireland; they often accompanied a leading temperance advocate and his followers at public forums. Catholic newspapers reported on well-attended parades in public areas, which often emphasized military-style uniforms and displays. In 1888 the members of the Sacred Heart Parish temperance society participated in a parade in which "[its] banner, the soldierly bearing and natty uniforms of the Cadets elicited the admiration and praise of all who saw them." Their uniforms had lavish detailing and military insignias, and the "cadets" were armed with battle axes, "which they wielded with such ease and dexterity in various ways as to excite the wonder and admiration of military experts and gained them many friends."[49] These parades, along with uniforms, were an important recruitment device for young Catholic men.

Many of the Catholic Total Abstinence Union conventions featured a torch-light parade in their opening ceremonies. By 1910, seven "regiments" of the CTAU had been formed in Boston. They had modeled themselves on the Wilkes-Barre, Pennsylvania, regiment "as a means of winning converts." The 500-member Wilkes-Barre regiment held an annual "encampment" in Cambridge's Russell Field. That an Irish Catholic organization should emphasize military practices is significant. Because so many of the men involved in temperance activities were immigrants or sons of immigrants, the majority would not have participated in the Civil War, nor would their forebears have participated in other organized military efforts, such as the Revolutionary War. Following the Spanish American War, such martial events became even more popular among diverse groups of American men as an expression of masculine patriotism. While this military regiment was in part an extension of the parades and bands that were indigenous to Father Mathew's campaign, these rituals had been translated into more current and American cultural practices.[50]

The Father Mathew Total Abstinence Society, North Billerica, Massachusetts.
(From Dinneen, Catholic Total Abstinence Movement)

Catholic total abstinence societies also served as de facto fraternal organizations. Because the Catholic Church prohibited membership in secret societies, practicing Catholics were effectively barred from joining many existing fraternal organizations. Consequently, some Catholic men relied on temperance societies for some of the functions of a fraternal club. Indeed, in at least one society, members addressed each other as "brother." They shared aspects of fraternalism with unions and associations such as the Ancient Order of Hibernians and the Catholic Order of Foresters.[51]

Members used sports and other manly amusements as an inducement in order to increase membership in their societies. The members of the Father Mathew Total Abstinence Society of Sacred Heart Parish in East Cambridge debated over whether the society could afford to repair the pool table cloth and purchase new equipment for their hall. They also proposed starting a baseball team and establishing socials every Saturday evening. Baseball became so popular that twelve societies formed a league in 1888. Baseball attracted younger members of the Irish Catholic population; by incorporating the sport into the total abstinence movement's program, the movement adapted to late-nineteenth-century urban American culture while essentially serving the same ends as Father Mathew envisioned. Boat rides and other excursions also served as attractions. Members of temperance societies in St. Louis, for example, took a boat ride on the Mississippi in conjunction with the visit of the secretary of the Illinois Total Abstinence Union. One reporter noted: "[E]verything in the passage of the boat from and back to the city, in the pleasant grove of the Illinois shore, in the smiling faces of the ladies was such as to render the day and evening an occasion of real enjoyment."[52]

Many groups provided material comforts and benefits to their members. Father Mathew had made reading rooms a cornerstone of his movement. He envisioned a place in which "[w]orking men could sit at the bright fire of the reading-room without risk of temptation, hearing the news, discussing the topics of the hour, or glorying in the cause from which they were taught to expect honour and lasting advantage to their country. These reading rooms [w]ere long assumed an important feature in the movement and became one of its most effective means of practical organization."[53]

Father Mathew's vision was replicated in the United States, but as one of a series of practical activities of the movement. The temperance hall was often a focal point of activity and a place in which to hold dances and other celebrations. In some instances, the hall was lavishly furnished by contemporary standards. One temperance society in Charlestown planned to erect a hall "in the Romanesque style of architecture" for $30,000. The building was to be constructed of "faced brick, with freestone trimmings and terra cotta enrichments," would contain a hall for 1,000, a gymnasium, a spacious library, and rooms for officials of the society, and would be "lighted by the incandescent system." Reporting on the new hall of the Lawrence, Massachusetts, society, an observer stated: "At first those who interested themselves in the cause were considered fanatics, but, happily, this has been lived down." He noted that the hall provided "rooms for gentlemen" and featured a piazza, library, and a chandelier, adding, "The temperate man shows how he can enjoy himself better after his day's work than the man who feels as though he 'must have a glass.'" In Philadelphia, the largest total abstinence society in the country had a fund for burials, a sick fund that had paid out $23,000 in benefits, and a hall "purchased and fitted up at a cost of $21,000," as well as a circulating library.[54]

While cultural uplift was a component of these temperance halls, in general, fraternalism and militarism, as well as sports and recreation, were more heavily emphasized than libraries and lectures, in part because of a fear of the charges of unmanliness and Puritanism, but also because there existed a separate movement to form Catholic literary societies and other education-based groups. While the furnishings and attractions of many temperance halls served as an inducement for members who lived in modest and crowded

The Catholic Total Abstinence Union Centennial Fountain, Fairmont Park,
Philadelphia, ca. 1877. (Courtesy of The Library Company of Philadelphia)

homes and apartments, too strong an emphasis on cultural uplift activities
would lead many potential members to remain wary of these societies.

Another activity of the societies was to raise funds to erect public monu-
ments or memorials in behalf of Catholic total abstinence. By locating a
monument in a public urban area, Catholics could challenge preconceived
notions about a city's Irish population, notions related both to their drinking
habits and their economic status. One Philadelphia society alone contributed
$7,000 for a Catholic Total Abstinence Union Centennial Fountain in Fair-
mont Park. That monument was the only one erected in conjunction with the
1876 Centennial Exposition to remain a permanent fixture. During the centenary of Father Mathew's birth, many societies erected statues in his honor, including one in Salem, Massachusetts, once a "stronghold of Puritan prejudice." Perhaps the most important centenary event in the United States was
the establishment of a Father Mathew chair at Catholic University in Washington, D.C.[55]

Choosing appropriate organized activities became crucial to recruiting and
publicizing the cause of temperance to a group of men who did not wish to be

branded as fanatics, unmanly, or lacking in conviviality. That temperance advocates stressed a code of masculine sociability in their efforts to sustain their movement suggests that they tacitly accepted aspects of the stereotype of the Irish American character but sought to transform that stereotype into a more benign form than that of a drunkard or even a ward politician. Furthermore, in some instances total abstinence promoters replaced a Catholic stereotype of temperance advocates—that of the Puritan fanatic—with a more appealing image.

Women and Catholic Temperance

In the last decade of the nineteenth century and the early twentieth century, Catholic temperance advocates sought to incorporate women into their movement; however, women never became more than a minority in temperance organizations, and they often remained segregated at the local level. Although some leaders of the movement had encouraged the earlier inclusion of women, they never joined in significant numbers, nor did they emerge as leaders until the 1890s.

Beginning in the 1870s, Irish Catholics had defined their temperance movement as male in order to challenge the negative stereotypes of males resulting from their status as members of a religious minority group. Catholic women, however, became more involved in social reform issues as increasing numbers of Catholics attained middle-class status. During the 1890s women gained a foothold in other social reform efforts within the Catholic Church, including settlement houses and other charities. This transition to middle-class status and to women's involvement in reform was accompanied by shifting opinions about the role of Catholic women.

Catholic women's prescribed role in the total abstinence movement was primarily to exert influence upon their male relatives in the home. In 1892 Thomas Conaty discussed the role of mothers in temperance activity: "By word and example she ought to teach the children to love and to practice the holy virtue of temperance; she ought to be the first to practice what she teaches; to banish from her home everything that tends to encourage intemperance." Implicit in this comment was the notion that a mother should also forbid her husband from drinking in the home.[56]

The attitudes of temperance advocates often reflected the commonly held American middle-class belief that women were more virtuous than men and that a woman could change her family's actions by exerting her influence

Female members of the Hibernian Total Abstinence Association, Boston.
(From Dinneen, Catholic Total Abstinence Movement*)*

while remaining at home full-time. While most Irish Catholics had not yet attained middle-class status by the end of the century, it represented an ideal model toward which they might strive. Moreover, because the majority of Irish women left the workforce following marriage, arguments based on domestic ideology appealed to those women who remained at home. A writer lauded the increasing participation of women at the national CTAU convention in 1898 but added: "Yet it will always be the chief aim of far-seeing temperance workers to reach the boys and the men first of all, inasmuch as the temptations in their way are so much greater and their example so much more influential. Virtues involving denial of the appetite are comparatively easy for women." He concluded that women could promote temperance by providing good cooking and a home environment, so that men will "crave neither artificial stimulation nor dangerous company."[57]

While there was little basis for the assertion that it was comparatively easy for women to deny their appetites, among Irish Catholics in the United States it was clear that the reputation of males was decidedly worse than that of females and far more threatening to the image of the group as a whole. Total abstinence promoters therefore sought to influence males, more of whom drank heavily. Moreover, because Catholics continued to emphasize moral suasion, their strategy was to transform the individual first, by encouraging him to "take the pledge," and then to change the customs of society as a whole. As a result, at the same time that Protestant women moved away from justifying their involvement in the public sphere as a home protection measure, Catholic women's nascent social reform efforts were being supported in terms of domestic ideology.[58]

Female drinking never became a major issue among either Protestant or Catholic temperance groups, although some total abstainers expressed concern over its perceived increase. In fact, Father James Walsh's diary entries mention several cases in which women had drinking problems. Drinking and alcoholism among women were less visible to those outside the family, because women usually did not frequent saloons and other public drinking places. In 1894 Edmund Phelan, the temperance columnist for the *Pilot*, acknowledged the existence of women's drunkenness and deplored the "growing custom [of providing] facilities for women drinkers, such as side doors, whereby they may enter and depart unobserved."[59]

In 1891 the Boston CTAU submitted an unsuccessful petition to a committee of the state legislature urging a ban on the sale of liquor to women. This contradicted its support of moral suasion arguments and went farther than temperance activities on behalf of local restrictions on the sale of liquor and more stringent licensing regulations. Advocating prohibition exclusively for women suggested a growing concern with female drinking behavior and ironically contradicted the argument that women had the unique moral influence necessary to prevent liquor use within their families. Even when the CTAU began to include women in its membership ranks, however, it did not incorporate the issue of female problem drinking into its public platform.[60]

As third vice president of the CTAU for several years, Leonora Barry Lake became the only major female national leader, just as she had risen to prominence as a high-ranking woman in the national leadership of the Knights of Labor. Born Leonora Kearney in 1849, she had immigrated with her parents from Ireland to a farm in Pierrepont in northern New York. In 1871 she married William B. Barry, an Irish immigrant; they had three children, one of whom died just months following her husband's death in 1881. Before her second marriage, to Obadiah Lake, a printer, Leonora Barry worked for the Knights of Labor in the 1880s. She first joined the organization while an unskilled hand at a clothing factory and later became the "master workman," or head, of her upstate New York assembly. She then served as leader of the district assembly and, finally, became a general investigator for the Knights. Barry wrote reports documenting child labor and sweatshop conditions in factories, which she submitted to the union's general assembly; she also worked to secure passage of the 1889 Pennsylvania factory inspection act. As head of the Knights' women's department, she traveled extensively and therefore was separated from her children in that period. While the Knights welcomed women into leadership positions to a much greater extent than did other national unions at the time, Barry nevertheless encountered hostility from some male leaders, including John Hayes, the Knights' secretary-treasurer, who proved antagonistic to several women leaders in the organization.[61] Barry's views on women's rights, however, were complex, if not contradictory. Like many other Irish Catholic immigrant women in the late nineteenth century, she had been forced by economic circumstances to enter the labor market upon her husband's death. Nevertheless, she maintained that mothers should not work outside the home unless it was essential to their families' economic well-being.

After ostensibly leaving the Knights to return to domestic life after her second marriage, Leonora Barry Lake lectured widely in behalf of women's suffrage and later for the total abstinence cause, speaking in church basements and mission churches. In fact, between 1897 and 1898, she gave 131 speeches on total abstinence; the following year she gave 160 speeches, traveling over 20,000 miles by train to do so.[62] Her life as a Catholic reformer in many ways replicated her stint as a Knights organizer. Her speaking skills resulted in a near doubling of at least one local ladies' total abstinence society's membership. She also was an outspoken critic of the lack of support given to total abstinence efforts by both priests and bishops in many areas of the country. That criticism, along with her unparalleled position as a female leader in the national Catholic temperance movement and overtures she made to the WCTU, resulted in prejudice against Lake among some in the movement. In particular, she encountered resistance from Archbishop John Glennon of St. Louis, a temperance advocate who was deeply opposed to the participation of women in the movement.[63]

Women were increasingly establishing new societies at the local level, and by the early twentieth century a few societies had been integrated by sex. By 1910 women had a greater participation in general total abstinence events and joined men on committees to arrange preparations for the CTAU national convention. Although men still predominated, women filled 141 of 375 committee slots and served on all eighteen committees, even those pertaining to traditionally male activities, such as Athletic Sports and Competitive Drill.

Women in total abstinence societies also became involved in activities that had not been part of male temperance organizations. In the St. Theresa Society of Boston, established in 1900, women under the leadership of Mary Molloy visited women who were sick or "fallen," "combining the work of St. Vincent de Paul with [that of] Father Mathew." In Stoughton, Massachusetts, the St. Mary's Society presented a drama at the town hall and held benefits for needy families. Others instituted libraries as a component of their "practical organization."[64]

The shift toward greater inclusion of women, along with Leonora Barry Lake's enthusiastic leadership in the CTAU, paved the way for the CTAU and WCTU to endeavor to improve their relationship. The highlight of this relationship was Frances Willard's short address to the CTAU convention in August of 1891, which she attended with other officials of her organization. In her closing remarks, Willard invited a delegation of the CTAU to attend the WCTU convention and pointedly encouraged them to include a woman, as well as a priest. A *Pilot* editorial on the WCTU convention in Boston praised the efforts to meet on "common ground" and stated: "Earnest Catholics and non-Catholics are at one in recognizing the magnitude of the evil of intemperance. . . . They differ only as to methods."[65]

Despite the problems that Father Mathew encountered in forging alliances with Protestants in both Ireland and the United States, those in the movement had never completely ignored their Protestant counterparts or supporters in the United States. The CTAU on at least one occasion accepted Protestants into a local society in a rural area, and its members generally welcomed Protestants at total abstinence lectures. They reacted favorably when their group received the support of Protestants, including Theodore Roosevelt, who spoke at the national convention in 1895. Leaders in the organization also held up Protestant-based temperance groups as examples of superior organization. Despite substantial disagreements with Protestant-oriented groups, and the fear that Catholic stereotypes of "Puritans" would undermine their efforts, abstinence leaders also recognized that Protestant support would lend legitimacy to Catholic temperance goals. Yet it was easier to accept Protestants who joined the CTAU and to invite Protestant speakers to their conventions than to forge long-term alliances.[66]

Following the WCTU delegation's appearance at the CTAU convention, some Catholics accused the members of "fraternizing with the Committee of One Hundred[,] Knownothings, the British Americans and kindred associations." Because the decade of the 1890s, like the 1920s, was a period of increased nativism and anti-Catholicism, Catholics were sensitive to perceived anti-Catholic activity. Despite the desire of Leonora Barry Lake and Frances Willard to overcome the deeply held divisions between their groups, most members remained reluctant to do so, and the two were unsuccessful in their attempts to convince members to pursue the relationship between the two groups.[67]

In Boston, local temperance groups sought to include children in their movement in the first decade of the twentieth century through the formation of a Holy Family League. Concurrently, the temperance movement in Ireland had been resuscitated by the Pioneer movement, which sought to instill the values of temperance in children before they reached drinking age. However, while the Pioneer movement achieved success, and its program survives today, in the United States similar strategies and organizations never became significant at the national level. Instead, membership in total abstinence societies declined precipitously in the early twentieth century. Catholic total abstinence movements' continued strategy of moral suasion was rendered obsolete by the public's growing support for the Protestant-oriented prohibitionary strategy that eventually resulted in the constitutional amendment against the manufacture and sale of liquor. Additionally, Irish Americans had obtained greater economic gains and increased urban political power by the early twentieth century, so that the original impetus for organizing temperance societies became less compelling.[68]

· · · · ·

The Catholic total abstinence movement in the United States developed separately from Protestant efforts to fight alcohol abuse. The movement drew upon Father Mathew's Irish legacy and traditions as its base. Its adherents defined the American movement as male by establishing a system of predominantly male societies that emphasized fraternal cultural practices and by gaining support through a network of labor leaders, such as Terence Powderly and Leonora Barry, and Irish nationalists, such as Alexander Sullivan, to attract new members. With some exceptions, the movement maintained its strategy of moral suasion, even while most other groups had gravitated toward prohibition and other legal means of addressing alcohol abuse.

Temperance activities among the Catholic laity cannot be attributed simply to a strong position on the subject by those in the American hierarchy, nor to enthusiasm for it among their parish priests. As the frustrations of various members of the PTAL reveal, much of the clergy and hierarchy remained either ambivalent or opposed to total abstinence activities. The movement had the crucial support of Bishops Ireland and Ryan and benefited from the work of several active priests such as Thomas Conaty of Massachusetts, Morgan Sheedy of Pennsylvania, Peter Cooney of Indiana, and James Cleary of Wisconsin. In Boston, however, where societies were numerous in the late nineteenth century, Archbishop John J. Williams remained relatively muted in his support and did not assume a national leadership role on the issue of Catholic total abstinence.

Despite these developments, and despite the use of arguments that appealed to a religious and ethnic minority in the United States, the movement could not exist independent of Protestant-based temperance efforts. Indeed, while the movement sought to combat pernicious stereotypes of the Irish Catholic male, generalizations were not one-sided. Catholics' negative stereotypes of Protestant "temperance zealots" predisposed them to apply those same views toward Catholic efforts in this arena, and consequently total abstinence advocates portrayed themselves as a positive alternative to Protestants who supported compulsion over suasion, denial over substitution, dourness over sociability.

As we shall see in Chapter 4, Catholics involved in social reform feared the role of Protestants in their charitable efforts and believed that many Protestants sought to proselytize urban Catholics to either Protestantism or secularism. In response, they took defensive measures to counter this influence. In contrast, Catholics in the temperance movement believed the major threat from Protestants was against the Catholic reputation; they had few fears that Protestant-oriented temperance groups would appeal to Catholics in large numbers. Instead, they sought to appeal to their coreligionists by remaining distinct from, and even opposed to, existing temperance efforts, by highlighting ethnic and political ties between Ireland and the United States, and by drawing on the legacy of Father Mathew while adapting his movement to American circumstances.

The Friendly Hand
& the Helping Purse

• • • • •

Catholic Immigration
and Rural Colonization
Programs

As a significant group of middle-class lay Catholics emerged in the late nineteenth century, increasing numbers of them embraced social reform efforts. Those reforms often addressed the perceived needs and circumstances of newly arriving European immigrants. Although some of those efforts transcended ethnic divisions, reformers and their programs tended to target immigrants of their own ethnicity. The reformers assisted immigrants in two distinct ways. First, some promoted rural colonization, a movement designed to help urban Catholics, particularly those from Ireland, resettle into agricultural environments. Second, a movement emerged in Europe and later in the United States to assist immigrants destined for urban areas.

Reformers worked to make the transition of immigrants to the United States more systematic, more rewarding economically, and less dangerous—both physically and morally—especially for those who did not immediately join relatives or friends upon their arrival. Catholic groups also feared that without direction and immediate contact with the American church immigrants would turn away from Catholicism and toward either Protestantism or secularism. Moreover, they expressed concern that the continued poverty of large numbers of urban Catholics impeded the church's ability to gain acceptance from the larger society and to attract new members. Initially, reformers sought to accomplish their goals by encouraging Irish immigrants to settle collectively in rural farming communities established through Catholic programs at the lay and hierarchical levels.

An examination of immigration programs illuminates the nature of migration patterns among Europeans entering the United States during the late nineteenth century. To some extent, chain migration obviated the need for such assistance programs, because relatives and friends often initiated newer arrivals into the community, helping them to procure jobs and housing. The church sought to become a link in this chain by providing information to immigrants as well as by presenting them with opportunities to settle in rural areas in groups rather than as individuals.

Rural colonization programs had close ties to Irish nationalism. In fact, a major figure in the early Catholic rural colonization effort of the mid-nineteenth century, Thomas D'Arcy McGee, had been an Irish nationalist in the Young Ireland movement.[1] Just as in Ireland, the concept of land as a means for economic and political independence was crucial to the American colonization movement of the 1880s, the decade in which support for the Land League was at its height and in which famine had recurred.

Catholic newspapers in the United States and England played a significant role in rural colonization efforts. Immigrants of various nationalities had access to information to assist them in their decisions to leave their original countries. In fact, in addition to promoting colonization in their publications, journalists and editors were active participants in immigrant assistance programs in the United States. Patrick Donohue, editor of the Boston *Pilot*, played a significant role in supporting early efforts at rural colonization, while John Boyle O'Reilly, who later served as *Pilot* editor, became a member of the board of directors of the Irish Catholic Colonization Association. Dillon O'Brien, the editor of a Catholic paper, *Northwestern Chronicle*, assisted Bishop John Ireland in his Catholic Colonization Bureau.[2] In addition to these lay perspectives, Father James Nugent's *Liverpool Catholic Times* also covered immigrant assistance programs in detail.

After colonization efforts in midcentury and the early 1880s failed to alter significantly the concentration of Catholics in cities, reformers increasingly launched localized, urban-based programs for Catholics by the early twentieth century. These efforts sought to assist immigrant arrivals by providing them with advice, such as on locating relatives and job opportunities. This shift in focus coincided with the increasing urbanization of American society, the growth of industrial capitalism, and the mechanization of agriculture. As a result of these changes, by the end of the nineteenth century, Catholics increasingly recognized that economic opportunities for the vast majority of Americans would be concentrated in urban centers rather than in rural locations. Ultimately, their localized efforts were integrated and expanded, first under the auspices of diocesan bureaus and then under the National Catholic Welfare Council.

A recognition of the problems of urbanization and industrial capitalism was further reflected, during the late 1880s and early 1890s, in Pope Leo's decision not to condemn the Knights of Labor as a secret society and by his issuing of *Rerum Novarum*, the encyclical on capital and labor. The social changes occurred in tandem with the maturation of the American Catholic Church, which was now better prepared, at the lay and hierarchical levels, to address the needs of urban Catholic immigrants. Catholics became increasingly reconciled with the idea that the American church was essentially an urban institution and would have a greater presence in the urban North and Midwest than in the South or other rural areas.

Indigenous port programs in the United States at the local and national levels had fewer direct ties to nationalist causes than the rural colonization efforts had, but such ties did exist. Port programs arose in large part from concerns about proselytizing and the increasing willingness of lay groups and the diocese to take greater responsibility for the care of their coreligionists. Port programs were established in Boston and New York as a direct result of the efforts of lay activists, including Peter Cahensly and Charlotte O'Brien. O'Brien's father was a well-known Irish nationalist, while O'Brien herself was a strong supporter of Charles Parnell and the Land League. Rural colonization programs, O'Brien's efforts, and the later port programs all stressed the importance of providing assistance in order that immigrants could become economically self-sufficient in ways that had eluded them in Europe.

Because they addressed shared concerns and similar goals, immigration assistance reformers constituted an international social reform movement. Reform leaders in this era often cooperated with one another and became involved in several Catholic social reform efforts. William J. Onahan, for example, the layman and comptroller for the city of Chicago who organized the Columbian Catholic Congress of 1893, also helped to found the Irish Catholic Colonization Association (ICCA), hosted O'Brien on her American tour, and promoted temperance issues. Charlotte Grace O'Brien became active in immigration issues primarily within Ireland, but while in the United States she worked with Onahan and others in the Catholic hierarchy and laity to promote similar programs in New York and Boston. Both worked in tandem with Father James Nugent and Bishop Ireland. Newspaper editors such as John Boyle O'Reilly, who corresponded with O'Brien and urged her to expand her efforts to American ports, advocated and reported on immigration protection and rural colonization, as well as Land League activities. These diverse reform efforts also suggest the extent to which immigration issues were a two-way, or even circular, phenomenon. Because immigrants sometimes traveled to or resettled in a third country, such as England, before arriving in the United States, concern for immigration was not confined to the receiving communities, as illustrated by the development of several immigration programs in Europe.

A decade earlier, in 1870, Father James Nugent of Liverpool began a nine-month tour of the United States and Canada. Lecturing on behalf of "nobody's children," the destitute orphans and street children of Liverpool, he sought to place them, a few at a time, among lay Catholics in Canada and the United States. Father Nugent, a well-known figure in Liverpool, committed himself to addressing a myriad of social issues facing destitute Catholics, most of whom were Irish immigrants, until he was well into his eighties. Nugent, the eldest of nine children, had been born in Liverpool in 1822 to an Irish father and a Catholic convert mother. In addition to his roles as temperance activist and publisher of the *Liverpool Catholic Times*, Nugent served as chaplain at Walton Gaol for twenty-two years, opened institutions and developed programs for street children and orphans, and supported programs for unmarried mothers. His niece later became a nun in St. Paul, Minnesota, home of Bishop Ireland. Ultimately, each of these reformers became acquainted with, and influenced, the others, and their various reform efforts strongly complemented one another.[3]

Immigration assistance initiatives constituted an important development in the emergence of a group of reform-minded, urban, middle-class Catholics. Many laypersons active in these programs had immigrated themselves, and they often drew on their own experiences in developing or running the programs. In addition, these efforts signaled a growing sentiment of concern among middle-class and wealthy Catholics for the welfare of their less fortunate coreligionists. This sentiment provided legitimacy to their improved economic status by demonstrating that they had the means to provide assistance to those with few resources.

The creation of a Catholic reform network, however, did not always occur easily. Proponents of rural colonization experienced difficulty in raising sufficient funds for their projects, although they had few problems in attracting interest from Catholics of modest means who sought to participate in the efforts. The plan only gained momentum after its proponents, including

Bishop Ireland and General O'Neill of Nebraska's Greeley County colony, undertook widespread lecture tours throughout urban centers in the East. The Charitable Irish Society, founded in 1737 with the intention of helping unfortunate Irish immigrants and their descendants, had allowed such programs to lapse for almost a century, while members turned their efforts to ceremonial activities. In the late nineteenth century, moreover, Land League agitation captured the interest of many Catholics and diverted their attention from the situation of Irish Americans. Thus a sense of noblesse oblige did not occur naturally among Catholics with their entrance into the middle and upper classes but rather had to be nurtured. The impulse often arose when Catholics compared their charitable efforts with those of other groups, particularly those of Protestants, but also those of Jews. Like Catholics, Jews had experienced tensions within their community between cultural preservation and acceptance by the majority, and middle-class members of both groups had initiated efforts to assist their communities' poor.[4]

This chapter focuses first on the rural Catholic colonization movement. It discusses the arguments used for the promotion of colonies in the West and then its practical organization, including the formation in 1880 of the Irish Catholic Colonization Association. Second, it examines the activities of early port programs, focusing on Charlotte Grace O'Brien and her specific concerns over the welfare of immigrant women. Finally, it analyzes the various port programs run by lay groups, including those of the Charitable Irish Society and St. Vincent de Paul Society, and their eventual submergence under the aegis of the National Catholic Welfare Council in the early 1920s.

Rural Catholic Colonization

Late-nineteenth-century attempts to develop Catholic colonies and encourage the migration of Catholics westward and into agricultural pursuits were not the first of their kind. Catholics of various nationalities had organized efforts from the late eighteenth century to the early to mid-nineteenth century, including the settlements of Loretto, Pennsylvania, and Benedicta, Maine. Shortly after his consecration as the first bishop of Dubuque, Iowa, in 1837, Mathias Loras developed several Irish- and German-dominated Catholic colonies in that state. He was supported by contributions from the Vienna-based Leopoldine Society, a Catholic mission society that often assisted immigrants, and through publicity from the recently organized Irish Emigrant Society in New York. In 1834 Reverend William Horstmann brought a small group of eight colonists from Westphalia to Putnam County, Ohio, and established a settlement there after purchasing land from the federal government. Six years later, the settlement had grown to a community of almost 600 Catholics.[5]

Mid-century nativism and Know-Nothing activity served as an impetus for the establishment of many small colonies during the peak of German and Irish immigration to the United States. Many native-born Americans, especially in urban areas, feared the intense concentration of immigrants and their growing tendency to vote in blocs.[6] Although Lyman Beecher and others spoke about the need to keep "popery" out of the West, and some in Congress sought unsuccessfully to restrict Homestead Act benefits to citizens, the bulk of anti-Catholic and nativist activity in the mid-nineteenth century occurred in the urban Northeast. Many proponents of the early colonization efforts seemed to view it not only as a means for immigrants to escape nativism and anti-Catholicism, but also as a way to diffuse criticism of immigrants and the Catholic Church. Other Catholics, however, both those in the church as well as political leaders, remained wary of widespread colonization efforts. Having gained widespread support from a concentrated urban Catholic population, they argued that the development of immigrant and Catholic institutions in urban areas could protect immigrants from anti-Catholicism, safeguard the faith of immigrants, and allow Catholics to exercise some political power.[7]

While the establishment of modest Catholic colonies throughout the West proved at least partly successful, early efforts to establish a large-scale movement were not. In the late 1850s a group of laymen, priests, and a few members of the hierarchy met in Buffalo at an Irish Immigrant Aid Convention. Thomas D'Arcy McGee, an Irish nationalist and journalist who had launched night schools and other programs for Irish immigrants in New York, served as the catalyst for this organizing effort. He soon came under sharp personal attack from Archbishop Hughes of New York, who distrusted his political motivations. Earlier, the two had split over the Young Ireland movement. McGee had been involved in this movement before leaving Ireland as a political exile, while Hughes had supported, but later disavowed, it from the United States. McGee later published articles critical of the church hierarchy's role in the suppression of the Young Ireland movement, and Hughes responded by banning McGee's publication among Catholics. Consequently, Hughes adamantly opposed colonization efforts and accused McGee and others active in the movement of profiting from land speculation. Objecting to the concept of colonies, Hughes railed against such efforts by drawing an analogy between "Irish towns" and Mormon settlements, a comparison that exaggerated the extent of ethnic exclusivity in Catholic colonies.[8]

Other historians have suggested that Hughes's opposition was more complex than is usually recognized. For example, Henry J. Browne has argued that Hughes's objections stemmed in part from his fear that organized colonization efforts that were ethnically homogeneous would inhibit Irish immigrants from integrating into the larger American society, and that he felt that some of the proponents of colonization efforts were impractical, given the capital and skills needed for western life. Moreover, Browne states that Hughes had a more optimistic view of Irish immigrants' future in urban areas than did those meeting in Buffalo. Browne argues that Hughes did not oppose Irish settlement on the frontiers per se, but only those organized by the church, which would reflect poorly on the church's reputation if they failed.[9]

Surveying the development of Catholic colonization efforts, Bishops John Ireland of St. Paul, Minnesota, and John Lancaster Spalding of Peoria, Illinois, both cited Hughes's early opposition to colonization as a setback for the status of Catholics in the nineteenth century. Browne contends, however, that other factors proved more important to the failure of colonization efforts to take hold, including the unwillingness of most Irish immigrants to enter farming, the gradual demise of the Know-Nothing Party by the late 1850s, and the increase in railroad grants that decreased the availability of cheap western land.[10]

Advocates of rural colonization in the late nineteenth century focused on the superiority of rural life over that of the city. Supporters of the movement described the benefits of farming in economic, political, physical, and moral terms and criticized many of the conditions prevalent in the urban United States. Those involved in colonization organizations promoted the view that, to improve their status, poor immigrants and Catholics who had failed to prosper in urban settings would have to gain a stake in American society through land and property ownership outside metropolitan areas. Yet reformers feared that if immigrants moved to rural areas where few others from their ethnic or religious backgrounds lived, and where no Catholic institutions existed, they would lose their religious identity. On the other hand, Catholics who moved to settlements that were founded as Catholic communities and had established Catholic schools and churches would be able to preserve their religion. Supporters of colonization thus believed that Catholic immigrants would have to settle in rural areas collectively rather than individually. By encouraging permanent settlement by Catholics in rural areas, those reformers also hoped to appeal to potential new members of the church and to expand their religion's base in the United States both numerically and geographically.

Although these reformers understated the risks of agricultural life, their vision of an agrarian society for Catholics was far from utopian. Those advocating colonization envisioned a society in which immigrants continued their traditional roles as agriculturalists, while benefiting economically and morally from an improved environment. Because a significant percentage of most nineteenth-century European immigrant groups, including those from Ireland, had rural backgrounds, colonization efforts offered them opportunities to continue farming. Proponents of rural colonization believed that the availability and relatively low cost of land, combined with an abundance of resources, could insure that a family's hard work would result in success. This scenario contrasted with Irish farming life under the constraints of colonial rule and tenancy laws. It also differed from life in urban America, where limited economic opportunities meant that hard work did not necessarily result in improved living standards for immigrants and, indeed, often rendered them dependent upon employers and vulnerable to depressions, "which affected the mechanics and laboring classes to a degree as never before, at least in America."[11]

In an essay promoting rural colonization, Bishop Spalding used biblical and classical references, as well as the writings of Ralph Waldo Emerson, to argue that an agricultural existence ranked superior to others, for both physical and moral reasons. He maintained that "the farmer's life, I know as well as any man, is not ideal; no human life is so. . . . The farmer must learn to be content with hard work and small gains. . . . But in return he is nature's freeman, dependent upon God's providence and his own strong arm. He is no man's hired servant."[12] In contrast, Spalding portrayed the city as the locus of immorality, exploitation, and ill health. To bolster his argument, he cited higher rates of death, insanity, and immorality (using the example of out-of-wedlock births in Europe to measure the latter) in cities as compared with other areas. He asserted: "The benefits which accrue to the great body of people from the cheap and suicidal labor of the operatives are undeniable and real. It is mere declamation to affirm that machinery is the slave of capitalists and works in their interest alone." Spalding further argued that city life contributed to the breakdown of traditions, of families, and of economic independence.[13]

Some of the arguments put forth by advocates of Catholic colonization recalled early nationalist debates over the relative merits of agriculture and manufacturing as the economic basis for American society. Support for these colonization efforts echoed the Jeffersonian concept of the independent yeomanry, a central tenet in the economic and political ideology of the late eighteenth and early nineteenth centuries. Indeed, Spalding's vision of the industrialized city evoked the Jeffersonian critique of Hamilton's economic plan of industrialization.[14]

Other rhetoric surrounding Catholic colonization suggested the later "Free Soil, Free Labor, Free Men" Republican ideology of the 1850s and early 1860s, which at the time had held little appeal for urban Catholic immigrants. Indeed, Eric Foner has noted that advocates of free labor ideology had often criticized Irish immigrants for their lack of industriousness, comparing them unfavorably to Germans, who had "become either artisans or cultivators of their own land at once."[15] As if to challenge that decades-old stereotype, an article on colonization in the Boston *Pilot* echoed the free soil slogan in its subtitle: "Free Air, Free Homes, Free Men." Like those who had earlier advocated this ideology, Catholic reformers extolled the virtues of producers over those of commerce and emphasized the opportunities available to those of modest means who were committed to work hard and eschew active social lives. Yet, as Spalding's critiques of urban society suggest, advocates of Catholic colonization tended to be more critical of employers and of capitalism than free soilers had been.[16]

While anti-Catholicism was a major impetus for the creation of Catholic colonies in the antebellum era, the perception that Irish Catholics were not as economically mobile as other groups served as an important catalyst for organizing the later movement. Members of the Irish Catholic Colonization Association, as well as Catholics involved in earlier efforts, sought to counteract the overwhelming propensity of Irish Catholic immigrants to settle in large cities, primarily on the eastern seaboard. Chain migration patterns encouraged newly arriving Irish immigrants to settle in established Irish neighborhoods where friends or relatives had previously located. Because of these connections, there was little incentive for them to move to new territories, where they knew no one. The ICCA received the active support of three members of the church hierarchy—Bishop Ireland, Bishop Spalding, and Bishop James O'Connor of Omaha.[17]

Proponents of rural colonization among the Irish emphasized German and Scandinavian models as examples. They highlighted the fact that their proposal to promote rural settlement was not unique. The *Catholic Citizen* commented: "Thriving German and Scandinavian land companies are to-day operating in this fashion at Chicago and Milwaukee. They arouse and direct the immigration of their countrymen. And nobody doubts that they work an immense good; the service to their element and nationality being incalculably greater than their financial gains, considerable as they are." Colonization advocates looked to the patterns of German and Scandinavian immigrants who settled in the Midwest and Plains regions as models for building rural communities while preserving ethnic and religious ties distinct from those of the majority. Another writer, noting that of 2 million Irish immigrants, 800,000 lived in cities, concluded that they were not able to "keep pace with the Anglo and Germanic constituents in the mighty strides that our American population is taking."[18]

J. Hector St. John de Crèvecoeur had noted German immigrant success in American agriculture in 1783, well before the large-scale Irish and German immigration of the mid-nineteenth century. Crèvecoeur, a French consul to America in the late eighteenth century, later settled as a farmer along New York's Hudson River Valley before returning to France in 1790. In *Letters from an American Farmer*, he commented: "How much wiser, in general, [are] the honest Germans than almost all other Europeans. . . . Whence the difference arises I know not; but, out of every twelve families of emigrants of each country, generally seven Scotch will succeed, nine German, and four Irish." He expressed admiration for Germans' industriousness, their success despite language obstacles, and the hard work of German women, in particular. In contrast, Crèvecoeur attributed the relative lack of success of the Irish to their love of drink, fondness for quarreling, ignorance of husbandry skills, and history of colonial rule.[19]

German immigrants who settled in American cities in the nineteenth century also tended to be more economically successful than their Irish counterparts. To some extent that proved true because more of them arrived with skills appropriate for industrial production. In further contrast with the Irish, Germans tended to settle farther west, on farms, in Milwaukee and St. Louis, or in cities with relatively small populations, where opportunities for economic advancement were good. The wave of nineteenth-century German immigration to the United States originated among freehold farmers, artisans, and shopkeepers from southwestern provinces such as Bavaria, Baden, Württemberg, and Rhenish Prussia and Palatinate. In the first decades of the nineteenth century, these Germans often left their homes as a result of poor harvests. As potato rot and famine led to depressions by midcentury, increasing numbers of immigrants from the central provinces also left. That wave was more likely to have drawn farmers from lower economic levels than previous migrations. Although some were "forty-eighters," leaving Germany after the failed revolution of that year, this group never formed a substantial percentage of midcentury immigrants.[20]

Between the Civil War and 1880, German Catholics in the United States experienced an opposite problem to that of Irish Catholics. Following the Homestead Act of 1862, the large number of German Catholics migrants moving west to avail themselves of inexpensive lands led to a shortage of clergy in western Catholic communities. That situation was not fully anticipated by the American hierarchy nor alleviated sufficiently by recruiting German-speaking priests to German parishes.[21]

In the 1870s the shortage of German-speaking priests was somewhat lessened by a crisis in Germany, which led many clergy to emigrate to the United States. Otto von Bismarck's Kulturkampf (struggle of civilizations), a series of repressive policies supported by German liberals, began in 1871 with his rise to power and remained in effect until 1887. The Iron Chancellor sought, at the time of German unification, to strengthen German nationalism by weakening the political power of the Catholic Church, whose members constituted almost half of the new nation's population. The policy emerged in the years following Pope Pius IX's 1864 encyclical *Syllabus of Errors*, which denounced secular ideas such as progress and liberalism, and his subsequent pronouncement of the doctrine of infallibility. Both declarations caused major controversies in Germany, especially among liberals. Bismarck's policies also emanated in part from the erroneous assumption among German leaders that the number of Germans joining religious orders had increased substantially in the 1860s and 1870s. The German government first banished Jesuits, and later most other Catholic religious orders, and required state inspection of Catholic schools. In 1873 the legislature passed a series of bills, collectively known as the May Laws, which allowed the government to veto the appointment of a parish priest and to require priests to obtain German citizenship and to pass a series of exams on German culture. Bishops and clergy who failed to conform to those laws faced imprisonment. In all, an estimated 1,800 priests had been exiled or jailed.[22]

The Kulturkampf met with strong resistance by Catholic bishops, clergy, and laity alike, either through individual acts of defiance or collective action, including street protest. Due to weak administrative enforcement under Adalbert Falk, however, the policies were not uniformly carried out. Germany's

Center Party, a political party comprised of Catholics and a major target of Kulturkampf policies, managed in 1844 to increase its representatives in the Reichstag to ninety-one from sixty-three. Ultimately, instead of creating a more unified German culture, the Kulturkampf led to heightened divisions between Catholics and Protestants, both culturally and geographically. As will be discussed in subsequent chapters, it also led German Catholics, both in Germany and the United States, to became wary of the centralized power of the state.[23]

Members of the American Catholic hierarchy became increasingly concerned about the fact that the Irish had not been able to replicate German immigrants' success. With help from like-minded lay activists, they began to address ways to promote the idea that Irish immigrants would improve their economic opportunities if they changed their migration patterns once in the United States.

In contrast to Germans and Scandinavians, who were far more likely to establish their own farms and to take advantage of Homestead Act provisions, famine-era Irish had fewer resources than other groups, so that even relatively inexpensive land remained unattainable for them in the late nineteenth century. Irish colonization societies had thus concluded that the Homestead Act was insufficient to accomplish an urban-to-rural transition among Irish Catholics. Moreover, rail and other transportation to the Midwest and West proved beyond their means as well. Other considerations also contributed to Irish Catholics' reluctance to move outside the urban Northeast. First, unlike most immigrant groups, many Irish arrived young and unmarried rather than in families, and by the late nineteenth century, unmarried women predominated. Such demographics were not conducive to family-based agriculture. Second, the enormous growth of American cities in this era created immediate job opportunities for domestic servants, manual laborers, and factory workers.[24]

Commentators argued that the Irish sought out enclaves as a result of their gregariousness. For example, Bishop Spalding noted the tendency of Irish immigrants to congregate in urban areas; he also exhorted the Irish to resist the temptation to accept with passivity their economic circumstances. "It is so natural, too, when one has wandered far from home and meets with old acquaintances in a strange land, to make pause and stop with them, above all when these old friends urge us to stay." He also noted that English policy and famine in their homeland had created a distaste among the Irish for pursuing agriculture once in the United States.[25] Implicit in the discussion of Irish immigration patterns was the view that the Irish in America needed to adopt a more individualistic economic and social outlook better suited to capitalism.

The solution, however, was not to break this migration chain, nor to dissolve communities, but to redirect immigrants to agricultural areas. In fact, rural colonization remained dependent on word-of-mouth and newspaper publicity for its success. The *Pilot* asserted: "It may be assumed that every man that comes is a forerunner of a few more, and that few in turn insure the coming hither of a few other persons in their wake." Thus the same qualities that had characterized Irish immigration in the past, such as chain migration patterns and a tendency toward establishing strong communities, could prove as beneficial for rural as for urban migration.[26]

Rural colonization reform appealed to positive ethnically based interests as well. There were several parallels between the goals of the Catholic total abstinence movement and colonization efforts. William Onahan and others active in both movements stressed the economic and moral uplift aspects of their efforts, targeting those Catholics, often the "sober and industrious" poor, who sought to improve their status in society through a program of self-help. Such qualities might manifest themselves in the creation of farms as well as in the practice of abstinence from liquor. Indeed, the adjectives "sober" and "industrious" were often linked in descriptions of ideal colonists. Moreover, both reforms sought to improve the reputation of Catholics as a whole by changing the circumstances that gave rise to the negative stereotypes that many Americans held of them. Saloons were banned from colonies established by Bishop Ireland as well as those of the ICCA. Father James Nugent of Liverpool, a proponent of both rural colonization and immigration assistance programs, also actively promoted total abstinence through the League of the Cross.[27]

· · · · ·

As with other social reform efforts within the American Catholic Church, colonization efforts were contemporaneous with, and related to, Land League agitation in Ireland, an issue that held great appeal for many Irish American Catholics in the 1880s. The Land League, known formally as the Irish National Land League, was established in Dublin in 1879, and had been modeled on the local National Land League of Mayo. Its founders were the charismatic Charles S. Parnell, a Cambridge-educated Irish Protestant landlord from Avondale, County Wicklow, who had been elected to Parliament, and Michael Davitt. Davitt, whose background could hardly be more different from Parnell's, was an Irish-born activist who grew up in poverty in Lancaster, England, where his parents had immigrated after being evicted from their land in County Mayo. He began work at a cotton mill at the age of ten, and his right arm had been amputated following an industrial accident. Davitt had been jailed for his role in the Fenian uprising of the 1860s and 1870s. The Fenians had led an unsuccessful revolutionary movement that sought to gain Irish independence through physical force. In contrast, the Land League initially concentrated its efforts on the issues of landownership and improved tenants' rights by addressing Irish landlords' high rents and the high eviction rates among tenants. The Land League used constitutional means to achieve its ends and sought support from more radical nationalists, who had not closed the door to physical force as a means for achieving Irish independence. Parnell's American tour in 1880 was important in garnering crucial financial and political support from Irish Americans, and many Irish newspapers closely monitored the activities of the Land League for their readers.[28]

The issue of land tenancy in Ireland had come to the fore in the late 1870s and early 1880s as a result of a mild famine. That famine never reached the magnitude of the devastating Great Famine of 1845–50, which resulted in the deaths of almost 1 million people (one-eighth of the population) and the immigration of 1.2 million others. Some areas of the country experienced a staggering population decline of over 30 percent between 1841 and 1851. Through death, emigration, and a drop in birth rates, a country of about 8 million people prior to the famine shrank to 5.8 million by 1861. While far less severe, the later famine of 1878–80 left 600,000 Irish in desperate need of food following two bad potato harvests, hitting seventeen western counties particularly hard. The situation improved following the harvest of 1880, but problems persisted until 1886. In fact, immigration rates from 1881 to 1891 increased by 24 percent over the previous decade. The later famine, widely covered in the Irish American press, created an interest in the work of Charles Parnell and the Land League and led to successful fund-raising efforts among Irish Americans.[29]

The Land League had been formed following the development of the Home Rule Party in the 1870s. That party emerged from a movement led originally by Sir Isaac Butt, who organized to promote a separate parliament for Ireland, although one that would remain dependent on imperial rule by England. Parnell, who supported home rule, although not the gradualist approach of Butt, took over leadership of the movement from him. Parnell then sought to bring attention to the issues of home rule and land reform through his strategy of obstructing parliamentary procedure. In 1880 he supported Prime Minister William Gladstone and England's Liberal Party but withdrew his support following Gladstone's backing of the Land Act, which was intended to address tenants' rights in Ireland. In the Irish nationalists' view, the Land Act was weak, in part because it did not address the plight of tenants with plots over one acre and did not relieve tenants who were in arrears with their rent payments. The Land Act, however, did ease some of the pressures felt by Irish tenants by allowing for greater security of land tenure, the right to gain a profit from improvements upon vacating, and the right to arbitrate rents through a judicial body.

In response to the passage of the Land Act, the Land League called for a rent strike against Irish landlords by their tenants, and soon most league leaders were jailed in England under the Coercion Act. After Parnell secretly agreed to stop his rent strike plan and support the Liberal Party's efforts to achieve greater political power for Ireland, he was released from Kilmainham jail. Soon after, he was confronted by the murder of the secretary and undersecretary for Irish affairs in Dublin by a militant revolutionary group, while tensions with Davitt occurred over the direction of the movement. Following Parnell's release, the Land Act was amended to address some of the inadequacies of the original law.[30]

By that time, the movement had moved its focus away from the issue of land reform to that of home rule. Largely due to the impact that the Coercion Act had on its leaders, the Land League had dissolved by the end of 1881; the Irish National League had arisen in its place the following year, with the home rule issue at its core. In 1885 Gladstone, needing Parnell's support in the House of Commons, introduced a home rule bill that would create a legislature in Ireland. Whether Ireland would retain its representation in the English Parliament under such a law remained unclear. Yet the measure remained a far cry from granting Ireland political independence, since such a body would not have the power over trade, customs, and other issues reserved by England. The bill was defeated as a result of many defections from the Liberal Party and brought down the Gladstone administration.[31]

In 1889, however, Parnell lost substantial support from his Irish Catholic constituents and fellow leaders when his affair with Katharine O'Shea, the wife of a fellow Irish member of Parliament, became widely publicized during the O'Shea divorce proceedings. That revelation led to a major controversy among his largely Catholic supporters and severely weakened his political reputation. Gladstone, once again serving as prime minister, wrote a letter requesting that Parnell resign from his party leadership position in exchange for Gladstone's support of a new home rule bill. Some of Parnell's closest allies also withdrew their support, and ultimately the bill was defeated. In 1891, three months after marrying O'Shea, Parnell was dead at age forty-five. The Irish nationalist movement was badly wounded as a result of internal strife, violence, and controversies that arose in response to the Parnell crisis. Yet, despite his failings, Parnell became widely known as the "uncrowned king of Ireland" for his leadership of the nationalist movement.[32]

• • • • •

Both the Land League and the ICCA stressed the importance of landowner-ship as a step away from the economic exploitation of employers and land-lords and toward social legitimacy as well as economic and political freedom. There were distinct parallels between the two organizations. Beneath a *Pilot* article on colonization efforts, for example, ran another on a Land League meeting addressing "the best means of obtaining Irish land for Irish men," a statement that perfectly described the ICCA's agenda.[33]

A writer in the Milwaukee *Catholic Citizen* harshly condemned Irish Americans who supported the Land League without pursuing its principles in their own lives. "All Irish-Americans who rent farms or live in city tenements have no business to boast of their Land League principles unless they are making conscious efforts to own some property. Talking against Irish land-lordism and yet helping to build up American landlordism is hypocrisy and treachery united." In a similar vein, Onahan discussed the need to direct some of the "patriotic zeal and oratory and money" used in Irish national and benevolent associations "towards aiding and befriending the Irish emigrant on his arrival in America." Onahan continued: "Surely the Irish peasant farmer, when he lands in America, perhaps friendless and helpless, is no less an object of our sympathy, and appeals no less strongly to our friendly aid, than his struggling countryman at home."[34]

That Irish Catholics chose to identify their rural resettlement programs as "colonization" efforts was on one level ironic, given the use of the term to describe the system of English political and economic dominance over Ire-land. Of course, the term "colonization" at that time carried with it the more benign connotation of the process of developing new settlements in seven-teenth- and eighteenth-century North America. In fact, the ICCA was a joint-stock corporation, a form that had been used by the English to establish several of the American colonies, including Virginia.[35] The ICCA could therefore claim that its goal—settling immigrants on new land in order to build communities while expanding economic production—was a typically American enterprise.

The farmer ideal portrayed by colonization reformers embraced American images of the importance, and indeed superiority, of agrarian life, as well as the view that farming was a natural extension of the economic role of the Irish when freed from the constraints of tenancy. Underlying support for the Land League, Catholic temperance, and rural colonization were many of the same precepts: sobriety, gaining independence from exploitative employers and landlords, respectability, and self-improvement.

The ICCA sought to encourage and assist urban Catholic immigrants to re-settle in rural communities, primarily those established in Minnesota and Nebraska, by providing them with both economic assistance and loans. The idea for establishing the organization grew out of the St. Patrick's Society of Chicago, of which William Onahan was a member. That group held a national conference in 1879, which led to the ICCA's foundation the following year. In addition to its charitable goals, the ICCA was intended, as a joint-stock corpo-ration, to provide a profit for its principal investors—wealthy Catholics who sympathized with the plight of their coreligionists. Despite its status as a profit-making venture, Onahan emphasized the fact that the ICCA was "more than merely a joint stock company." In addition to benefiting those "classes who ought to make homes for themselves on the land," the effort should draw support from "those whose duty it is to give practical encouragement and aid to this movement by investing a portion of their wealth in enterprises which are not only safe, but which are besides opportunities that invite co-operation in the noblest work of religion and philanthropy."[36]

Onahan also added that, unlike previous immigrants, incoming settlers were knowledgeable about the West and its resources but "need[ed] the friendly hand and the helping purse of their more fortunate country man" in order to take advantage of them. But while the rhetoric encouraging support of the ICCA's goals suggested benevolent intentions, implicit in the coloniza-tion efforts was also the recognition that uplifting the immigrant poor would improve the status of the Irish American community as a whole. By contrib-uting to the relief of their poorer coreligionists, the Irish in the middle and upper classes could also demonstrate how far they had come in society since their forebears arrived in the United States. The organization bought large tracts of land both from the government and from railroad companies and sold them to immigrants who learned of the program through newspaper articles, lectures, or brochures. It also protected immigrants from unscrupulous land speculators and provided them with assurances that the land they selected would be conducive to profitable farming.[37]

The ICCA modeled itself on the Catholic Colonization Bureau, established by Bishop Ireland in Minnesota in 1876. In contrast to the Catholic Colonization Bureau, however, the ICCA relied heavily on lay participation—it placed lay members on its board of directors, appointed a lay secretary, and raised funds through wealthy and middle-class laity. Rather than limiting its colonization efforts to Minnesota, as Bishop Ireland's organization had done, the ICCA sought to extend these efforts on a national scale.[38]

The ICCA founded two major colonies in Greeley, Nebraska, and Adrian, Minnesota. The latter was a smaller colony established with land it bought from Bishop Ireland's Catholic Colonization Bureau. In addition, the ICCA invested in a less successful Arkansas venture, St. Patrick's colony. In the last case, the ICCA did not purchase the land outright but served as a de facto agent for the railroad by arranging for favorable terms of sale to prospective Catholic settlers.[39] The ICCA had an authorized capital stock of $100,000, and by 1880 the association had issued certificates to 294 individuals in the amount of $65,000, an average of $221 per shareholder.[40]

Greeley County, Nebraska, served as a model settlement of the ICCA. In 1877 two coal miners, Patrick Hynes and Michael McCarthy, headed west to Nebraska from Pittston, Pennsylvania. After meeting in Omaha with Bishop O'Connor, who told them that he intended to form a Catholic colony in Nebraska, they chose to settle in Greeley County upon the suggestion of a government surveyor. The next settlers arrived from Boston and Woburn, Massachusetts; they in turn arranged for more family members and friends to relocate there the following autumn. Patrick Hynes became immigrant agent for the area, and new settlers from Massachusetts used the immigrant house, located on his farm, as a transitional shelter until they could build sod houses for themselves. Other colonists arrived directly from Ireland. General John O'Neill, an Irish immigrant who had served in the Civil War, established the town of O'Connor, within the Greeley County colony. O'Neill worked closely on the project with Bishop O'Connor, gave speeches on the East Coast, and, along with other lay supporters of this movement, helped to organize the ICCA. To promote this colony, the ICCA sent out 10,000 pamphlets on the Greeley settlement alone. By 1900, 165 families in the town of Spalding belonged to the Catholic Church. Three-fourths were Irish, and the remaining families were German or Belgian. Belgian families had also settled in Bishop Ireland's most successful colony, in Ghent, Minnesota.[41]

Writers of rural colonization literature explicitly aimed their promotions at male heads of household and assigned to women the role of helpmeet on the frontier. With poor men, colonization would prove beneficial by "lift[ing] them up to independence without lowering their manhood; to relieve their want without bestowing alms on them."[42] In pamphlets and other publicity, colonization proponents addressed men, warning them that they would need to enlist the assistance of their wives in order to be successful, and that they should hesitate to embark on the venture if unmarried or if their spouses objected to the plan. Colonization associations recognized that isolation for both men and women was a danger. Bishop Spalding noted that the ICCA planned its colony so that houses would be built a quarter mile apart, and thus "social intercourse of neighbors [would be] greatly facilitated and the loneliness of country life diminished." In addition, cooperation between neighbors would be encouraged by herd laws of Nebraska and Minnesota, which did not require fencing around individual farms.[43]

Proponents of rural colonization viewed women as supplying a moral voice of the family by encouraging their husbands to improve their economic circumstances. Bishop Spalding noted, "Now there are thousands and tens of thousands of just such strong, courageous, pure, self-denying Irish girls, who are laboring for others, and who will allow some cowardly young man to take them into a tenement house to die there after a life of poverty." He urged them to go west where they could own a home, stating: "[W]e have found that no class of people sympathized more with us than the Irish Catholic young woman. . . . [M]any of them have invested their savings in [the ICCA] and it is a good work for them." This trend would be consistent with the practice, noted by other historians, of Irish women saving substantial amounts of money and remitting part of their savings to relatives in Ireland.[44]

In discussing colonization, Charlotte O'Brien concurred with the image of the woman as helpmeet. "A young man going out to Bishop Ireland's Colony with £100 and a wife—a wife is essential—may look forward to being, perhaps in a few years, the principal citizen of a young and rising town. . . . But young men who go out without wives, do not succeed as a rule, I hear. The life is so rough that men who have no home fail, and the woman is as essential in the farming business as a man."[45]

Although the initial objective of the ICCA was to address the needs of the industrious poor, sparse funds prevented the group from assisting large numbers of those without capital. The ICCA divided the written inquiries it received into three categories: those of limited means who sought a home in the West to provide their children with further opportunities; a larger number who possessed fewer means who had "toiled for years in public employments, or in shops and factories"; and the greatest number, "poor, laboring men, who though perhaps in steady employment, scarcely have anything to put by." Onahan suggested that more efforts needed to be put into the class of "deserving and suitable poor," while recognizing the limited resources available to the ICCA to accomplish this. The leaders of the ICCA warned prospective immigrants and migrants to the colonies that they should have at least $400, but preferably $600, in cash available to settle their families on the farm. According to a local history of Greeley County, those who settled there initially were relatively poor, but by the 1890s, the county's settlers included those of "considerable financial means, people who were accustomed to comfortable and oft times luxurious living."[46]

Two rural colonization projects—the Sweetman colony and the settlement of Connemara immigrants—illustrate the limitations of assisting poor immigrants rather than those of modest means with prior farming experience in the United States. The Sweetman colony, in Murray County, Minnesota, was founded by John Sweetman, a wealthy Irish philanthropist who bought 20,000 acres adjacent to the Avoca colony after hearing about the successes of the Catholic Colonization Bureau and the ICCA in this area. Sweetman established a colonization company in England, the Irish-American Colonization Society, and appointed English and Irish Catholics to its board. Individual board members themselves paid for some of the colonists' passage, although the society itself did not have sufficient resources to fund settlers's transportation. Other philanthropists donated land and money to build a church. The program limited colonists' holdings to eighty acres; the settlers began repayments eighteen months after their arrival in the colony. The financial arrangements of the Sweetman colony therefore differed from the other Catholic colonization settlement efforts in Minnesota.[47]

Bishop Ireland gave the Sweetman colony his approval but voiced several reservations. He acknowledged that Sweetman and his directors addressed the issue that most concerned the "Christian Economist": "[h]ow to unite capital with labor to the mutual advantage of both." But Ireland criticized Sweetman's decision to include colonists (and their families) who had not invested their own money in the venture; he felt that these circumstances failed to provide colonists with sufficient incentives to remain on the land when they encountered setbacks. He noted that of the seventy families who settled in the town of Currie in the Sweetman colony, fifteen had left for Minneapolis or St. Paul, adding that these had all come to the colony directly from Ireland. In contrast, the success rate of migrants who had come from within the United States was much higher.[48]

A second, widely publicized, controversy occurred with the transplanting of 200 emigrants from Connemara, in the west of Ireland, who "were among the poorest in Ireland" and suffered from the effects of the ongoing famine. Their material possessions were meager—none of the children and few of women had shoes. The fact that the emigrants spoke only Gaelic was yet another obstacle to their success. Father James Nugent had raised the funds to pay for their passage and requested that the ICCA arrange for the families to be placed on farms. The Land League denounced the effort as "assisted emigration" and argued that assistance should be provided to allow the farmers to stay in Ireland. The ICCA declined to help, but Bishop Ireland took responsibility and arranged for the group to settle near the Graceville colony in Minnesota. It soon became clear to Bishop Ireland, Dillon O'Brien, and others that the Connemara colonists had little farming experience. In addition to requiring further financial assistance, they had difficulty in getting along with neighbors and, in the estimation of some, were unwilling to work to make their farms successful. Critics charged that the Connemara colonists had become dependent on charity because they had received it from the time they left Ireland. Moreover, some observers asserted that the colonists had failed largely because they had not immigrated on their own initiative, but rather as a result of Father Nugent's goodwill gesture.[49]

Rural colonization provided a safety net for poorer immigrants who could benefit from "squatters' rights," a situation that was readily promoted in information disseminated by the colonization programs. This situation contrasted with the precariousness of tenants' rights in Ireland. Dillon O'Brien, who had helped arrange the settlement of the impoverished Connemara immigrants in the Minnesota colony, claimed that "if [the land] should revert back to the government, as it is very likely to do, these emigrants will own it by the right of the squatter."[50]

Reformers active in rural colonization drew sharp distinctions between their efforts and those of the English government, which during the 1880s launched a policy toward the Irish that was termed "assisted immigration." That program provided £5 to each Irish family who agreed to leave Ireland for the United States. The *Pilot* reported an incident in which the writer asserted that the English government had paid the passage and provided each of the twenty immigrants, who had formerly lived in poorhouses, with $3.50 for expenses until they secured employment. Other reports suggested that such accounts were inaccurate.[51] Proponents of immigration programs, both those pertaining to colonization and the port programs, emphasized that they did not seek to encourage immigration among people who were able to remain in their country of origin, and in fact most colonization efforts sought to resettle Irish immigrants who lived in urban America. Reformers sought to deflect any potential criticism that might portray them as contributing to or condoning English policy.

The Catholic rural colonization movement of the late nineteenth century failed to change significantly the geographical distribution of Irish immigration, nor was it able to relieve the economic conditions of those it had originally sought to assist—the "sober and industrious poor." The movement was plagued by too few resources and, perhaps, by overly ambitious goals. Its proponents also had to compete with the Irish Catholic middle class's support of Land League activism, directed toward the homeland, and to demonstrate that its program was not intended to substitute for long-term economic and political change in Ireland. Moreover, the critiques of urban society employed to appeal to potential supporters of rural colonization efforts might not have resonated with the growing population of urban middle-class Catholics, who had little reason to be convinced that farming was the best route to upward mobility. While industrial laborers led precarious lives in urban centers, many Catholics recognized that farming, too, was fraught with risks.

Yet, by providing incentives and publicity, the ICCA encouraged Catholics to settle in Minnesota and in Greeley County, Nebraska, in larger numbers than they otherwise would have. In fact, the movement generated significant interest from those seeking to become colonists, although relatively few of them could realize their goal of owning a farm. The efforts further reflected a recognition among some Catholics that the church needed to expand beyond its traditional urban perimeters and an acknowledgment that there were economic and other reasons that most Catholic immigrants remained in cities.

As a result of the inability of Catholic reformers to garner widespread support for their colonization initiatives, and after some well-publicized failures, reformers turned their attention toward more practical efforts to assist immigrants in the cities in which they would live and work. They began to recognize that a program aimed at fundamentally altering the immigration patterns of Catholic immigrants and urban poor was unrealistic, due in part to the limited resources of the church and the well-established patterns of immigrant networks and enclaves, as well as the availability of jobs, however low-paying, in urban areas. Moreover, those involved in immigration reform acknowledged that the church's growing influence in cities enabled Catholics to engage in greater urban reform efforts.

Charlotte Grace O'Brien and Female Immigrant Protection

In the early 1880s, Charlotte Grace O'Brien launched what would soon become an international campaign for the "protection of female immigrants." As part of her effort she established an emigration program in Ireland to advise and prepare girls and women for the conditions they faced as immigrants in the United States. Shortly afterward, she toured the United States to promote the creation of programs for women at incoming ports. O'Brien viewed immigration as fraught with danger for young female immigrants. Irish culture had few constraints against women's immigrating alone, and by the late nineteenth century women comprised the majority of Irish immigrants.[52] Yet O'Brien and others active in immigrant welfare efforts expressed their concern that unsuspecting and naive women would be trapped unwittingly into prostitution or other immoral activities by sailors and other men aboard ship or later by unscrupulous men offering them transportation, employment, or lodging.

O'Brien's activism in Ireland and later in the United States highlighted the need for programs for female immigrants in the Irish American community and ultimately led to the establishment of immigrant assistance programs under the auspices of the Catholic Church. Reformers established policies to influence immigrant women's experiences based on middle- and upper-class Victorian notions of gender relations. Those within the church hierarchy supported those efforts as part of a larger effort to shape Catholic immigration patterns in the United States.

The port assistance programs established in the late nineteenth century arose during an era in which concern over the behavior of young, single, wage-earning women, especially those living apart from their families in urban areas, came to the fore in both Europe and the United States.[53] While O'Brien's activism on that issue ultimately benefited many immigrants, the programs regulated and monitored the behavior of female immigrants in particular. In some cases port agents called upon the state or federal government to intervene in individual cases, a fact that could ultimately lead to institutionalization or deportation.

Charlotte Grace O'Brien was born into an aristocratic Irish Protestant family in Limerick, at the beginning of the famine in 1845. Yet her family background was atypical for a member of the Irish gentry. She was the daughter of William Smith O'Brien, a celebrated Irish nationalist who had once been sentenced to death by the English government for his political activities in the Young Ireland movement. After his death sentence was commuted in 1849, O'Brien was transported to Tasmania; he was finally pardoned and subsequently allowed to return to Ireland in 1856.[54] Charlotte O'Brien converted to Catholicism in her forties. Both of her parents had died before she was twenty, and she never married. In her youth she lived mainly at the family's estate, Cahirmoyle, and in early adulthood she continued to reside there with her eldest brother, Edward, and his family. She cared for her brother's children after the death of their mother but had an uneasy relationship with her brother. Around 1880, following Edward's remarriage, he decided to close the house, and O'Brien then moved to Ardanoir, a home she had built along the Shannon River. She wrote poetry, essays, and fiction, including a novel about the Fenian uprising of 1869, and her interest in natural history was furthered through her correspondence with George Rolleston, a professor at Oxford University. Late in her life, she spent most of her time in Dublin, where she socialized with such people as Douglas Hyde, leader of the Gaelic League, who would become the first president of Ireland, and the painter William Osborne. Her nephew and biographer, Stephen Gwynn, noted that despite her family's wealth and position, the independent O'Brien "had something of a peasant woman's dignity in her carriage" and gave little attention to her appearance or domestic surroundings.[55]

O'Brien was an ardent supporter of the Land League and of Parnell, who had, like herself, been born into the Protestant landowning class. After her conversion to Catholicism, she continued to defend him during the controversy over his role in the O'Shea divorce. Stephen Gwynn stated: "In a class war she took the side of her nation against the interest and the judgement of those nearest to her, those whom she had the best right to respect."[56]

Despite her correspondence with political figures, her vociferous support for nationalist causes, and her writing, O'Brien refrained from embarking on a life of public activism until 1881, when she was in her mid-thirties. Her activism on the issue of immigrant protection arose following a tour of a steamer in Queenstown (now Cobh, County Cork) during a visit with her brother Charles's widow, Mrs. William Dickson, who had married an officer in the Royal Irish Constabulary. In a short article in London's *Pall Mall Gazette*, entitled "Horrors of the Emigrant Ship," O'Brien reported on conditions in the steerage of the White Star Line's ship *Germanic*, which, she argued, led to moral and physical degradation. Single immigrant women in steerage class, she asserted, had no alternative but to share quarters with married couples, and therefore "if they remove their clothes it is under his [male] eyes, if they lie down to rest it is beside him." She also noted that despite the limit of 1,000 passengers, the steamer had at least once carried as many as 1,775. To address these problems, O'Brien advocated that women serve as inspectors because they would be less likely than men to find such conditions acceptable. She concluded: "Governments protect and inspect property of various kinds. Should they not above all protect defenceless human beings, especially women and children?" O'Brien had also objected to the lack of sanitary facilities in steerage and to the poor ventilation, although she did not discuss those concerns in her article.[57]

Within a week, the publicity surrounding the issue led Joseph Chamberlain, president of the Board of Trade in London, to launch an investigation. O'Brien's allegations ignited controversy amongst steamship operators, who in letters to the editor of the *Pall Mall Gazette* vigorously denied that the assertions were accurate. After inspecting other steamers, O'Brien conceded that she had drawn some inaccurate conclusions based upon having seen only one ship, but she asserted nevertheless that her fundamental criticisms had merit. She also wrote letters to the Board of Trade outlining the problems she had written about in the *Pall Mall Gazette* article. Chamberlain, however, chastised her in a parliamentary report for writing "sensational letters" when some transatlantic steamers later proved to have better conditions than those she had described.[58]

O'Brien's concern over the failure of some immigrant steamships to segregate the sexes reflected her adherence to the middle- and upper-class Victorian view of sexual propriety, which contrasted the essential innocence of young women with male sexual aggression. Although O'Brien allowed that rural Irish women routinely had shared close quarters with male relatives, she feared the effects of unregulated contact between strangers of the opposite sex. Indeed, the specter of "women adrift" in urban areas, without family members or friends to turn to, proved to be a major source of concern to social reformers of the era. While O'Brien's critique also seems to contradict her advocacy of domestic service occupations for immigrant women, in which they would live in the households of others, she most likely assumed that middle-class male employers posed less of a threat to female virtue than did sailors or working-class men. In fact, there were well-publicized cases in which urban women were raped or forced into prostitution against their will, and illegitimacy rates rose during this era as increasing numbers of Europeans migrated into urban areas. Ultimately, by the early twentieth century, American and European authorities undertook widespread efforts to addressing the issue of international white slave traffic. Thus O'Brien's concerns, while exaggerated, were not unfounded.[59]

Although it remains difficult to determine to what extent out-of-wedlock births were an issue, it is probable that they were underreported in official statistics. Hasia Diner has argued that Irish society in the postfamine era was characterized by a rigid segregation of the sexes in both private and public spheres, even within marriage. This situation arose in response to demographic pressures and land scarcity, which required a reduction in population. Diner has further concluded that as a result of these developments, premarital sex and illegitimacy were rare—and that Ireland had the lowest illegitimacy rate among fifteen countries in 1890. Consequently, she asserts, the Irish placed confidence in the power of internal constraints against sexual activity and entrusted unmarried women to guard their own chastity.[60] In the United States during the late nineteenth century, members of the Catholic hierarchy echoed that view of women by regularly praising unmarried Irish Catholic women workers for their virtuousness, their selflessness, and their religious devotion.[61]

Recent scholarship has suggested, however, that while perhaps not widespread, premarital sexual relations, out-of-wedlock births, and prostitution among Irish women in Ireland and the United States caused significant concern among reformers in the nineteenth century. In nineteenth-century Ireland, middle- and upper-class women, including nuns, directed much of their earliest reform effort at women whom they classified as "fallen." Some were sent to institutions, such as the Magdalene asylums established in several Irish cities and towns.[62] Out-of-wedlock births and prostitution tended to be urban issues, however, because community norms in rural areas insured that pregnant women would quickly marry whenever possible and made prostitution less common and less visible than in cities.

Young Irish women were much more likely to immigrate outside of nuclear families than were women of other ethnic groups.[63] Yet the receptiveness to O'Brien's message among Catholic reformers in the early twentieth century reveals that some Irish and Irish Americans were not entirely confident that cultural constraints against premarital sex and, to a lesser degree, prostitution would survive outside traditional Irish communities and kin networks, especially because the migration process usually ended in large urban centers.

Following the controversy over steamship conditions, O'Brien expanded her efforts on behalf of immigrant protection. She opened a boardinghouse in Queenstown, a major port for emigrants departing from Ireland for the United States. She embarked on this project only after failing to convince the Catholic clergy to launch such a program itself and relied mainly on her own funds to maintain the house. O'Brien resided there and oversaw it herself. The Emigrants' Home had the capacity to accommodate as many as 105 emigrants—during one year alone over 3,000 people stayed in the house. She charged emigrants two shillings a night for "a good supper, bed, breakfast, and thorough protection." From her base in Queenstown, she was also able to inspect the steamships periodically and to convince their operators to enact some of the reforms she had advocated.[64]

O'Brien became part of a transatlantic network of reformers concerned with assisting Irish immigrants. She received support in this endeavor from Father James Nugent of Liverpool, the major immigrant advocate there, who had earlier arranged for the group of Connemara famine victims to settle in Minnesota colonies in 1880. Father Nugent was also an acquaintance of William Onahan, who had lived in Liverpool as a youth. In fact, Onahan recalled serving as an altar boy for Nugent at Sunday mass at St. Nicholas Church while living in Liverpool. Both men, and O'Brien herself, worked with Bishop Ireland on the issue of immigrant assistance. As part of her efforts, O'Brien interviewed prospective emigrants about the conditions they faced and advised them about which lines they should travel on. In addition to protecting immigrant women, O'Brien's boardinghouse program offered them advice on the conditions they would encounter in the United States.[65]

O'Brien recommended to immigrant women that they work in domestic service positions rather than in factories, stating that "[p]rivate service is safer than factory work everywhere." Her justification for that conclusion is not entirely clear.[66] In early nineteenth-century England, factory work for women was generally viewed as degrading, although Ireland itself had relatively few factories. O'Brien might have felt that domestic service would provide immigrant women with a workplace and residence that was less dangerous than factories because employers, both male and female, would serve as substitutes for parental authority in the household, and male employers would

Charlotte Grace O'Brien,
overseeing the Emigrants'
Home she established in
Cobh, County Cork, 1882.
(From Gwynn, Charlotte
Grace O'Brien*)*

pose less of a threat to the chastity of women than factory foremen and male workers. O'Brien likely viewed household work as an occupation that could be easily reconciled with the Victorian-era view of female roles. She may have concluded that it was best suited for single women immigrating on their own because they would not need to pay rent or live alone. It is also likely that she viewed the work, the leading paid occupation for Irish women in the nineteenth century, as good preparation in the skills required for marriage and motherhood. She probably also recognized that domestic service was a position that was in high demand in the United States, but one that relatively few white, native-born women would accept.

While her advocacy of domestic service for young immigrant women had some merit, O'Brien's confidence in the occupation reflected her own upper-class upbringing and not necessarily the realities of most rural immigrant women's backgrounds or the conditions of employment. While some aspects of domestic employment held advantages over factory work, women domestic workers generally endured more constraints on their personal lives than women who worked in factories. There is evidence that some servants were able to save a good deal of money and that their daughters were able to move up economically; many immigrants also had prior experience as domestics. Yet the long hours and the restrictions placed on servants isolated them from many social interactions, especially romantic ones, and provided few opportunities to interact with others as equals. Moreover, older women servants found it more difficult to obtain new positions as domestics, and there was no guarantee of job security in illness or in old age. Even if a servant married eventually, many of her employment skills would not prove especially useful in a working-class home.[67]

In 1882 O'Brien left Ireland to tour the United States, in order to promote the issue of immigrant protection and to convince American Catholics of the necessity of establishing immigrant assistance programs at major ports. When she decided to tour the United States she closed her house temporarily, reopening it in 1883 after her return. Although O'Brien had not yet converted to Catholicism, she nevertheless viewed the church as the appropriate institution to undertake and expand the type of work she had begun in Queenstown. It was while working at the Emigrants' Home in Queenstown that she came to recognize that establishing programs at ports of entry in the United States was vital to the success of immigrant protection efforts.

Charlotte O'Brien successfully forged alliances with Americans in order to advance her reform efforts. Stephen Gwynn noted that although at the outset of her visit she had no friends and few contacts in the United States, she was well received by Catholics there. In New York and elsewhere, she toured immigrant tenements to gain a firsthand view of their conditions. She wrote to Lady Monteagle, a relative by marriage: "I have established intercommunication between different points and travelled about 4,000 miles of American soil, so that I have a good general notion of the country." Bishop Ireland, Onahan, and others active in the Catholic rural colonization movement were particularly receptive to her call for port reform, and the two issues reinforced one another.[68] In fact, O'Brien saw her efforts in Queenstown, rural colonization, temperance, and future port programs in American cities as an integrated system of Catholic reform: "I believe it may be a result of my work to start here, or rather to consolidate here, one of the greatest movements that has ever worked for the Irish people—a movement for systematically exporting the people to the West the moment they touch American shores, and doing this in connection with the temperance movement—Bishop Ireland at one end of the rope, Father Nugent and myself at the other, the Lines vying in improvements as they are—societies here at the ports."[69]

In the United States, her father's reputation brought O'Brien large audiences that otherwise might not have been receptive to her message. A lecture in Minnesota on behalf of immigrant assistance programs drew 2,000–3,000 people. During her visit to Minnesota, O'Brien met with, and found an ally in, Bishop Ireland. It was through their meeting that the idea for a mission at New York's Castle Garden (the forerunner of Ellis Island) developed.[70]

Working from the recommendation of the Catholic bishops, Cardinal McCloskey of New York appointed Father Joseph Riordan to head the Castle Garden mission on behalf of English-speaking immigrants after it opened in 1884. Our Lady of the Rosary for the Protection of Emigrants served as an auxiliary organization to provide the mission with funding. Local branches of the St. Vincent de Paul Society also provided financial support. The mission later moved to Ellis Island when it opened in 1892. That year, in praising the mission's work, the Boston *Pilot* cited an incident in which mission workers had assisted a young immigrant girl who found that her sister was "the keeper of a notorious dive, and had sent for her . . . to be used for the fiendish purpose which characterized [her sister's] own life." The mission took her in, and "at her own request" she returned home.[71]

O'Brien's speech in Boston before the Charitable Irish Society (CIS) brought attention to the dearth of port activities in that city. Her activism led the CIS to initiate a port program in the early twentieth century that focused particularly on the protection of immigrant women. O'Brien called on the Boston Catholic laity to establish a program similar to those in Philadelphia.[72] She also outlined seven activities that port programs should undertake, including telegraphing relatives of illiterate immigrants; organizing offices to provide information on jobs, lodging, and housing; helping immigrants move out West; and providing poor immigrants with funds to help them get established. Although O'Brien directed her attention exclusively toward the problems of Irish immigrants, she believed that her programs could be successfully expanded to assist other groups from Europe. She also reported that her efforts to improve steamship conditions had been heeded by some steamship lines. O'Brien appeared at the CIS speech with Emma Carey, a Boston Catholic convert who was a member of the Massachusetts Prison Commission and the founder of a Catholic society at Radcliffe College, which suggests that she was forming alliances with Catholic laywomen as well as with members of the hierarchy and laymen involved in rural colonization.[73]

Despite her concerns for the safety and morality of women, O'Brien viewed immigration neither as inherently dangerous for female immigrants nor as a panacea for economic problems. In fact, she believed that in some cases women fared better than males economically once in the United States. To highlight her point, she mentioned the expanding opportunities available to women in department stores in Philadelphia. She also emphasized the importance of assistance from relatives and friends: "If girls have good friends to go to in America, I do not discourage them to go. In the West they do very well, and everywhere with good home friends to advise them on whom they can fall back, they have a fair opening." Indeed, in her article in the *Pall Mall Gazette*, she had noted that "my countrywomen hardly go singly, but in batches of from six to twelve 'neighboring' boys and girls." It was outside of these types of relationships that O'Brien thought single women faced physical and moral dangers. Citing the dangers to younger immigrants, including the health problems associated with tenements, she stated: "America is not the land of gold it is represented. It is a fine country, . . . but if I had children whom I loved, I would rather rear them on potatoes and salt at home than risk their lives by taking them immature to America." In contrast to Bishop Spalding, who criticized Irish immigrants for their propensity to congregate in urban enclaves, O'Brien believed that existing chain migration patterns generally served as a positive force for Irish immigrants, rather than as an inhibitor to their economic mobility. Yet she acknowledged the benefits of rural colonization as well.[74]

After her return to Ireland, a second controversy concerning O'Brien's reform efforts erupted over persistent accusations that she was working to support the English policy of "assisted immigration," a characterization she emphatically denied. John Boyle O'Reilly, editor of the Boston *Pilot*, sent her a strongly worded letter: "I beg of you to write me at once, if the report that you are associated with the Government agents is untrue. . . . Your influence, marvelous and beautiful as it was, will die in one moment if it be known that you act as the agent of the [English] Government."[75] O'Brien had already addressed such reports, and she further asserted that the English policy was intended to deflect attention from the major issues of land reform, industrial policy, and self-government. O'Brien did, however, accept "assisted immigrants" into her boardinghouse. In an 1883 letter to the American press, O'Brien justified her role in immigration issues by stating that the recent famine, the attractiveness of the United States, and British policy rendered immigration inevitable. She stated: "Remember that the emigrant of to-day may be a soldier in the battle of freedom to-morrow. . . . Every man who leaves Ireland will be a greater strength to Ireland in America than ever he could be at home." She suggested, then, that Irish nationalism was being exported to the United States through the steady flow of immigration. After that exchange, O'Brien increasingly retreated to private life, trying to cope with her growing deafness and bouts of depression; she died of heart failure in 1909.[76]

O'Brien's American tour elicited support among Irish Catholics in the United States for the establishment of port assistance programs to help incoming immigrants with practical problems. These issues had been largely ignored by Catholics prior to her tour. Her notion of the particular dangers facing immigrant women also became incorporated into subsequent immigrant assistance efforts. Although O'Brien entered the reform field almost by accident, she came to view her work as part of a systematic transatlantic effort among the church laity and hierarchy to improve the condition and economic status of immigrants.

Port Assistance Programs in New York and Boston

By the 1880s immigrant protection programs among Catholics in American cities had begun to take hold. In New York, in addition to the Our Lady of the Rosary for the Protection of Emigrants Mission, a branch of the German Catholic St. Raphael Society had established a port program in 1883 in order to address the needs of immigrants. Peter Paul Cahensly, the German layman later at the center of the Americanist controversy, had created the St. Raphael Society in 1871, the year that Germany was unified and the Kulturkampf began. The impetus for the port program's organization derived from the fact that by the late nineteenth century, four of five immigrants from Europe were Catholic. Many Catholics argued that there was a tremendous rate of "leakage" as those immigrants left the church; later, however, those concerns proved to have been overstated. On a trip to the United States in 1883, Cahensly had noted that other religious groups had significant numbers of agents, and that Lutherans in particular had sponsored numerous free lodging houses for immigrants.[77]

The St. Raphael Society placed agents in ports throughout the world, particularly in countries where emigration and immigration of European Catholics was most prevalent, including Germany, the United States, Italy, South America, and Canada. The society also became interested in other immigration issues, such as the plight of Italian workers in Germany. Like Charlotte O'Brien, Cahensly also agitated for better ship conditions for emigrants, including the segregation of sexes. Under Bismarck, however, the

German government was reluctant to support immigration reform lest it be perceived as encouraging emigration. Cahensly's initial efforts in 1868 to interest New York's Archbishop John McCloskey in the reform also proved unsuccessful.[78]

The St. Raphael Society gradually became less reliant on the laity for the administration of port programs. From 1883 to 1884 it assigned Joseph Kölble, a layman, as its agent for Castle Garden in New York. The Central Verein had employed Kölble as a port agent for German Catholics in New York since 1868, and he had traveled to Germany that year to speak to Catholic groups about his work. In 1885 the society replaced Kölble with a priest, Reverend John Reuland of Ettelbrück, Germany, who visited its port programs in Europe before assuming his assignment. That change in leadership occurred at the behest of Reverend Peter Schlösser, a St. Raphael's agent in Bremen, after he visited New York. Schlösser had recommended that a priest be appointed in order to achieve greater support among American Catholics for the modestly funded work of the society, and presumably to underscore that the program had a spiritual as well as a material mission.[79]

The society provided immigrants with assistance by offering religious services, informing them of employment opportunities, and writing letters for them, as well as dispensing other aid. When Reuland was first appointed in New York, Father Joseph Riordan of the Our Lady mission objected to having a second Catholic port program at Castle Garden. Riordan argued that Reuland should be appointed as his assistant instead. But the hierarchy concluded that too little was being done to assist German immigrants and overruled his suggestion. In 1898 the St. Raphael Society became part of Caritas, the German hierarchy's welfare and charity organization. Monsignor Lorenz Werthmann, a friend of Cahensly's from his hometown of Limberg and founder of Caritasverband, the German Catholic charities association, took over the administrative activities of the St. Raphael Society as Cahensly became older. In New York, Leo House opened in 1887, named in recognition of the pope's support. The St. Raphael Society sponsored the building, supplemented by funds from the pope, German priests, and numerous small donations, after the major port of immigration moved from Castle Garden to Ellis Island. Reverend Urban Nageleisen headed Leo House, and members of the Sisters of St. Agnes ran it; its board of directors included eight priests and seven laymen.[80]

Strong leadership by Cahensly and O'Brien resulted in successful port programs in Cobh, Bremen, New York, and Boston. Without their leadership, the port assistance programs they advocated would not have been established. Both Cahensly and O'Brien sought to promote their reforms through two channels: government regulation and the auspices of the Catholic Church. By initiating these programs, they opened a new arena for Catholic involvement. While is not clear that O'Brien herself was directly influenced by Cahensly's work, many Catholics in Europe and the United States began to recognize the benefits of expanding immigration efforts. Indeed, in 1881 Bishop Ireland, who later emerged as one of Cahensly's most vocal critics, praised the work of the St. Raphael Society, as he would later encourage O'Brien to develop efforts in the United States. Although immigrant protection work among German Catholics would ultimately be turned over to the clergy and the hierarchy, Cahensly's support and organizational efforts were critical in bringing the reform issue to the fore.[81]

In 1882, in conjunction with Charlotte O'Brien's visit to Boston, John Boyle O'Reilly, editor of the *Pilot* and supporter of rural colonization efforts, noted that Boston's Charitable Irish Society had lost sight of its original goal. This society's mission, articulated in its preamble, was to support "countrymen in these Parts, who might be reduced by sickness, Shipwrack, Old age and other Infirmities and unforeseen Accidents." O'Reilly further noted that these charitable efforts had been overlooked for approximately a century. Instead, the society's activities centered around lectures, parades, presidential visits and balls, support of the Gaelic League, and other ethnic interests of its middle- and upper-class members.[82] In the early 1880s William Onahan also criticized the modest efforts of Irish groups in caring for new immigrants when compared to the activities of other ethnic groups, some of which had arrived relatively recently. "In Chicago I can point to German, Bohemian and Scandinavian Immigrant Aid Societies. . . . I certainly hope this reproach will not be permitted much longer rest."[83] Those involved in Catholic rural colonization efforts viewed the expansion of such port programs as a logical extension of the work they had begun.

In Boston, efforts to mobilize immigrant protection efforts finally came to fruition. In 1882 the *Pilot* reported that the Charitable Irish Society had "begun a too long neglected work" on behalf of Irish Catholic immigrants arriving at the port of Boston. It further noted that Irish Americans had too long assumed that immigrants would rely on friends and relatives for assistance, while British, Scottish, and German groups had established port programs in Boston and New York. The need for port assistance programs for the Irish had been greatest in the famine era of the 1840s; by the time the CIS and other groups of middle-class Irish Catholics belatedly launched their port programs, immigration from Ireland had slowed substantially and stronger chain migration patterns had developed to allow friends and relatives to better care for recent immigrants.[84]

By 1910 the CIS had joined forces with the St. Vincent de Paul Society to fund the hiring of an agent at the port of Boston. To a large degree, that initiative came as a result of the issues articulated by Charlotte O'Brien. Each group contributed about $200 toward a common port assistance program. Although the CIS was an ethnic society rather than a Catholic lay organization, its cooperation with both the Archdiocese of Boston and the St. Vincent de Paul Society demonstrates that it served as an affiliate of the Catholic Church. The two groups employed an agent, Julia C. Hayes of Brookline, who met arriving steamer ships in order to assist incoming immigrants; prior to this joint endeavor, she had worked for the St. Vincent de Paul Society, "for some years past." Before joining the CIS port program as an agent, Hayes was employed as a stenographer and lived as a boarder on Sycamore Street in the Roslindale section of Boston.[85] Later, through its Catholic Charitable Bureau, the Archdiocese of Boston launched a program whose primary purpose was to insure secure marriage rites for Italian immigrants. By 1914 the St. Vincent de Paul Society had turned over full responsibility of the Boston port program to the CIS. Bernard Kelley, of the St. Vincent de Paul Society, indicated that this decision occurred as a result of changes "in our office force," most likely as a result of financial constraints. In 1922, upon the resumption of immigration after World War I, the Catholic Charitable Bureau requested that the CIS contribute $300 to the archdiocese's newly created Immigration Welfare Bureau in order to fund the port work among incoming Irish immigrants. This was an effort to consolidate the previously separate ethnic organizations' efforts among Catholics and to bring this work under the supervision of the archbishop.[86]

One implicit function of the CIS agent's role was to diminish the potential for proselytizing among Catholics by the numerous Protestant groups that already employed agents at the port of Boston. In addition to the CIS, fifteen other ethnic and religious organizations had placed agents at the wharf. Jewish societies had two agents, Scandinavian church groups had a total of nine agents, the Young Men's Christian Association (YMCA) and Young Women's Christian Association (YWCA) each had two agents, and the Italian St. Raphael Society had two.[87] Moreover, the North American Civic League, a conservative organization founded in 1908 by native-born businessmen in response to concerns about the negative effects of immigration, employed three agents at the dock. Because approximately one-quarter of all immigrants arriving in the port of Boston in this period came from Ireland, Irish Catholics could no longer afford to ignore the need to develop a port presence.[88]

Julia Hayes, the society's agent, wrote regular immigration reports, which provide several insights into the extent of Irish immigration, and remigration, during this period and into the nature of assistance the port program provided. Her reports suggest that many immigrants had, by the early twentieth century, established complex networks of friends and relatives in the United States who assisted them in financing their passage and providing them with jobs upon their arrival.[89] This pattern of chain migration was especially pronounced among the Irish arriving in the early twentieth century. The reports also reveal the precariousness of aliens' status in the United States and the ease with which immigrants could be detained and deported by the Immigration Commission for a variety of problems, including illness, old age, youth, feeblemindedness, and lack of employment, even after having lived in the country for an extended period.

Many immigrants experienced difficulty in locating relatives or friends who had moved after last corresponding with them, demonstrating the high residential mobility rates of the working class in this era. Hayes attempted to insure that newly arriving immigrant females were met by relatives or friends, or that, if their final destinations were outside Boston, they had telegraphed their relatives and had the means and information necessary to arrive there. She routinely provided them with fares for trains and local transportation. Those who needed to stay overnight in Boston before traveling to their eventual destination were accommodated in the Immigrant's Home. Another point at which Hayes intervened was when an immigrant was detained by immigration officials. She tried to locate his or her relatives prior to the immigration hearing, because the scheduling of a second hearing "often results in hardship to the relatives especially if they have come from distant points and must take lodgings in this city and perhaps lose a couple of days wages besides." Hayes also helped to organize and pay for a party at Christmas for ninety detained immigrants forced to spend their holidays at the immigration office.[90]

Occasionally, the CIS provided passage money for immigrants who sought to return to Ireland due to chronic unemployment, illness, or old age, or because they needed to care for elderly relatives there. This seemed particularly necessary for women, perhaps because so many remained unmarried and lacked family members in the United States to care for them when they were no longer able to work. In some instances, the CIS helped to provide passage for families to repatriate. The society often obtained a "charity rate" from the steamship lines, which led many to seek such help. Over the course of sixteen visits, Hayes arranged for a sixty-eight-year-old woman to return to Ireland. According to Hayes, the woman had spent most of her twenty-five years in the United States in charitable institutions, hospitals, and at the Temporary Home for Women in Boston until a family took her into their home temporarily. The woman finally decided to return to her native Cork in order to open an apple stand in a marketplace. Through various fund-raising efforts in her behalf, she received $50 and a year's supply of clothing for her return.

The Archdiocese of Boston requested that the CIS write to the British Embassy on behalf of Mary Sheehan, an immigrant woman who, due to illness, sought to return to relatives in Ireland after spending two years in the United States. Another unmarried woman desired to return to Ireland to be cared for by relatives, and the CIS agreed to pay for her passage to Donegal. Anna Cassidy wrote the CIS requesting a reduction in the fare so that she could return to Ireland after less than a year in the United States to help care for her elderly parents. In closing, she confessed, "I have no friends here and it is awful." Michael O'Kelly wrote to the CIS for help in getting money to return with his wife to Ireland because he could not get a job as a teacher. Although the CIS declined to help O'Kelly return, John Keenan, its secretary, informed him that he had spoken to a man who had agreed to provide him with a job.[91]

Through her informal relationship with immigration officials at the port of Boston, Hayes also negotiated the release of detained immigrants, often by arranging employment for them. In one case, Hayes agreed to take on responsibility for a young man who had been detained and found him work on a farm in New Hampshire, although she made it clear that the CIS could not accept responsibility for him "in case of sickness or any other trouble." She also provided employment advice and positions to other incoming immigrants. Hayes generally placed Irish immigrant women in domestic service positions within private households.[92]

Through its immigration protection efforts, the CIS and its agent intervened in several cases where women had engaged in activities that were generally considered immoral or inappropriate and advocated that three of the women be deported. In all but one of these incidents, it was unlikely that the women were deported for having engaged in criminal behavior, nor were they unable to work. Instead, the women, all of whom had initially worked as domestic servants upon their arrival, and three of whom had sisters in the Boston area, had transgressed against some aspect of morality or mode of acceptable behavior prescribed for women.

The first case was that of Delia Burke, an unmarried eighteen-year-old immigrant women who had left Ireland to join her sister in Somerville, Massachusetts, after becoming pregnant. With the help of her sister, she secured a position as a maid with a family there. Before she could receive medical help, she went into labor at the Somerville police station. The baby, a girl, died later that week. Immigration officials were then notified, and Burke entered the hospital after having what was characterized as a nervous breakdown; she was later transferred to a psychopathic hospital after being diagnosed as "feeble-minded." The publicity surrounding the case evoked sympathy from "at least 1000 persons" who offered her employment. One man, who signed his letter "An Irishman," remarked that the Burke case was "a pitiful state of affairs. I hope you will help the unfortunate girl." Nevertheless, although she visited Burke in the hospital, Hayes strongly opposed having the CIS intervene on the women's behalf during her deportation process. Hayes noted that if the CIS did serve as her advocate, it would have to provide a bond for her release in the amount of $500 to $1,000. Immediately prior to Burke's scheduled deportation, it was reported that she had voluntarily agreed to return to her family in Ireland.[93]

Hayes's comment that Burke's case "is one of many such cases and owes its notoriety to the press" suggests that while the particular circumstances of this situation were unusual, it was not uncommon for a young unmarried Irish woman to immigrate to the United States when she became pregnant. In fact, a second case brought to the attention of the CIS involved an unmarried Canadian woman of "Irish parentage" and her two children, who were deported because the children's father could not be located. Presumably, without his wages, the family would become a public charge. A third case involved a nineteen-year-old mother and her child who had experienced difficulty in joining her family, now living in the United States, despite the fact that "there were four wage earners in the family and the net income was $32 per week." A fourth case involved a detained woman who was hospitalized with her seven-month-old infant daughter, ill with bronchitis. It is probable that the mother was unmarried and without financial support, because Hayes reports, "Eventually, they will be deported."[94] Therefore, while pregnancy among single women proved the exception among Irish immigrants in Boston, the port agent's view suggests it was by no means rare.

In addition to cases involving single mothers, Julia Hayes reported on her investigations of four other young women who had been living in the United States for periods of six months to over a year. Two had "given relatives and friends considerable trouble." One eighteen-year-old woman had worked as a nanny but was removed from her employers after being injured in an accident when she was sent on an errand to purchase alcohol. According to Hayes, the woman then drifted to various hotels, had a relationship with a married Italian man "of questionable character," kept late hours, smoked cigarettes, drank alcohol, and defiantly told her sisters she could take care of herself. Hayes referred the case to immigration officials, who recommended that the woman be deported due to feeblemindedness.[95]

Hayes reported on a second woman, "of weak character," who quit or was fired from several positions as a domestic worker, failed to contribute board or housework when she moved into the house of an acquaintance, and instead spent her money on clothes and jewelry. Hayes noted that immigration officials had asked her to "keep track of [the woman] and report the case if she gets out of work." Hayes briefly mentioned another woman whom she had placed in a domestic service position; the woman had then moved to New Hampshire and a year later "had a bad reputation at the factory where she worked." Hayes noted that this woman had "succeeded in getting herself in the newspapers," was taken from a "questionable house," and would soon be deported "as a woman of bad character." The account suggests the strong possibility that the woman had become a prostitute.[96]

Another case ended more happily, but only after the threat of deportation had been raised. A young immigrant woman who had arrived a few days earlier had returned to the Immigrant's Home "very much under the influence of liquor," after having made new acquaintances who claimed to have come from her hometown. The matron of the home called on Hayes to speak to the woman. Hayes reported that "[a] half hour's talk failed to make the girl realize that she must not go with these people who had become relatives in the course of conversation, and the agent was compelled to threaten to turn the girl over to the Immigration Department as an undesirable alien before she became amenable to reason." She was thereafter allowed to remain at the Immigrant's Home, where the matron "spoke so favorably of the girl and her method of working that the agent had no hesitation about placing her in a private family."[97]

These cases moved significantly beyond discerning whether, upon entry, an immigrant would become a public charge, investigating the case of an ill or missing relative, or intervening on behalf of an immigrant detained by immigration officials. Nor did Hayes seek merely to protect these female immigrants against unscrupulous agents, employers, or others. Instead, she monitored their behavior long after they had arrived in the United States and, in some instances, instigated investigations by immigration officials into their circumstances. In some cases, such as that of the inebriated woman or the woman who lived in "a questionable house," Hayes's intervention might have forestalled future encounters with the criminal justice system or problems with unemployment, because these woman either did not have family members present to intervene or did not have relatives able to address those problems.

Unfortunately, the immigrants' perspectives have been occluded from the historical record because the women, who were generally poor and lacking in education, were often encouraged to leave the country voluntarily rather than face official deportation proceedings and thus would have been dealt with informally rather than through the legal system. Moreover, as port agent, Hayes also served as the program's record keeper and would therefore have discouraged the women's views from being expressed. Many of their names or ages were not recorded in the CIS records, making their cases impossible to trace further.

Hayes's reports also suggest a propensity for diagnosing women as feeble-minded for behavior that today might be classified as shock, postpartum depression, or rebelliousness. It is likely that authorities used this classification as a legal mechanism enabling them to deport immigrant women in accordance with the provisions of the Immigration Act of March 3, 1891, an immigration law that reinforced an earlier one, passed in 1882. The 1891 act permitted the deportation of several classes of immigrants, including "all idiots, insane persons, or paupers."[98] A letter from John Trant, the British vice-consul, to John Keenan, secretary of the CIS, alludes to the practice of classifying women as feebleminded for violations of the moral code. Trant discussed the case of a woman from Mitchelstown, County Cork, who had been committed to the Massachusetts State School for the Feeble-Minded, "confined by reason of her low mentality, which is given as the reason for her having become the mother of an illegitimate child about two years ago." He continued: "[I]t appeared on investigation that there was nothing radically wrong with the girl beyond the fact that she had become an offender against society, and having no means of her own was placed in a State Institution."[99]

The relationship between the immigration office and the CIS and St. Vincent de Paul Society's port assistance program was interdependent. Indeed, Hayes characterized the agents of private immigrant aid societies as "auxiliary workers [who] supplement the work of the Commissioner and his subordinates."[100] As Americanization programs became increasingly important during and after World War I, the port program was enlisted in this movement. George Creel, of the Committee on Public Information, wrote to John Keenan of CIS, asking him to register with the agency as a group involved in Americanization work in Boston. Activities the agency defined as Americanization included instruction in civics, "counteracting anti-American propaganda," and "adopting safeguards against alien enemy activities." During the war, however, immigration had come to a virtual standstill, and by the 1920s immigration from Ireland had slowed considerably from prewar levels. Julia Hayes had left her position as port agent in 1918 to begin a job in Washington, and by 1922 the CIS port assistance efforts were limited to helping fund the Archdiocese of Boston's newly created Bureau of Immigration, which directed the bulk of its efforts toward Italian immigrants. In light of the CIS's prediction of a precipitous decline in Irish immigration in the future, the society moved to establish an employment bureau as part of its charitable efforts.[101]

The port program of the archdiocese's Immigration Welfare Department (IWD), a component of its Catholic Charitable Bureau (CCB), expanded the work initiated by the St. Vincent de Paul/CIS program in Boston to all significant incoming groups of Catholics. The director of the program boasted that Boston was the first diocese to have established such a program, noting that even the Archdiocese of New York had not done so. The Archdiocese of Boston sought to centralize the efforts of all societies and bring them under Cardinal O'Connell's control. O'Connell's secretary, Monsignor Richard Haberlin, directed the CCB's Father Michael Scanlan: "See to it that all Catholic agencies doing any form of immigration work become affiliated with the bureau and not overlap." Although the CIS had already left the field, the St. Raphael Society had continued its program. Apparently Father Rafaele D'Alfonso, a priest from an Italian parish, had objected to a plan in which he would have had to cede supervision of the St. Raphael's program to the IWD.[102]

Following the model of the CIS program, the director of the IWD emphasized the importance of hiring women as agents, because the department's efforts were directed primarily at female immigrants. The sole full-time salaried agent was a woman, Mary Cotter, but the CCB also sought out women employees who were fluent in Italian, Polish, Portuguese, and German to assist immigrants who spoke those languages. These decisions reflected the concerns articulated by Charlotte Grace O'Brien several decades earlier.[103]

O'Brien's reform efforts sought to insure that Irish women emigrating to the United States would be protected from the potentially dangerous actions of male strangers in the same way that their parents and the larger community would regulate social interactions in their home towns and villages. To do that she enlisted the assistance of the steamship lines and, ultimately, members of the Catholic hierarchy and laity in the United States. While the port assistance programs that arose from O'Brien's activism often provided a social welfare net for immigrants, there were also harsh consequences for those women who deviated from gender norms. The reform effort was certainly double-edged: the reverse side of protection was a punitive form of social control, often occurring well after the immigration process had ended. Ultimately, if the state intervened, women faced deportation or institutionalization for their actions. Moreover, while O'Brien's Victorian views located the threat to young immigrant Irish women in their innocence, those in charge of the Boston port assistance program tended to deem the women morally culpable. The church's support of those programs implicitly acknowledged that urban life remained appealing to immigrants because it allowed them to re-create communities and to ease the perils and hardships of immigration. Those who promoted such programs hoped that they might smooth the transition for those who could not readily depend on relatives or acquaintances for support upon their arrival. Finally, the reform effort illustrates how fluidly many Catholic-based reform efforts permeated national boundaries and highlights the existence of an international network of reformers who worked on a range of social issues, from immigration assistance to temperance to charitable efforts, by adapting existing models to suit particular circumstances in the United States.

· · · · ·

National Catholic Welfare Council Port Programs

Following World War I, the newly established National Catholic Welfare Council launched a program that would soon eclipse the localized immigration programs organized through the activism of Charlotte O'Brien and others. Ironically, the new initiative occurred immediately following a period in which immigration from Europe had virtually ceased as a result of the war and in a decade that ushered in a wave of immigration restriction laws.

Just as the cis program was eventually overshadowed by that of the Archdiocese of Boston, the new ncwc intervened in the archdiocese's efforts and provided its program with substantial financial assistance. In its first year, the ncwc provided the Archdiocese of Boston's iwd with $1,000 because the archdiocese did not have sufficient resources to establish a program of its own in Boston.[104]

By 1920 the ncwc, based in Washington, D.C., had established a comprehensive national immigration bureau with satellite programs at European departure points, such as those in Danzig (present-day Gdansk) and Warsaw. Although the ncwc continued to rely on support from the local ethnically based groups, the port assistance program became increasingly centralized, as had many other social welfare functions formerly under the control of local lay groups or archdioceses.

The ncwc founded its Bureau of Immigration in 1920 as "the equal of other immigrant aid organizations, both sectarian and non-sectarian." The annual report for 1922–23 noted that "these privileges were received only by means of careful and diplomatic negotiations by our Bureau necessary to overcome opposition, resulting from petty jealousies of other groups." The ncwc launched its programs on an international scale by establishing, in addition to its Washington headquarters, branch offices on Ellis Island and in Philadelphia and smaller stations in Warsaw and Danzig. In fact, its Ellis Island station alone employed nine workers. The ncwc also initiated a Mexican border program in El Paso and Juarez and cooperated, in conjunction with the local conference of the St. Vincent de Paul Society, with the immigrant assistance work concerning a group of Filipino Catholics in Seattle. The extension of immigration work to non-European immigrants signaled a recognition of the increasing diversity of immigrants and an acknowledgement of changes in international politics. Unlike other Asians, Filipinos were not excluded from the United States before 1938, because of their status as U.S. nationals following the Spanish-American War.[105]

The NCWC also broadened significantly the scope of Catholic immigrant assistance programs. As a large national organization it was in a far better position than previous Catholic groups to lobby for changes in immigration regulations and station conditions and to intervene on behalf of detained immigrants. It also participated in a variety of committees and panels pertaining to the subject of immigration, including the National Conference of Social Work, the General Committee for Immigrant Aid at Ellis Island, and the New York Joint Legislative Committee to Investigate Exploitation of Immigrants. In the year ending June 30, 1923, 328 immigrants requested that the NCWC Bureau of Immigration represent them at appeals hearings before the U.S. Department of Labor. The bureau represented 243 of the immigrants and succeeded in obtaining favorable decisions in the majority of those cases. While agents for both the CIS and the Archdiocese of Boston had intervened in the cases of detained immigrants, the appeals process became much more formalized under the NCWC's aegis.[106]

The NCWC's program placed a heavy emphasis on its role in limiting the proselytizing effects of Protestant groups. Although it had been one concern of those running prior port programs, this aspect of the NCWC's work permeated accounts of its activities. The NCWC nevertheless sought to build a cooperative relationship with the various religious groups working at the ports in order to lobby for improvements in immigration law and policies for the protection of immigrants, and to sponsor joint conferences on these issues. The NCWC supported a House of Representatives bill that would allow for the reunification of immigrant families under a provision that established a non-quota class of immigrants for relatives of U.S. citizens. In 1923 the NCWC had declined to take a public stand on the immigration restriction issue. The Reed-Johnson bill, debated in 1923 and 1924, would have greatly reduced immigration from southern and eastern Europe and virtually eliminated Asian immigration. By 1924 the NCWC had decided to oppose this immigration bill, and the bureau's director, Bruce Mohler, lobbied against its passage.[107]

Although the NCWC greatly expanded the scale and comprehensiveness of Catholic immigrant port programs, it retained a concern over the status of immigrant females in particular. As in the other programs, women served as agents at many of these ports. Other details of the NCWC program also echoed the concerns expressed earlier by Charlotte O'Brien. In Juarez, for example, the NCWC established separate toilet facilities for males and females. The bureau also noted that the program provided assistance when medical examinations or delousing occurred "in a manner which proves harmful or embarrassing to girls and women, including [women] religious."

Despite its size, much of the "routine work" performed by the NCWC's Bureau of Immigration replicated the activities that local groups such as the CIS had undertaken a decade earlier. That work included arranging for telegrams, supplying food and clothing, arranging marriage ceremonies, and providing tickets for rail transportation.[108] In fact, local ethnically based port programs continued to supplement the NCWC's immigration work. The National Alliance of Bohemian Catholics, the Polish Aid Society (or Somopomoc Polska), and the Italian Gens Society all retained their programs, and in some cases hired social workers, but agreed to operate according to conditions approved by the NCWC's Bureau of Immigration. Other ethnically based Catholic groups agreed to forward to the NCWC the names of their cases for follow-up purposes; these included the St. Raphael Society and Leo House. Yet the NCWC never fully realized its ambitious plans for following up on immigrants' cases after they had left the bureau's stations.[109]

The NCWC's international programs on behalf of immigrants had two main objectives: to counter proselytizing and to prepare local Catholic groups to assume its functions in the future. The NCWC reiterated local complaints about the insidious effects of Protestant groups and their programs on the Mexican border and in Poland; it was especially agitated over the work of the YMCA and YWCA, although the latter group eventually discontinued its programs in both locations. Polish Catholic societies had also entered port assistance work; the NCWC "insisted that all contact of this group with the Y.W.C.A. be severed and is hopeful that both Catholic groups in Poland will, through the efforts of our Bureau, be united as the one body—the Polish Emigration Bureau." The NCWC bureau also intervened on the Mexican border to stop the practice of Mexican officials and a local lawyer taking bribes from immigrants seeking fewer delays in immigration. Although it did not establish stations in Great Britain, the NCWC forged alliances with women's lay groups in England, Ireland, and Scotland to insure that deported or remigrating immigrants would receive assistance upon their return from the United States. In Liverpool, for example, the Catholic Women's League ran a hostel at which immigrants were accommodated. This effort proved similar to Charlotte O'Brien's efforts to assist immigrants at the point of departure, during the crossing, and at the point of entry.[110]

Thus, while Catholic port assistance work under the NCWC became far more influential on a national and international scale and was able to help far more immigrants than previous programs, the NCWC's Bureau of Immigration greatly eclipsed local programs. That change coincided with larger Progressive-era trends in America toward bureaucracy, efficiency, and the professionalism of social welfare. Yet, despite these developments, aspects of these NCWC programs reflected both earlier efforts by local groups and the concerns articulated by Charlotte O'Brien.

The bureau's work finally began to wind down in response to increasing financial pressures in 1926, when it decided to close its station in Philadelphia. This move coincided with the precipitous decline in European immigration that resulted from the immigration restriction laws enacted during the 1920s.[111]

· · · · ·

Catholic lay efforts to assist incoming immigrants in the late nineteenth and early twentieth centuries emanated in part from a growing identification with an urban middle class on the part of these program's supporters, but it was not an easy task to convince other Catholics of the importance of sponsoring such work. These efforts occurred in the context of an international reform network, extending from the American West to Liverpool, Cork, Bremen, New York, Boston, and later to Mexico and eastern Europe. Several of these efforts also coincided with, and to some extent were related to, both Land League agitation and famine in Ireland. These two events highlighted the importance of land in a population's self-determination and economic independence and would seem to complement rural colonization efforts in the United States as well as the move to improve conditions among new immigrants. But these developments also left reformers in these areas open to the charge that they were subverting the possibility of change in Europe by encouraging immigration, thus limiting their programs' appeal.

An examination of these reform efforts also reveals the pervasiveness of chain migration patterns and remigration among immigrants—providing later arrivals with networks and advantages that were not available to original waves of immigrants. Reformers viewed such patterns as either beneficial (in O'Brien's and Hayes's case) or detrimental (in the view of rural colonization promoters). Port program records demonstrate that immigrants' status was often precarious even after they had lived in the United States for several years. Without relatives, many immigrants were forced to return to Europe.

There is no doubt that many immigrants benefited from rural colonization and port programs established at the turn of the century. Yet immigrant protection efforts sometimes moved beyond extending "a friendly hand." Some middle-class or upper-class reformers sought to assert authority over their poorer immigrant coreligionists by invoking particular provisions in immigration law. In part, their intervention intended to improve the status of the religion as a whole by rendering some behavior unacceptable.

Finally, we have seen how small, locally based Catholic assistance programs became larger, more bureaucratic, and more formalized during the first two decades of the twentieth century, as well as farther removed from the hands of the laity. Concurrently, these newer programs became increasingly concerned with the proselytizing effects of Protestant-based efforts. Many of the activities taken on by the port programs of the Archdiocese of Boston's Immigrant Welfare Department and the NCWC reflected the concerns of Charlotte O'Brien and the activities previously initiated by local lay groups. Even in the earlier programs, Catholic reformers sought to systematize the process of immigration and, in doing so, to improve the social and economic status both of incoming immigrants and of Catholics already residing in the United States.

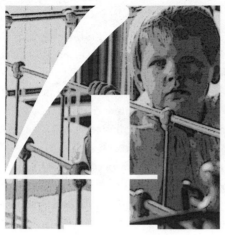

Poverty & Proselytizers

• • • • •

Lay Catholic Charitable and Settlement Work

In the late nineteenth and early twentieth centuries, the Catholic laity expanded its involvement in charitable and settlement house work for several reasons. Catholics engaged in reform efforts in part as a result of their fear of proselytizing by Protestant groups. Their participation also resulted from a growing sense that their involvement in charity would strengthen the reputation of the church in the United States and would illustrate the increasing presence of Catholics in the urban middle class—and the accompanying sentiment of noblesse oblige. By enlarging their participation in charity, lay Catholics could also broaden their interaction and influence with members of new immigrant groups. A deeper understanding of the relationship between Catholic charity givers and their recipients can illuminate attitudes toward poverty and social reform as well as the relationship of Catholics to the larger American society. That dynamic differed from that of Protestant-oriented groups whose members belonged to the dominant social class. Members of Catholic charity groups generally had not attained a social status equal to that of their Protestant counterparts. In fact, many of the laity in charitable organizations bemoaned the fact that wealthy Catholics in the United States remained reluctant to become involved in their efforts. At the same time, like Catholic temperance reformers, middle-class and wealthier Catholics involved in charity needed to distance themselves from the stereotypes typically associated with their poorer coreligionists. That motivation was absent in the relationship between Protestant charity givers and their Catholic recipients. Catholic settlement house workers in particular felt compelled to intervene between the Catholic poor and the Protestant majority by establishing alternative institutions rather than initiating programs where none existed.[1]

Catholics often portrayed themselves as uniquely equipped to care for the urban poor, a majority of whom were Catholic, on the basis of their common religious and European ties and their more enlightened attitude toward immigrants. To some degree, that claim was valid. Catholics regarded new immigrants as an important base within an expanding church rather than as a threat to American society's stability and ethnic composition. Moreover, Catholic reformers were not as concerned by the new immigrants' European traditions or religious practices, both sources of suspicion among many Americans, to the same degree as other charity providers.

Catholics did, however, categorize the poor according to their circumstances. For example, lay groups sometimes deemed particular sectors of society as worthy poor and others as not worthy. Moreover, providers often concluded that the poor lacked values such as thrift and sobriety, as well as home management skills. Therefore one might characterize the approach of some lay Catholic charitable activities as "mediating," as their leaders sought to intervene between the dominant class and poor Catholics. Although many charitable efforts benefited the Catholic Church as a whole, lay charities operated with several disadvantages, such as a shortage of material assistance, relative to other groups. As members of a religious minority, their tenuous status sometimes led Catholic reformers to adopt positions similar to those of Protestant-oriented charitable organizations.

Catholics promoted the view that religious groups held "proprietary" rights to care for their members. The idea that members of religious organizations had a particular responsibility for their poor coreligionists was highlighted by the praise that Catholic charity workers expressed for the work performed by Jewish organizations on behalf of the poor in "their" community. For example, a Mr. Mallon, a member of the St. Vincent de Paul Society in Brooklyn, commended the work in New York of some "of our Hebrew women [who] organized a committee and appealed to their wealthy co-religionists for funds to enable them to pension widows and children so that it would not be necessary to take the dependent little ones from their mothers and hand them over to strangers." Robert Hebberd, secretary of the New York State Board of Charities, stated in a speech reprinted in an 1898 issue of the *St. Vincent de Paul Quarterly* that Jews "vie most successfully with their Christian brethren in deeds of unostentatious charity, and . . . in their benevolent administrations they omit neither race nor creed, although, of course, as may readily be imagined, very properly giving especial attention to those of the household of their own faith."[2]

Such praise contrasted sharply with the Catholic perspective on charity provided across religious lines and highlighted the view that religious communities had proprietary rights to care for their own. There was little fear among Catholics that Jewish charitable groups, who represented a small religious minority, would extend their programs beyond their own community. Moreover, in that era, Orthodox Jews did not seek converts to their faith. Simultaneously, though, Catholics boasted that the St. Vincent de Paul Society, as well as other Catholic charities, did not discriminate against the poor based on race, creed, or nationality. That policy sometimes led Catholics to provide assistance to those outside their own religion. Catholics further contrasted their policy with that of some Protestant institutions, which they accused of treating Catholics poorly, or not at all.[3]

Catholic rhetoric surrounding issues of poverty and its causes in the nineteenth and early twentieth centuries differed from that of many Protestant-oriented charities, such as the Charity Organization Society. Ironically, despite their differing forms, Catholic lay charities and Protestant settlement workers launched similar critiques of the proponents of "scientific charity" and its methods.[4] Although Catholic charity workers could not eradicate their prejudices against the poor, both the St. Vincent de Paul Society and the Catholic settlement house movement exemplified modes of charity that differed substantially from the prevailing attitudes of most Protestant-oriented charities in the late nineteenth century.

There were, however, limits to the extent to which the shared religion of charity providers and their recipients allowed them to transcend traditional relations between the two groups. First, differences of class and values created tensions between Catholic charity givers and recipients in almost all situations in which the poor were assisted. The belief that the poor should be cared for without condescension or judgment thus competed with the notion that some poor were worthy while others were not.

Second, Catholics as a group needed to portray themselves defensively in order to stave off potential criticism that they were promoting non-American values, or at least tolerating them within their church. This was especially true given the fact that during World War I the loyalty of German Americans and Irish Americans, a significant portion of the U.S. Catholic population, came into question.[5] Settlement workers, whether Catholic or non-Catholic, often had more tolerance for the European traditions of immigrants than did traditional charity providers. But the Americanization programs for immigrants administered by native-born settlement workers did not emanate from a need to prove themselves as loyal Americans—with the exception of those reformers who had socialist or radical political views.[6] Some Catholic charity workers, however, felt compelled to institute Americanization programs in the late teens and early 1920s as a defensive measure.

Third, many of the laity involved in Catholic charitable activities, whether working, middle, or upper class, strove to challenge negative stereotypes of their coreligionists. Therefore their sense of obligation extended beyond a sense of noblesse oblige as they sought to gain respectability for the religion as a whole. In significant ways, the relationship between lay Catholic charity providers and their recipients paralleled that of German American Jews and newly arrived eastern European Jews. By the late nineteenth century, both religious groups experienced widening class divisions among their members, and each suffered from stereotypes that lay leaders sought to eradicate by engaging in charity and uplifting the status of their coreligionists. The two religious communities also sought to preserve their religion in an often hostile environment.[7]

This chapter focuses on two major types of lay charitable work by examining the organization and efforts of indigenous chapters of the Society of St. Vincent de Paul, a predominantly male charitable group, and the Catholic settlement house movement, whose charitable activities, like those of its Protestant and secular counterparts, were defined as appropriate for upper- and middle-class women. Both efforts emanated from a belief that the poor needed more than material relief and should be treated as equals rather than looked down upon. Yet this ideal was often challenged in the daily practice of charity.[8]

In the mid-1840s, Catholic laymen in the United States began forming American chapters of the Society of St. Vincent de Paul, an international charitable organization begun in Paris in 1833 by Frederic Ozanam. The group, whose membership was limited to men, was the oldest and most extensive lay Catholic charitable organization in the United States in the nineteenth century. Although its total American membership remained modest, it had numerous chapters at the parish level and served as a model for later charitable activities among the laity, including women. Until the early twentieth century, much of organized Catholic charity remained in the hands of women religious who ran a variety of Catholic institutions, such as orphanages and homes for the elderly.

In addition to the St. Vincent de Paul Society and the work of women religious, new charitable efforts emerged by the early twentieth century, including a settlement house movement. The second half of this chapter discusses the importance of Catholic settlements in the development of lay charity, concentrating on two major examples: Madonna Center, founded initially as the Guardian Angel Mission on Chicago's West Side in 1898, and St. Elizabeth Settlement in St. Louis, which was established in 1915 and funded by both the Catholic Central Verein and the Catholic Women's Union. Those efforts resulted in part from *Rerum Novarum,* issued by Pope Leo XIII in 1891, which provided further impetus to the expansion of charitable activities by the laity as well as other groups in the church by emphasizing the importance of economic relations between workers and business and rejecting socialism as a valid path toward a more equitable distribution of wealth. The settlement house efforts were also partly a response to the proliferation of Protestant and secular organizations' charitable programs targeted toward poor, urban Catholics, many of whom were immigrants.

Catholics at the lay level recognized the dearth of their own settlement house and charitable efforts and devoted their energies toward building urban programs to counter perceived proselytizing by non-Catholic groups. This fear was especially strong with regard to newly arriving Italians, who were often seen by their coreligionists as especially susceptible to Protestant proselytizers. Members of the hierarchy and clergy drew such conclusions based on their perceptions that Italians were lax about church attendance compared to other Catholics, because of widespread anticlericalism among Italians, and because they viewed critically many aspects of Italians' religious worship, which emphasized street festivals, feast days, and the veneration of the Madonna. As Robert Orsi has suggested in his studies of Italian American religious practices, prior to the 1930s, Italian Catholics did not always tie their religious worship to parishes or other church institutions.[9]

The chapter further explores both the ways in which these groups drew on particular European influences and organizations and also the ways in which their efforts paralleled those of other charitable groups operating in urban America. These efforts did not simply appropriate the strategies and views of those non-Catholic groups. Instead, lay Catholics sought to infuse their charitable efforts with Catholic and European influences, using both defensive and offensive strategies to distinguish their programs from others. The chapter also analyzes the ways in which lay Catholic charitable activities became defined as appropriate for men or women and the ways in which those perceptions changed from the late nineteenth century to the 1920s.

Although concerns about proselytizing permeated many of the laity's social reform efforts in this era, nowhere were they more apparent than in the area of charity. Catholic charity providers viewed the YMCA and the YWCA as especially dangerous to the status of poor, urban Catholics because of their extensive social and recreational programs with insidious Protestant instruction. One Catholic publication asserted that among Protestant organizations "[e]verywhere the object is the same, to de-Catholicize and to Americanize." Settlement houses and other neighborhood centers and programs also served to consternate Catholics. Despite their harsh criticism of Protestant and "humanist" charitable efforts, however, Catholics involved in the field repeatedly sought to legitimize their efforts by garnering the approval of non-Catholics.[10]

While exaggerated, the Catholic fear of proselytizing by those engaged in charitable and settlement house work was not unfounded. Several Protestant denominations sponsored programs that expressly sought to convert poor Catholics to their churches, although predictions by some Catholics of immense "leakage" among the newer immigrant groups did not, in the end, prove true. It is also not surprising that during the 1920s, a decade of renewed anti-Catholic sentiment, Protestant groups (and secular ones whose members came from largely Protestant backgrounds) became the object of suspicion among some Catholics. In several instances, settlement workers did seek to convert Catholic immigrants to Protestantism. Moreover, the fact that settlement house programs were targeted at children in particular often created tensions between immigrant parents and their second-generation children and angered parish priests in their midst. The Protestant-oriented curriculum in the public school systems also led to fear that Catholic children were being taught beliefs that ran counter to Catholic teaching.[11]

Writing on the YMCA in a question-and-answer format, Reverend Monsignor Thomas Bona, of St. Mary's of Perpetual Help Church in Chicago, noted in 1927 that the organization posed a threat to the Catholic Church by its "clever proselytizing" and "sly propaganda." He asked, "Do our Catholic boys belong to the organization?" and responded, "Large numbers of them." Bona asserted that Bible classes were held in the YMCA buildings and that Protestant ministers gave talks to members. He also maintained that singing classes sometimes were brought to Protestant churches to perform and conjectured that Catholic boys had access to "almost any anti-Catholic book" on the association's bookshelves. In an unflattering assessment of Catholics, he further criticized the YMCA for conducting "high brow" discussions that raised questions that "an ordinary Catholic cannot answer." In contrast, Bishop James Griffen of Springfield, Illinois, in a letter to Cardinal George Mundelein that same year, concluded that the YMCA did not pose a significant threat to Catholics in his diocese and had lost popularity since the war.[12]

Those involved in Catholic charitable efforts in the late nineteenth and early twentieth centuries emphasized that spiritual needs were as, if not more, important than material ones. That assertion extended to the providers of charity as well as to the recipients. In general, the majority of Catholic charity providers in this period focused on seeking individual solutions to the problems of poverty rather than placing it in the larger context of social reform. There were exceptions to this pattern, however. Father John A. Ryan, a priest active in labor issues and social causes and a major Catholic supporter of New Deal programs, viewed poverty in the context of a larger framework of social relations and actively supported labor issues. William J. Kerby was another crucial figure in the field of Catholic charity. A priest and professor of sociology at Catholic University, Kerby authored *The Social Mission of Charity* and worked toward the professionalization of social work among Catholics. Ryan and Kerby were among those who promoted a larger critique of American society and industrialization and emphasized the need for a more equitable relationship between capital and labor.

Both men feared that socialism would draw away members of the Catholic working class unless the church made significant and sincere efforts to address major social and economic issues of the day. Ryan therefore supported Progressive-era legislation such as the Child Labor Amendment. As discussed below, however, increasing numbers of Catholics in the field of charity in the early twentieth century gradually accepted the notion of "preventative charity." That concept recognized that circumstances surrounding poverty often resulted from external forces such as industrial accidents, disease, and economic downturns rather than individual vices or practices. Yet lay Catholics remained wary of the state's role in eradicating poverty.[13]

Catholics contrasted their conception of charity with that of other groups, who, they argued, had been moving gradually toward a more materialist view of social problems. This critique of materialism and individualism echoed that of Catholic women's groups, discussed in Chapter 5. Catholics also emphasized that charity's value was not limited to the poor but extended to the givers of spiritual, emotional, and material assistance as well, because they would receive eternal rewards for their efforts. Catholic charity improved the life of the provider as well as that of the recipient because it would clarify the former's values and priorities.

The Society of St. Vincent de Paul

Frederic Ozanam founded the Society of St. Vincent de Paul while a student at the Sorbonne in Paris. Ozanam had been born in Milan, where his father studied medicine and established a thriving practice before the family repatriated to Lyons. As a young man, Ozanam, who displayed academic promise and a gift for languages, moved to Paris to study law, the profession that his father had encouraged him to pursue. Ozanam and six other members chartered the Society, named in honor of St. Vincent de Paul, a French saint born in 1581 who was renowned for his involvement in charity, and particularly for his efforts to organize men into charitable groups. While university students formed the core of the Society in its early years, Ozanam remarked that by the end of the 1830s they had been joined by many elites, including a peer of France, noblemen, government clerks, army generals, lawyers, engineers, physicians, and "distinguished" writers and artists, as well as "small shop-keepers and even shop-hands."[14]

Although by 1911 only 12,000 of the St. Vincent de Paul Society's world-wide membership of 200,000 resided in the United States, the organization's influence within the American church was greater than that number suggests. As many as 500 conferences had formed at the parish level, with a priest serving as spiritual director of each. Moreover, in 1909 the Society in the United States reported that in those conferences that had submitted figures, its members had undertaken a total of 148,419 visits and spent $278,600 on their charitable efforts.[15]

Two American lay Catholics, educated in France, had imported the Society to the United States. Bryan Mullanphy and Moses Linton organized the first American conference at the Old Cathedral Parish in St. Louis in 1845. A pamphlet writer summarizing the one-hundredth anniversary of the Society found it suitably symbolic that the first branch of the French Society had been established in St. Louis, which was "only recently part of France in the New World, a city French in foundation, French in name and French in culture."[16]

Mullanphy, the son of one of St. Louis's leading families, had been born in Baltimore in 1809 but was educated in France and England before settling permanently in Missouri. He had attended the Sorbonne and, according to one publication of the Society, had "apparently met Ozanam." Like Ozanam, Mullanphy had studied law. His father was John Mullanphy, an Irish immigrant born in Iniskillen, County Fermanagh, in 1758, who had moved with his family from the East Coast to St. Louis when it was barely more than a village. After moving west, he acquired substantial landholdings and became successful in trade. He and his wife, Elizabeth, from County Waterford, sent their children to school in France. John Mullanphy's wealth allowed him to contribute generously to various charities, and he is credited with establishing the first Catholic hospital west of the Mississippi. Bryan Mullanphy, who never married, carried on his father's charitable tradition by establishing the St. Louis Conference of the St. Vincent de Paul Society and supporting the city's Irish Emigration Society. Described by some as eccentric for the stipulations he attached to his gifts, he was also characterized as hardworking and kindhearted. He later practiced law, became involved in Democratic politics as a city alderman, and received an appointment to the St. Louis Circuit Court. He died in 1851, leaving his considerable estate to the city of St. Louis to assist needy immigrants.[17]

The cofounder of the St. Louis branch of the Society, Dr. Moses Linton, a Catholic convert who had also studied in Paris, was born and raised in Kentucky. In contrast to the Mullanphys, the Linton family was of modest means, but Moses earned enough money to study medicine with a Springfield, Kentucky, physician and received a medical degree from Transylvania University. After marrying Ann Booker, a judge's daughter, he moved to Edinburgh, Scotland, and later to Paris for additional medical training. After returning to Springfield, he converted to Catholicism and accepted a position on the medical faculty of St. Louis University. Linton was highly regarded for his knowledge of medicine, his keen intellect, and his community activism. He served as president of the St. Louis Conference until 1851, except for a two-year term filled by Mullanphy.[18]

The Society of St. Vincent de Paul emphasized two forms of charity. The major focus of its members' works involved visiting poor Catholic families in their homes to give friendship, spiritual guidance, and material assistance to those in need. Maintaining that "no charity was foreign to the Society," members also engaged in a variety of "Special Works" tailored to the current needs of the local community and its institutions. In general, Special Works entailed visiting prisons, reformatories, and other institutions where poor Catholics were present and undertaking juvenile probation work. But Special Works programs also promoted those values that, in the Society's view, would alleviate poverty. These included encouraging temperance, advising the poor to save money, providing leisure activities to working men, and teaching occupations and trades to orphans. In Philadelphia the Society cooperated closely with local temperance societies, "making the improvement in the home life of the poor more steadfast and enduring." Through their spiritual work, Vincentians, as the Society's members were known, encouraged the poor Catholics whom they visited to attend mass, to baptize their children, and to enter into Catholic marriages.[19]

The Society emphasized that one of its primary goals was to "preserve the family" whenever possible. Vincentians could foster that goal by assisting mothers to obtain employment so they could provide for their children, or by helping families in financial emergencies. One conference in Baltimore assisted a family with five children whose father had died of tuberculosis. The members "adopted this family with the full realization that it would have the help of the family for a period of from three to five years, until the older children would become wage earners. . . . [T]he family is practically being reared under the auspices of the society and is a happy illustration of the first principle of our work,—that a home should never be broken up, nor children deprived of the natural guardianship of the parents where the home life is morally sound."[20]

This emphasis on preserving the family wherever possible contrasted with the placing of children in institutions or in foster care, a situation that had caused a great deal of concern among Catholics throughout the nineteenth century. Partially due to a lack of adequate resources for child care in their own community, Catholic children whose parents could not care for them were frequently placed in Protestant environments.[21] The Society recognized that there was often an "indifference" toward children among their coreligionists that needed to be rectified.[22]

Despite the fact that Frederic Ozanam and the Society's cofounders were university educated, the socioeconomic profile of most American Vincentians tended to be far more modest. This difference arose in part from the fact that in France Catholicism was the majority religion, as well as the religion of most elites, while in the United States Catholics were both a minority and largely non-elite. Although the Society's rules indicated that membership was intended for young, educated Catholic laymen, in the United States the members did not always meet that description. While establishing the socioeconomic profile of the Society's members is difficult, on the whole they seem to have been skilled workers striving for respectability or middle-class status rather than the wealthy elite. Their status contrasted with that of wealthier Catholic reformers engaged in settlement work or the members of Boston's League of Catholic Women.

Vincentians also differed in social status from the members of many late-nineteenth-century Protestant-oriented charities, who tended to come from the upper classes. In Pittsburgh, for example, most Vincentians belonged to the working class. Similarly, wealthy men rarely belonged to the Society in Brooklyn, although some of them provided financial assistance. In 1865 the Brooklyn Society stated that its members were "for the greater part, men who have themselves struggled, when newcomers here, to earn their living and attain the comparative ease they now enjoy, and which is within the reach of all who strive for it." It is probable, however, that Vincentians measured their members' status against their Protestant and secular counterparts rather than against fellow Catholics, who tended to be poor. The unwillingness of wealthy American Catholics to join the Society, in contrast to the practice in France, was a frequent refrain among those members speaking on the subject of the Society and its goals.[23] Their lament echoed that of Irish Catholic Colonization Association members.

There were examples, however, of successful and well-educated members. The ubiquitous American layman, William Onahan, was a member of the Holy Name Conference in Chicago, while John F. Fitzgerald, the mayor of Boston and maternal grandfather of future president John F. Kennedy, told a national meeting of the Society that he had once belonged the St. Stephen's Parish conference. And Thomas Dwight, Parkman Professor of Anatomy at Harvard University, served as president of the Central and Particular Councils in Boston's Society during the early twentieth century. A Catholic convert from an established Boston Protestant family, Dwight was born in Boston in 1843 but spent his childhood in Paris. After graduating from Harvard Medical School, he studied anatomy in Munich and made significant contributions to the field. Dwight's wife, Elizabeth, served as president of the League of Catholic Women in Boston. Poor men were explicitly barred from membership in the Society because its founders asserted that it would be difficult for them to minister to the poor if their economic circumstances remained inadequate. Implicit in this rule was the notion that poor men would have more difficulty in uplifting those of their own class.[24]

Vincentian leaders outlined a strategy for increasing the influence of the Society among non-Catholics that entailed recruiting wealthier Catholics into the organization. At one national conference in 1886, delegates considered the following proposal placed on the agenda: "Efforts should be made to recruit the Conferences largely from young gentlemen of education and means." F. W. Dammann, president of the Particular Council of Baltimore, acknowledged that putting forth such an issue "presupposes that they [Vincentians] are not, generally, composed of this class of persons." He noted that this situation presented a problem "to be regretted in regard to this class of persons as on account of the conferences themselves." But Dammann's subsequent remarks belied such a sentiment. He asserted that if each conference could successfully recruit a few Catholic men of means and education, their "influence would draw them to it, and be felt in outside [society], even Catholic Society . . . [and] give it more standing in society."[25]

William Onahan viewed the more egalitarian membership of the Society in the United States as its strength rather than its weakness. In his Golden Jubilee address to the Society, Onahan recounted that in France, England, and Ireland many men from the professions, the military, and commerce as well as gentlemen of the "highest social rank and position count it as a privilege to be enrolled." In contrast, he noted that in the United States membership in the Society was not limited to a particular class or condition but was based instead on one's conduct and behavior.[26]

Although Vincentians feared the effects of proselytizing as much as any other Catholic charity providers, the Society also sought approval from secular and Protestant groups for its work and viewed its activities, and the composition of its membership, as ways to gain greater acceptance for the Catholic Church as a whole. The *St. Vincent de Paul Quarterly* remarked: "Our church as its stands in this country, in the eyes of many is an alien." But the author suggested that Vincentian charity work would lead to greater acceptance among Americans. Another report emphasized that "[o]ur greatest desire is to see the Society established in new fields as, by this means we may look for a greater extension of its power for good among those of our own faith, and an increase among non-Catholics of respect and good-will for Holy Mother Church."[27] By recruiting more college-educated men into its ranks, then, the Society would gain increasing prestige for the church and its activities among non-Catholics.

In the late nineteenth and early twentieth centuries a tension existed within the Society between the international nature of the organization and the desire of some members to create a tighter network among its American chapters. An example of that tension was reflected in the controversy that emerged over the decision to publish an American *Bulletin* rather than rely-ing on the *Irish Bulletin*, the Society's official English-language publication. The position supporting the establishment of a national journal finally won out. Another Vincentian argued that there was "little or no union of action" among the branches of the Society in the United States and that it was "an unnatural arrangement" that, in order to discover what their fellow mem-bers in Louisiana or Missouri were doing, American Vincentians should "be obliged to go to Dublin or Paris." The speaker noted, moreover, that "even the existence of western branches of the society is unknown to many of its mem-bers in the East."[28]

Despite these efforts to strengthen relationships between American chap-ters, the organization's international dimension remained important. Indeed, the Special Works of European conferences served as models for those Amer-ican councils that had not yet expanded into this area. An 1886 meeting emphasized the fact that the American assembly did not have the power to "make or amend the Rules of the Society or to construe them." That power rested with the Council General of Paris alone. At the Society's 1911 conven-tion, the opening speech declared that "[the Society] is not national, it is universal and it has its value in this: that it inspires men to love and help one another because all are children of God." The Society's international nature also benefited American conferences because immigrants, as well as mi-grants, were often familiar with the organization's work upon their arrival in a new city.[29]

Despite the Society's universalist outlook, some ethnic divisions emerged within the organization in the United States. Although a large percentage of its American members had Irish surnames, in many cities the Society's con-ferences had members from other ethnic groups. In both Milwaukee and St. Louis, German Americans had been instrumental in the Society's founding. In fact, Milwaukee's conference emerged following Bishop John Henni's 1848 visit to the Munich Conference. By 1930, Catholics in Milwaukee had formed separate conferences comprised of Czech, Italian, Polish, and Bohe-mian Catholics.[30] By 1893, African American Catholics had joined the Society in Boston, Indianapolis, and Washington, D.C. African Americans had earlier formed a conference in St. Louis that was active in 1886. While the St. Louis conferences were segregated, it is unclear whether or not African Americans routinely belonged to integrated conferences.[31] Links between ethnic Vin-centians and their countries of origin often remained strong, as illustrated by

the Boston port assistance program and the aid sent to Germans and Aus-
trians by Milwaukee conferences, through the Cologne Conference, following
World War I.[32]

Society members in the United States, however, did not emphasize specifically ethnic issues to the same extent as members of the Catholic total abstinence movement or those in the Catholic colonization societies, who viewed
alcoholism or landlessness in a nationalist and ethnic framework. Vincentians in the late nineteenth and early twentieth century refrained from discussing the relative attributes and tendencies of particular ethnic groups. In
part, this approach emanated from the Society's desire to promote the idea of
the universal, rather than specific, nature of the poor and their needs. The
emphasis on universality proved incompatible with the strategy of stressing
shared ethnicity as the basis for assisting the poor. Thus, while Vincentians
sometimes formed conferences along racial and ethnic lines and assisted
those of similar ethnic backgrounds, they did not view poverty through the
lens of ethnicity.

Members of the Society continually emphasized that its purpose extended
beyond the material needs of the poor and stressed their concern with spiritual, moral, and emotional issues as much as "alms-giving." They cautioned
against giving the impression to potential members that the Society was a
"mere literary, social or philanthropic organization." Even the latter term
seemed to connote a preoccupation with the material condition of the poor, to
the exclusion of their other needs.[33]

Vincentians emphasized the reciprocal nature of charity, demonstrating
the ways in which charity providers benefited from contact with the poor.
"Who ever properly and with the right feeling and ideas, visited the poor, and
did not come away a wiser and better man?" F. W. Dammann asked rhetorically. W. J. McAuliffe, president of Philadelphia's St. Stanislaus Conference of
the Gesu, lamented: "How many young men there are who frequently squan-
der their money, if not sinfully at least foolishly, who have never been brought
into direct contact with a real deserving case of destitution and want." The
work served yet another purpose: to engage younger Vincentians who might
otherwise be subject to temptations "in the shape of cheap theatres, dance
halls, free concert gardens, and in a thousand and one other forms."[34]

Vincentian leaders further emphasized that the poor had something to
offer the Society's members. In one *Quarterly* article, a London member
intoned, "I could give you tales of every virtue, practiced by our poor, which

ought to incite us, who are blessed with so much comfort, to imitation." In addition to character building, however, charitable work among the poor, when done according to the spirit of the Society, would lead to members' sanctification. As Frederic Ozanam said as he began organizing the Society, "The blessing of the poor is the blessing of God."[35]

The method and attitudes that Vincentians were to carry with them in visiting the poor contained an implicit contrast to, and criticism of, government relief, traditional private "philanthropy," and professional social work. Leaders of the Society and their spiritual directors stressed that visitors to the poor should not subject them to humiliation. "Go not as 'official' or an 'employe' but as a brother, friend, and benefactor." They invoked Frederic Ozanam's dictum of becoming personally acquainted with the wants of the poor, rather than carrying out their duties in a "perfunctory way." In an address commemorating the Society in Chicago, Arthur J. Murray criticized government's attitude toward charity and, specifically, the city of Chicago's failure to assist "the unfortunates" who remained following the World's Fair.[36]

Ozanam had earlier drawn a contrast between philanthropy and charity. Philanthropy, he asserted, "is a vain woman who likes to deck herself out in her good works and admire herself in the glass; whereas charity is a mother whose eyes rest lovingly on the child at her breast, who has no thought of self, but forgets her beauty in her love." His metaphor comparing philanthropy to a materialist woman foreshadowed the dichotomous view of idle, wealthy women and selfless mothers promoted by women's groups and other Catholics in the late nineteenth and early twentieth centuries, which I discuss in the following chapter.[37] In fact, the term "philanthropy," unlike "charity," connoted a secular activity deriving from eighteenth-century rationalism. Another difference that Vincentians cited between their work and that of other charities was that the Society did not expect immediate results from its activities on behalf of the poor but rather exercised patience in a Christlike manner.

Society members, as well as other Catholics discussing charitable activities, often expressed a similar stereotype of philanthropists, which was generally targeted at Protestant and secular groups. Philanthropists were portrayed as wasting their energies in record keeping, meetings, and other administrative matters intended toward greater efficiency but which in fact detracted from their immediate goal of caring for the poor. That view echoed one that Ozanam had articulated previously. A 1903 *Pilot* article drew a contrast between the quiet work of Vincentians with that of peacocklike philanthropists: "[T]here is nothing of that ostentatious fuss and feathers and intentional or unconscious attitude of patronage which too often robs 'organized charity' of the very essence of the virtue upon which it plumes itself." This stereotype of Protestant charity givers contrasted sharply with the Puritan image that Catholics ascribed to many Protestant temperance advocates. But it proved similar to the critique of the modern, frivolous, "new woman" who challenged traditional gender roles. That critique, which became increasingly popular among Catholics, also depicted both male and female charity givers as part of the nouveaux riches who sought to use charity as a measure of their wealth and influence in society.[38]

Society members further contrasted their methods with those of other groups by stressing the fact that almost all the money that they collected went directly to the poor, because their principal activity involved visiting the poor in their homes or in institutions. Vincentians raised money by secret contributions at their weekly meetings as well as by occasional fund-raisers. Members compared the Society's financial administration with that of city and other private charities, which they claimed spent a majority of their earnings on costs and salaries rather than on the poor. On several occasions, speakers noted that non-Catholics had praised the Society for its efficient distribution of funds to the poor. As volunteers who sacrificed their evenings after a long day of work, Vincentians portrayed their motives as purer than those of paid charity workers or of wealthy volunteers who had an abundance of leisure time.[39]

On the other hand, Catholics disputed the notion that the "modern" methods of charity popular in the United States at the turn of the century were recent innovations, arguing that such efforts were similar to the methods and aims of Frederic Ozanam and others within the church. They pointed out that the Catholic Church had always engaged in social work and other programs for the poor. A writer in the German Central Verein's *Central-Blatt and Social Justice* depicted Frederic Ozanam as a modern-day social worker, and the poor whom he visited as his "cases."

At the 1911 meeting of the Society, Thomas M. Mulry of New York took issue with the spiritual director's speech giving "credit solely to the modern social worker for the institution of this so-called 'Social Service' movement." Mulry claimed that "this particular species of social service work has been conducted by the St. Vincent de Paul Society for the last thirty years." Mulry was a leading member of the Society in the United States. He was born in New York City in 1855 to Thomas Mulry, an Irish immigrant, and Parthenia Crolius Mulry, a Catholic convert descended from some of New York's early Dutch settlers. Four of the Mulrys' fourteen children joined the Jesuit order and a daughter joined the Sisters of Charity. In contrast, Thomas followed his father into the St. Bernard's Conference of the Society and into the construction business. He married a fellow parishioner, Mary Gallagher, a Hunter College graduate and schoolteacher. They, too, raised a large family and saw three of their sons become Jesuits and a daughter join the Sisters of Charity. Mulry took courses at Cooper Union but never graduated from college. He became president of his parish's conference in 1880 and received encouragement from his brothers in the priesthood. As a leader in the Society, he focused on child welfare issues and on improving the brittle relationships between the Society and the Protestant and government agencies involved in charity. When Mulry died in 1916, his work was so widely recognized that Auxiliary Bishop Patrick Hayes delivered his eulogy at St. Patrick's Cathedral.[40]

* * * * *

Despite the Society's overall criticisms of non-Catholic charity, there were differences in Protestant attitudes toward the nature and principles of relief in the late nineteenth century. The Charity Organization Society (cos), a major late-nineteenth-century charity movement operating in many industrial cities in the United States, sought to organize the distribution of charity within cities without providing direct alms, because its members generally viewed almsgiving as creating dependency among its poor recipients. Josephine Shaw Lowell, a wealthy Civil War widow and sister of Robert Gould Shaw, the abolitionist who had commanded the Massachusetts 54th Regiment, moved from her native Boston to New York and rose to prominence in the cos. In Cleveland, cos board members included industrialists. The group's policies toward the poor tended to be punitive and its judgment of them harsh. Members of the cos generally viewed human nature pessimistically and blamed poverty on individual moral failure. Earlier in the nineteenth century, Robert Hartley had founded the Association for the Improvement of the Condition of the Poor, which also saw moral failure as the underlying cause of poverty and emphasized the need for investigation of the poor. Many cos and other upper-class Protestant-oriented charity leaders in the scientific charity movement sought to systematize charity by looking to business procedures as models. They also promoted the view that charity should be the province of private voluntary efforts rather than the responsibility of the state.[41] It would be the cos's model of charity that proponents of the Protestant Social Gospel would later seek to replace.

The cos sought to forestall a social revolution by the poor. As one cos member stated, "[I]f we do not furnish the poor with elevating influences, they will rule us by degrading ones." The organization further sought to replace the idea of "lady bountiful" benevolence with a more effective form of charity. Friendly visiting was undertaken to investigate the circumstances of the poor, to systematize relief, and to prevent abuse.[42]

In his history of charity, Roy Lubove reveals that the St. Vincent de Paul Society was one of the first organizations to institute house visits to the poor, in 1833. He stops short, however, of indicating that the cos and other Protestant charities modeled their efforts on those of the Society. Yet the friendly visiting undertaken by the cos differed in crucial ways from that of the Society because of the wider social gap and the lack of a common religion between cos visitors and the poor, as well as the cos's emphasis on keeping extensive records on the poor who were visited.

Some Protestants disagreed with the cos's view of poverty and charity. Critics such as James Huntington, a Protestant minister from New York, criticized the group for holding the poor to higher standards of truthfulness and virtue than those found in the upper class.[43] In Boston, Edward Frothingham, secretary of the Provident Society, entered into a disagreement in 1887 with Robert Treat Paine, president of the Associated Charities of Boston, a society that also emphasized scientific charity. Paine objected to the Provident Society's policy of giving basic necessities to poor families headed by able-bodied adults. The Associated Charities also objected to giving direct relief, on the grounds that it discouraged thrift and led the poor to view aid as a right. Such harsh critiques of prevailing views led to the development of a more sympathetic view of poverty among many liberal Protestants in the form of the Social Gospel movement and also influenced the development of the settlement house movement.[44]

By the 1890s, during the midst of a severe depression, those in the cos and other scientific charities increasingly came to recognize that environmental factors could not be ignored as causes of impoverishment. Robert Treat Paine began to question how to eradicate poverty's "prolific causes permanently at work," while Josephine Lowell had accepted the notion that many poor had little control over their unfortunate circumstances. In fact, Lowell later became a major advocate of labor reform and a leader of the National Consumers' League.[45]

· · · · ·

Among Catholics in the St. Vincent de Paul Society, there was a significant tension between the desire to serve the poor without judgment and the competing impulse to view some of them as more worthy than others. Members were cautioned against concluding that some of the poor were irredeemable, especially those who were "confirmed drunkards" or alcoholics. An article in the *Catholic Citizen* echoed this view by asserting that while many Protestants asked if recipients of charity belonged to their churches and if they are worthy, "[t]here is here [in the Catholic Church] no scrutiny into any previous condition of worthiness but on the other hand, care is given those who have abused the gifts of God and by such abuse have made themselves objects of charity." At the 1886 meeting of the Society, Reverend John F. Kearney of New York declared: "The same spirit of love must animate your words which animated the words spoken to Magdalen, which changed a sinner into a saint; the same spirit which animated the words spoken to a dying thief." Kearney's comments were not to be taken literally, as the Society forbade its members to assist any poor who were associated with houses of prostitution or other illicit activities, although, as part of Special Works programs, members could visit prisoners.[46]

The Society's ideal of treating the poor as friends, and without condescension, did not always erase the paternalist elements of charity. As with both the Catholic total abstinence movement and the Catholic colonization societies, the virtues of thrift, industry, and, most important, sobriety were continually emphasized. In fact, Catholics whose livelihoods were made in the liquor trade were expressly forbidden from membership in the Society, at least in the United States. That prohibition occurred in part so that members could bring moral authority to their tasks. Moreover, the tickets that Vincentians distributed to the poor for food could not be redeemed at grocery shops selling liquor. Such restrictions against alcohol were not universal throughout the Society, however. In Belgium, for example, Vincentians were encouraged to share tobacco and beer with the poor on their visits in order to establish a sense of camaraderie. This suggests that in the United States, the Society emphasized temperance in order to garner greater respect for Catholics from the society at large.[47]

In order to encourage thrift, Vincentians were warned not to undertake their weekly visiting responsibilities on a strict schedule. By avoiding the regularly scheduled provision of financial assistance, they would thereby force the poor "to economize and to look ahead." Society members were also warned against contributing their own money to the poor, because it would foster dependency. Yet, on another occasion, a Vincentian bestowed praise upon immigrants for practicing thrift and economy: "When they land on our shores, they are very, very poor, but in a few years, many of them raise themselves to a condition of independence, while Americans with the same and perhaps better opportunities, are to be found lagging behind."[48]

A *Pilot* article about the Society's work in San Francisco reveals much about Catholic perceptions of the worthy poor, as well as about charities. "Its members quietly search out those most urgently in need . . . who are by no means always the people who flock to the fore at the first indication of something being handed out free. They scrupulously avoid anything approaching gratuitous and offensive prying into the private affairs of the worthy poor." The author concluded that the truly deserving poor wait to be sought out, while those requesting assistance are often unworthy of aid.[49]

A controversy arose over the conferences' new practice of keeping records on the families who were visited. The system was instituted to make the Society more efficient and to prevent fraudulent claims by the poor. The Society in Ireland had first developed the method and put it into wide use. Some members objected strenuously to the innovation; they asserted that to deem potential recipients unworthy of assistance was incompatible with the tenets and spirit of the Society, even when those individuals used deception in order to obtain aid. That objection also implicitly criticized the Charity Organization Society and other groups that stressed record keeping as a means of preventing the poor from receiving long-term assistance or aid from more than one agency. Some members objected to record keeping on the grounds that recipients of assistance should remain anonymous, another principle of the Society. Supporters of the recording system countered this objection by pointing to the fact that in some cases those associated with prostitution had been assisted on more than one occasion; if the record-keeping mechanism had been in place, they asserted, such abuse would have been prevented.[50]

By about 1910, those within the Society widely promoted the concept of "Preventative Charity," which implicitly cast poverty as being caused by a myriad of external social ills, such as poor working conditions (leading to injury and unemployment), substandard housing conditions, communicable illnesses, and other "environmental" factors. This trend paralleled the more organic view of poverty that the cos and other Protestant groups had begun to embrace in the same era. In fact, a Dr. Sheehan, of Syracuse, offered a medical analogy for addressing the problem of poverty: "[W]hen we have made a proper diagnosis of the case, like the skilful medical practitioner, [we have to] adopt such curative measures as will not only cure the malady but will tend to eradicate it totally from the system." The environmental concept served as the clarion call of the 1911 annual meeting of the Society. One speaker at that meeting noted that a paper given at the convention eight years earlier had proved controversial then, but its precepts were now "almost universally acceptable." The paper, given by Edmond J. Butler of New York, had called on charity workers to address the causes of poverty rather than simply to ameliorate its effects and had argued that most causes were social ones whereby, in the words of Alexander Johnson of the National Conference of Charities and Correction, the poor had "no more control over them than over the rain or sunshine."[51] Vincentians also emphasized that for many recipients, poverty was a temporary condition. But some Catholics engaged in charity efforts still retained the notion that poor home management and spending habits were sometimes responsible for impoverishment.

Other Catholics' views of poverty increasingly extended beyond a critique of personal characteristics and practices. William Kerby viewed poverty as arising from larger systemic forces. Casting his analysis in religious terms, he noted that "[s]ins of employers, sins of wealth, negative and positive sins of lawmakers, sins of commerce and of trade are factors of poverty no less than wife desertion, deliberate immorality, hatred or lawlessness on the part of the poor themselves."[52] He further asserted that individualism had replaced religion in American society, further contributing to the persistence of poverty.

Louis Budenz, a journalist writing in the *Central-Blatt and Social Justice* in 1916, asserted: "The causes of modern poverty—and consequently its amelioration and correction—are connected with a thousand ramifications and entanglements." Noting that individual voluntary effort was insufficient to cure poverty, he called for "further system and organization," including increasing the number of trained social workers in Catholic charity efforts. Referring to the earlier controversy within the St. Vincent de Paul Society, he noted that "[r]eluctance to card index cases of charity, which arises from a worthy motive enough, must be discarded." Budenz later became an internationally known figure after leaving the Catholic Church in order to take an active role in the Communist Party. After serving as editor of the *Daily*

Worker, he renounced his involvement in the Party in 1945, returned to the church, and became a crucial witness for Senator Joseph McCarthy and other anti-Communists during the infamous Senate subcommittee hearings. Reflecting on the influences on his labor activism and involvement in the Central Verein, Budenz cited *Rerum Novarum* and his exposure to labor and social reform issues while growing up near Indianapolis.[53]

Although Vincentians condemned some philanthropies as bureaucratic and fixated upon efficiency rather than genuine charity, they did not completely shun new principles of social work. William Kerby urged Catholics not to disregard "scientific charity" simply because the concept had previously been associated with "un-Christian philanthropy." He viewed scientific charity, taken out of its association with the cos and other Protestant groups, as the "mastery of much information, insight into processes, thought and relations, application of the lessons of experience to the tasks in hand and careful supervision of the results." Moreover, Vincentians at the 1911 convention called for more studies on how to "prevent dependency and poverty."[54]

Despite the significant Catholic fear of proselytizing, and the different modes of interacting with the poor, there were distinct similarities between the Society and Protestant-oriented settlements in their approaches to the relief of poverty. As Mina Carson argues, Jane Addams and other settlement workers reacted against the practices of older Protestant charitable groups, especially the cos, which they felt often intruded into the lives of immigrants and other poor people through friendly visiting and other methods that sought to improve the morality and character of the poor. Like the Vincentians, settlements promoted the concept of "reciprocity" between charity workers and the poor, rather than viewing poverty as simply the result of moral failure. Settlement workers too desired to replace this condescending dynamic with a sense of neighborliness and friendship. Yet, while these settlement workers' approaches may have paralleled those articulated by the Society, Catholics also believed it was essential that such a principle be accompanied by a sense of spiritual assistance, a component that they charged was lacking in "humanist" programs such as those promoted by Addams's Hull-House.[55]

● ● ● ● ●

Although some Vincentians sought to enlarge the role of women within the Society, its rules continued to bar them from membership. Women could, however, serve as benefactresses or as auxiliary members. Auxiliary membership, instituted in 1902, gave women responsibility for visiting females at home, after members concluded that women would be able to handle some cases better than men could. In fact, in order to prevent scandal or the appearance of impropriety, men were specifically forbidden to visit the homes of poor women. As an additional safeguard, Vincentians undertook their task of visiting the poor accompanied by another member.[56]

The Society promoted an image of charity as a natural outgrowth of "true manhood" that echoed the male ideology of the Catholic total abstinence movement and its emphasis on "brotherhood." Thomas Mulry, president of the New York Council, urged his fellow Vincentians to "labor valiantly, for the honor of your manhood, your country, your society, your church demands of you." Another Vincentian referred to younger men as serving "apprentice-ships" in the Society. Yet such appeals to fraternalism did not pervade the Society to the extent that they did within the total abstinence movement. That difference occurred in part because charity was portrayed as a fundamental virtue among Catholics and needed little justification. Total abstinence, in contrast, was a voluntary action that ran counter to accepted cultural norms among Irish American males. Therefore, while both temperance and charitable activities could be seen as appropriately women's spheres, men involved in charity could portray their role as essential to their practice of Christianity with less defensiveness than men who gave up liquor.[57]

In his discussion of St. Vincent de Paul's attitude toward charity, Daniel McColgan, the Society's historian, suggested how men's and women's relationships to charity differed:

> This practical-minded, prudent saint realized that while women con-
> stitute the heart of the family—its source of love—men constitute its
> leadership, headship, and its source of strength. To insure the lasting,
> sound health of the family and of society at large, therefore, it is not
> sufficient to maintain the piety and purity of the women. It is also
> necessary to stimulate the virtue and Christian activity of the men.
> Personal service, both material and spiritual . . . would not only lighten
> the load on many a poor man's back; it would also serve simultaneously
> to preserve the faith and fervor of the benefactor.[58]

This statement of separate gender roles probably reflected early-twentieth-century Vincentian attitudes more than the views of St. Vincent de Paul. But McColgan and others did acknowledge the importance of a nun, Sister Rosalie, in introducing Ozanam and his fellow Vincentians to the poverty on the streets of Paris. Moreover, women religious had taken leadership roles in institutionalized and organized charity well before the Society had been established.[59]

By the early twentieth century, Vincentians as a group agreed that there was a role for women within their society, even as they continued to bar them from equal membership. Charles Souvay asserted, "[T]here are many things that men cannot do; there are conditions that they never know, because either it takes a woman's keen eye to detect them, or else they are confided only to the doctor or to a female confidante." He noted that women, working as friendly visitors or serving as benefactresses, could prove integral to the Society's work.[60] In 1904 James F. Wise of Boston, speaking at the annual convention in St. Louis, advocated that women should become members of the Society. Noting that Ozanam had restricted membership to men, Wise contended that "[t]he Catholic American woman labors under no such restraint as the French woman in the field of her activities." He added that "the rule which may be prudent there may be very imprudent here." Apparently his suggestion failed to garner widespread support, however.[61]

By 1911, women had formed twenty-five auxiliaries in Manhattan and the Bronx alone. In later years, local conferences of the Society employed many women as social workers, a fact that reflected the gender distribution of the field. In Milwaukee several women, paid and unpaid, worked on cases for the Society. Margaret Fanning, "never a woman of means," served as the Society's representative at the juvenile court, and Josephine Zimmerman served as a volunteer social worker who "was a pioneer in trying to help the colored people and did valiant work at a time when both personnel and facilities were limited." Sarah Barrett had been a social worker in England prior to moving to Milwaukee in 1919, when she began working for the Society, while Elizabeth Bergs, who served as an officer of the Wisconsin Frauenbund, contributed to the Society's efforts at the St. Charles Home for Boys.[62] The St. Vincent de Paul Society in Boston turned over its Special Works probation for female juveniles to the League of Catholic Women. Society members may have felt that a female influence would be more beneficial to the young women, but there may also have been an uneasiness over men's working with young girls. Despite the many constraints placed on women's involvement in the Society, Father Monaghan of Baltimore nevertheless wondered why "modern young women of leisure and influence . . . fail to grasp their opportunities for the performance of equally Christlike work?"[63]

Another role that the Society ceded to women pertained to their perceived

influence on the family and home. This situation arose in part as the result of
a general emphasis on domesticity among many American Catholics. The
women's organization working with the St. Vincent de Paul Society in the
Holy Cross Conference in Massachusetts, for example, "encourage[d] the
poor families to keep their homes clean," while many other auxiliaries and
women visitors offered advice on other aspects of home management. These
tasks included instilling pride in the home again after it "has been blunted by
innumerable hardships," making it more attractive, bettering the family's
wardrobe, and encouraging personal cleanliness. More than one Vincentian
asserted that some cases of male intemperance developed as a result of the
poor housekeeping skills and hygiene practices of their wives, presumably
because the men sought the comfort of the pub when it proved lacking at
home. In discussing visiting, another enjoined his fellow members: "Let us
encourage him to keep his little home clean and sweet, to open his windows
and to remove all those ornaments that might be unchristian in character or
in bad taste." Thus working-class and middle-class values of taste, respectability, and domesticity were to be taught to the poor as a strategy for improving their lives. Although women did not completely assume this role from
male members, instruction in housekeeping skills was increasingly delegated
to the auxiliary organizations.[64]

Protestant charitable efforts further motivated Vincentians to enlarge
women's roles within their organization. One member asserted that other
charities "had a score of ladies going around ferreting out the cases which
properly belonged to the Society." He continued by noting that, before criticizing these societies, one had to acknowledge that they were "more charitable than many Catholics." Just as with their increased participation in the
temperance movement, the involvement of Catholic women in the Society
came significantly later than Protestant women's activism in these spheres.

Settlement House Work

Settlement work among lay Catholics came in direct response to the successful and relatively well-funded efforts of Jane Addams and other Protestant
and secular-based organizations located in urban immigrant neighborhoods
in the late nineteenth and early twentieth centuries. It also became an extension of the enlarged role of women in the St. Vincent de Paul Society after
1900. The types of activities undertaken by Catholics tended to emulate those
already existing in social settlements. Yet the premises behind the establish-

ment of Catholic settlements differed significantly from those counterparts because of the shared religion of workers and clients and the minority status of American Catholics. This section compares the efforts of two such Catholic settlement houses established in the early twentieth century—Madonna Center on Chicago's West Side, which attracted mainly Italian immigrants, and St. Elizabeth Settlement in St. Louis, which assisted mostly eastern European and German immigrants. Mary Agnes Amberg headed the first effort, with the financial support of her family, while the Central Verein and its female counterpart, the Catholic Women's Union (CWU), financed the second house, staffed by women religious and professional lay social workers.

Within the church, settlement houses were viewed in the context of other charitable institutions, most notably those traditionally run by women religious. But unlike some reform movements undertaken by the laity, such as temperance, Catholic colonization, and the St. Vincent de Paul Society, settlements did not receive widespread encouragement from members of the hierarchy or clergy. Many in the church were reluctant to support an expanded role for lay women in charity and reform efforts, and settlement house work had already been defined as women's work in Progressive America. Instead, settlements depended on support from the parish priests in the neighborhoods in which they operated or on general praise from the hierarchy without their active interest. Another feature that distinguished settlements from the Society of St. Vincent de Paul was their greater emphasis on the ethnicity of recipients.

Catholic settlement house work failed to garner as much attention among Catholics as other charitable work. In a 1918 article in *The Catholic Charities Review*, Margaret Tucker noted that despite the fact that settlement work among American Catholics had begun thirty years before, the topic remained absent from the agenda of 1916 National Conference of Catholic Charities. Tucker further asserted that settlement work was not nearly as well funded by the laity as other charitable efforts within the church. Mary Agnes Amberg, of the Madonna Center settlement, also noted that the type of work in which she and her coworkers engaged could have "been a valuable adjunct of Catholic immigrant life everywhere in America had there been fewer intransigents among our clergy and laity."[65]

Catholics portrayed settlement house work as an appropriate charitable activity for women. This was not simply a result of emulating Protestant and secular programs, because there were several examples of men in those settlement organizations—for instance, Graham Taylor of Chicago Commons,

Robert Woods of Andover House, and Samuel Barnett, the Anglican minister who founded the original settlement house, London's Toynbee Hall. In her article, however, Margaret Tucker discussed settlements from the premise that it was a women's activity: "From the beginning, Catholic Settlement work was looked upon as the work of the Catholic laity. From the ecclesiastical as well as the lay point of view, those sincerely and intelligently interested in solving a problem, thought that the work should be turned over to the Catholic laywomen." She further contended that religious orders had been preoccupied with institutional charity and thus could not expend their energies in this new area. Therefore the assignment of settlement work to laywomen probably resulted in part from the fact that settlement houses contained many of the features associated with institutions run by women religious. Despite Tucker's assertion that laywomen were almost wholly responsible for settlement houses, women religious did in fact run many of them, and there was little reason that they could not have expanded their involvement in such programs.[66]

Yet Catholics also expressed a great deal of ambivalence about laywomen's ability to undertake such work. For example, in her discussion of Catholic social work, Tucker criticized the "average self-supporting woman" who might serve as a settlement worker and suggested rather impractically that a quasi-religious order or community of women be formed to take on settlement work within the church. This would "steer them past disrupting jealousies and ambitions—such women would have had a religious as well as a scientific training."[67] The convent analogy was also used by Mary Agnes Amberg to describe activities of the Guardian Angel Mission: "The workers were all volunteers activated by a spiritual impulse much as if they were religious men and women." Like convent life and non-Catholic settlements, Catholic settlement house work provided an alternative for middle- and upper-class women who did not marry and had limited career options.[68]

Laywomen had a significant history of activism in charitable work in both Ireland and England during the early- and mid-nineteenth century. In fact, sometimes work initiated by laywomen was later taken over by women religious. For example, in Liverpool a lay committee organized a home for female orphans in 1817 that was administrated by a matron until the orphanage moved to larger quarters and the Sisters of Mercy order took it over in 1845. A Miss Gordon ran the St. Elizabeth's Home for Girls in Liverpool, with assistance from Mrs. N. Roskell, its president, from 1854 until 1871, when the same religious order took over its administration. In Limerick, well-to-do Catholic laywomen organized the Magdalen Asylum, which was taken over by the Good Shepherd Sisters in 1848.[69] In the United States, however, nuns were heavily involved in Catholic charity prior to the emergence of a significant group of middle-class laywomen. Therefore, as women religious gradually developed a greater role in institutional charity in the Catholic Church throughout the nineteenth century, in some cases their activism eclipsed the charitable role that laywomen had previously held.

Women religious themselves also expressed concern over the role of lay-women in charitable efforts. Referring to a 1893 day nursery initiative in Jamaica Plain, Massachusetts, Sister Mary Agnes Sharkey remarked that the pastor of the parish "could not secure extra Sisters of Charity to take charge of this new venture, so he engaged a lay woman, but it was not very long before he found [that] the incipient institution, without Sisters in control, could not meet his expectations, and the 'Nursery' was closed." Perhaps the laywoman in question failed as a result of being overwhelmed with responsibilities, since the priest had apparently hoped to fill her role with more than one nun. Yet the tone of Sharkey's account suggests that some women religious feared that laywomen would usurp their own role as charity providers as well as their hard-won, but precarious, authority over aspects of charity within the church. Her remark further implies that laywomen were less competent at administration than women religious, and that the parish priest also had doubts about their abilities, perhaps because they were less accountable to church authority than nuns would have been.[70]

While the criticism of laywomen might have stemmed from the belief that women who had not taken religious vows were less committed to church-based charity, such concern was not commonly expressed about laymen involved in charity. The incident in Jamaica Plain was not unique. In 1921, the first year of its operation, the Holy Name Day nursery in upper Manhattan was run by a Miss Dwyer, a nurse, and Mrs. Francis Christenson, a public school teacher, with the assistance of a physician. A year later, for reasons that were not articulated, the pastor of the Holy Name Parish requested that the Sisters of Charity appoint two of their members to take charge of the nursery. The decision might have been motivated by financial considerations, if the nuns replaced professionally trained laywomen who required salaries. But, for a variety of reasons, some members of the clergy and hierarchy still viewed laywomen as less appropriate charity providers than either women religious or laymen.[71]

Even in the face of opposition, Catholic women had carved out a greater role for themselves in the area of charity by the early twentieth century. Two Catholic settlements funded by the laity—Madonna Center and St. Elizabeth Settlement House—illustrate a growing commitment among lay Catholics to become more intensively involved in addressing the needs of their poorer coreligionists, both to strengthen their church and to forestall reform efforts by those outside the church. Yet the two settlements further reveal that support for women's involvement in settlement work was not as strong as the support for the St. Vincent de Paul Society and other charitable initiatives.

Chicago's Madonna Center

In several ways the profile of the founders of Madonna Center proved similar to that of other female settlement workers of the Progressive era, who tended to be unmarried and from wealthy or middle-class backgrounds; unlike the majority of settlement house leaders, however, they were not college educated. Mary Agnes Amberg, born in 1874, came from a wealthy Catholic family in Chicago, where her father had successfully patented and manufactured office supplies. She spent her summers at Edgecliffe, her family's large Victorian summer home on Mackinac Island, off the coast of Michigan's Upper Peninsula.[72]

Amberg began her involvement in Catholic settlement work after helping her mother run the Guardian Angel Mission, a modest center on Forquer Street, between South Halsted and Desplaines, in an Italian neighborhood on the city's near West Side. The center was not far from Hull-House, which ran programs to assist Catholic and other immigrants. In 1913 Amberg decided to transform the mission into a settlement by moving into the building. She was joined by two female friends, Catherine Jordan and Marie Plamondon, who had both graduated with her from the Academy of the Sacred Heart. By the end of 1915, the mission/settlement boasted a "corps of sixty volunteer workers." In 1922 the center moved to a larger, well-appointed site on Chicago's South Loomis Street in the Union Park neighborhood, which included a large apartment for Amberg and her colleagues.[73]

Unlike many lay Catholic social reformers or other Progressive-era settlement workers, Mary Agnes Amberg was not part of a larger Catholic network at the national level. She did, however, communicate with others in the movement, such as Helen Montegriffo of St. Rose's Settlement in New York.[74] Her family's interest in establishing the mission emanated from their lay activism at the local level. A Chicago priest, Father Rosswinkle, suggested to a group of laywomen that they form a lay apostolate among Italian Americans.

Mary Agnes Amberg, ca. 1908.
(From Amberg, Madonna Center, 79; reprinted with permission)

Amberg noted that the effort was a "pioneering sort for Catholic women because the typical well-to-do Catholic matron, while fully social-minded, belonged to a very conservative tradition."[75] In later years, she assisted her sister-in-law in administering the Chicago chapter of the Washington, D.C., women's lay group, the Christ-Child Society, which provided clothing to the children of poor Catholic families. Although her father and his family had immigrated to the United States from Bavaria, Amberg's own ethnic background did not significantly influence her work. She did, however, comment on her father's reaction to the widespread prejudice toward, and poor treatment of, German Americans during World War I, which suggested that his German background might have influenced his interest in, and financial support of, mission work among recent Catholic immigrants.[76]

Amberg credited her interest in settlement house work in part to the influence of *Rerum Novarum*, asserting that "[o]ur church held and still holds a social gospel which, if not superior to, is certainly equal to that of any social-minded outsider." But she noted that, like many other American visitors to London, her parents had visited Toynbee Hall prior to organizing the Chicago mission. Thus the Ambergs' decision to establish a lay-run mission may have also been inspired by the Protestant settlement tradition.[77]

After assisting at the mission on Forquer Street for several years, and realizing that her aging mother could not continue to run the center indefinitely, Amberg considered whether she had the capacity and commitment to succeed her mother. Her decision to take over the mission as well as to transform it into a settlement house entailed a reappraisal of her priorities and values. Amberg spoke of her quest for good health, which had led her to various resorts and respites away from Chicago as a young woman: "Foolish and self-willed as my actions were, my self-indulgence did not blind me utterly." She decided to redirect her energies toward the administration of the mission and, later, the settlement.[78]

Amberg emphasized the importance of the laity in the social mission of the church. In a reference that alluded to her own realization, she drew on the parable of the rich man finding it harder to pass through the eye of a needle than to enter the kingdom of heaven to illustrate that wealth in itself was not sinful. Rather, "it was [a rich man's] stewardship of his wealth which mattered, and he failed in that stewardship if his wealth was only focused upon himself." Settlement workers at the center also employed the phrase "We are all laborers in His vineyard" to emphasize the role of the laity in the church.[79]

Amberg was well aware of the criticism directed at the Catholic settlement movement, presumably by coreligionists. "We were ridiculed as socialite settlement workers, exploiters of the poor Italian Americans we sought to serve, and charged with trying to isolate them from their fellow American citizens." That charge was related to the critique of wealthier Catholic women discussed in Chapter 5, as well as to distrust of laywomen's charitable efforts. Amberg addressed such criticisms by suggesting that some of those views were rooted in a belief in the inferiority of Italian Americans, derived in part from stereotypes of them as gangsters and for "the speedier tempo" and "gaudier" nature of their religious observances.[80]

Like many non-Catholic settlements, Madonna Center established several programs and concentrated especially on building a variety of activities and recreation for youth in the predominantly immigrant neighborhood. Previously, Amberg's mother had created a night school for Italian adults who wanted to learn English and had also developed a vacation program for children. The latter was patronized by children of several ethnic backgrounds and also served Jewish children in accordance with its policy of nondiscrimination. The center also offered catechism classes for Italian children. When the settlement was established, Madonna Center, like its non-Catholic counterparts, ran a day nursery for poor immigrant women who needed to earn wages outside the home. The settlement also provided medical care to the children who attended its programs, assisted those who suffered from malnourishment, and offered prenatal clinics for women staffed by "some of Chicago's best obstetricians and physicians." For boys, the settlement established a sports program and Boy Scout troops. Girls took domestic science courses and joined the Girl Scout troops. Both girls and boys availed themselves of field trips to museums and outdoor sites and became involved in plays and musical productions. Many of the center's events took place during the Christmas season.[81]

Neighborhood residents brought problems to the center and requested assistance from its staff. One teenage boy who had attended the mission's programs came to the center after he had gotten involved with a gang, while a woman asked for protection from her abusive husband. Others sought help for their children.[82]

In contrast to workers at the St. Elizabeth Settlement House, discussed below, those at Madonna Center rarely requested that the police or government agencies intervene on behalf of its clients. This reluctance extended to the public library system. Amberg's mother had created a library, and the city's librarian, Carl Rosen, expressed interest in assisting with it. Mrs. Amberg declined his offer because she would have had to relinquish her control over the collection, which specialized in Catholic literature.[83]

In order to address the success of other settlement houses, Amberg sought to portray her settlement, and the attitudes of the Catholic Church in general, as more tolerant and enlightened toward Italians and their culture. For example, she emphasized the Italian education of Father Edmund Dunne, a priest who worked among the Italians in the settlement's neighborhood, highlighting the fact that he spoke Italian fluently. Moreover, a fund-raising letter emphasized that during his theological training in Italy, Father Dunne "became thoroughly conversant with the characteristics, the habits and customs of the people of that sunny land; and consequently, when he assumed charge of the little colony of exiles on Forquer and neighboring streets, he was peculiarly fitted to cope with the difficulties surrounding those who work among them. For instance, he realized—as perhaps many of us do not—the unusual conditions that must seem to characterize even their religious life in this western world." The letter pointed out that because the church in Italy was traditionally supported by the wealthy, and few Italian clergy members immigrated to the United States, Italian immigrants' faith was "never dead but sadly dormant."[84]

Father Paul Ponziglione served as an exception to this situation. He was an Italian priest who came from Italian royalty but "sensed the hollowness" of luxury and became a Jesuit. He established the Guardian Mission School for immigrants in Chicago. Italian priests like himself, Amberg wrote, "were apostles of Christ and of Americanism. They taught their charges the new rules, the new speech, the new ways, while retaining a careful loyalty to the old." In naming the settlement Madonna Center, the Ambergs further emphasized the common religion of the settlement house and the Italians in the neighborhood and also acknowledged the particular importance of Mary in the Italian Catholic tradition.[85]

In addition to these sympathetic priests who were associated with the settlement, several Italian Americans worked at Madonna Center. For example, Frank Mentone, who had attended the center in his youth, headed the programs for boys there; Charlotte Pavese edited the center's newsletter, and Ed Scaccia worked at the center's library. The center involved members of the Italian community in its administration, rather than simply encouraging them to avail themselves of its programs.[86]

Like many in the settlement movement, Amberg held a romanticized notion of Italian immigrants. She discussed the irony of a situation in which Italians who were "strong working people of such proud lineage, excellent qualities, and high talent as these Italian Americans should have journeyed to the golden land of opportunity only to sink into the life of the slums." She asserted that Italians had a "deep attachment to the land" and "instinctively preferred to work outside, grow [their] own food, and supply [their] own needs, rather than grub in the dark veins of the city for [their] own money." But her romanticism of noble peasants simply replaced a negative stereotype of Italians with another, albeit less damaging, one.[87]

Amberg suggested that Madonna Center settlement workers had a more enlightened and less obtrusive manner than many other charity workers. For example, she emphasized that family visitors and workers at the Madonna settlement did not "upset a family's familiar bill of fare[;] it would be foolish to attempt to do so. If the family is not too poor, the mother always manages to prepare an appetizing and nourishing meal out of familiar Italian ingredients. Our workers know that Italian Americans as a rule possess healthier teeth and hair than the majority of their fellow citizens." This remark implied a contrast with those charity and settlement house workers who criticized the house-keeping skills of immigrant women and sought to get them to adopt American methods of cooking. Amberg also discussed how Italians, because of their different language and customs, had been "tagged as inferior" in the United States. Thus they looked to their families and to the Italian community for comfort, a situation that others might view negatively as clannishness.[88] When discussing her family's formation of a Chicago branch of the Christ-Child Society to provide clothing to poor Catholic children, Amberg stated, "There is no name and address of a well-off benefactor, no stab at the poverty of the poor mother, nothing but the heavenly lift of . . . 'From the Christ Child.'" Amberg, like the members of the Society of St. Vincent de Paul, emphasized the importance of performing charitable activities unostentatiously.[89]

While some aspects of Amberg's attitudes could be described as cultural pluralism, others tended to defy that description. Amberg did not believe immigrants needed to shed their ethnic identities to become part of American society. Yet there were limits to her contention that Italian peasant culture need not be replaced by American values. For example, in a letter requesting that a business donate a gas range to the mission, the writer noted that "we feel that a knowledge of domestic science would so materially improve the lives of these people."[90] Amberg also vigorously criticized the Italian tradition of spending a large amount of money on weddings, leaving families "saddled with debt." She further concluded that Italian funerals were "out of all proportion to the family's finances." Amberg's remark suggested her belief that the values of thrift needed to be reinforced among immigrants.[91]

Unlike some settlements and neighborhood centers, reformers at Madonna Center did not create a full-fledged Americanization program in the wake of the Red Scare following World War I. The center had already offered

English classes for Italians and assisted Italian immigrants in obtaining citizenship. Many of the entertainment programs, nursery schools, and other programs emphasized English skills, while the Scouts emphasized American values. Thus, while workers emphasized their tolerance for Italian traditions, there were limits to their acceptance of them.[92]

Madonna Center's programs, with the exception of its catechism classes, did not differ substantially from those offered by other settlements, including those of Hull-House. The center sought to offer an alternative to secular and religious settlements by replicating many of their features. Mary Agnes Amberg, however, portrayed its workers' attitudes toward its Italian clientele as far more enlightened than those of other reformers because of the shared religion between the two groups and volunteers' greater appreciation for Italian cultural practices and attitudes. Amberg, however, acknowledged that Catholic efforts in this arena compared unfavorably to the zeal, determination, and interest of secular initiatives, particularly those of Jane Addams. The fear of proselytizing, while largely directed at Protestants, also extended to the secular humanist efforts epitomized by Jane Addams's efforts at Hull-House. Amberg generally remained critical of Hull-House, maintaining that it was devoid of anything but materialist and secular values. The fear of socialism per se was not articulated by Amberg, perhaps because the threat of humanism or Protestantism loomed larger, although it was a frequently mentioned concern among Catholic reformers at the time and probably served as an underlying motivation for her lay activism.[93]

Amberg described her competition with secular and Protestant settlements as being in a "spiritual state of siege." She further challenged the characterization of social settlements as "proving grounds of the social spirit." Amberg asserted, "Families like the Pucciarellis in their bleak despair might have confused such social outposts with the true American way and unwittingly sold their Roman Catholic birthright for a mess of proselytizers' and humanists' pottage." Yet her view belied a lack of confidence that Italians would maintain their faith, as well as her fear of Protestant actions.[94]

Amberg also expressed frustration that nearby settlements were better funded, better housed, and had more programs than Madonna Center. The fact that Hull-House leader Ellen Gates Starr became a convert to Catholicism served to Amberg as a testament to the superiority of the Catholic attitude toward immigrants, and to the centrality of religion to their lives. She believed, moreover, that Graham Taylor, of Chicago Commons, proved less hostile to Catholicism than many other settlement house leaders.[95]

She further criticized "misnamed evangels" for promoting birth control, because they did not "realize that it were better for our country to encourage the prolific and substantial Italian-American parentage rather than to attempt to dam such valuable fecundity." She implied that those who advocated birth control did so out of prejudice toward poor Catholic immigrants rather than from a genuine belief that immigrants' lives would be improved through limiting the size of their families.[96]

Yet Amberg expressed a personal admiration for Addams, praising her energy and dedication to her cause, and her lack of racial prejudice. Despite Addams's irreligiosity, Amberg viewed her as "one of the most truly Christlike individuals I have ever known." Amberg noted that all of the Madonna Center residents attended Addams's memorial service. Moreover, in apparent conflict with her frequently expressed critique of non-Catholic settlements, Amberg arranged for Madonna Center to host a meeting of the Chicago Federation of Charities in the 1930s and also worked with the National Federation of Charities. That move toward secular associations suggests that the issue of proselytizing became less of a barrier to cooperation across religious lines by the 1930s than it had once been.[97]

The St. Elizabeth Settlement House

Established in 1915 on the south side of St. Louis, the St. Elizabeth Settlement House emerged as a German Catholic response to the proliferation of secular and Protestant settlements in that city. In contrast to Madonna Center, the workers at St. Elizabeth actively sought the intervention of government agencies, or advocated legal recourse, in many cases, including those pertaining to desertion, public health, poor housing, truancy, industrial accidents, and, in at least one case, sexual abuse. Three School Sisters of Notre Dame, a Milwaukee-based religious order, ran the settlement with the assistance of a lay social visitor, Stella Giess, and later Elizabeth Kuhlman. The need for such a community institution was apparently great—less than a year after it opened, the settlement boasted that it had cared for 632 children in a single month. The Central Verein founded the settlement, and along with the affiliated Catholic Women's Union, organized in 1916, provided most of its funding. In contrast to the St. Vincent de Paul Society, which minimized ethnic issues and emphasized charity to a greater extent than reform, the Central Verein emphasized issues of social and economic justice and advanced viewpoints ranging from conservative to quite liberal.[98]

Those active in the St. Elizabeth Settlement clearly drew many principles from Progressive-era reform, but they looked toward Catholic social welfare trends and reform principles popular in industrializing Germany more than those in the United States in shaping alternatives to Protestant or secular efforts. Germany had taken the lead in developing social welfare policies following unification in 1871. As industrial growth intensified, the Bismarck government embarked upon a web of social welfare programs to address the problems arising from modern industrialization, including education, public health, and worker safety. Under Bismarck, the German government introduced a compulsory social insurance system to cover illness, accidents, and old age. Bismarck supported such initiatives in order to forestall socialism and to strengthen the country's workforce and its position as an industrial leader. In doing so, he anticipated by a few decades the earliest successful efforts in the United States. As in the United States, German reform was not limited to the state. Catholics and Protestants, including middle-class laywomen, also organized separate voluntary groups to address issues arising from industrialization and influence policy making. That legacy inspired German Catholics, including those in the United States, to support social reform initiatives.[99]

German American Catholics began to focus on women's charitable roles in the years immediately preceding the formation of both the St. Elizabeth House and the Catholic Women's Union, the women's counterpart to the Central Verein. Prior to the settlement's founding, a series of articles on Catholic women's charitable efforts appeared in the Central Verein's monthly periodical, *Central-Blatt and Social Justice*. Authors of those articles compared the proliferation of organized charity efforts by German and other European Catholic women with the relatively inactive laity in the United States; one writer acknowledged that "[a]mong Catholics, in this country at least, the cooperation of women and young girls in active social work has been a sort of afterthought." Paul Gonzaga Rohr, S.J., proclaimed, "A veritable volume could be written on the various careers open to woman in the layapostolate." The authors of these articles also emphasized that settlement house work was a perfect opportunity for women. Writers discussing the aims of settlement work emphasized that the concept of *Nächstenliebe*, or neighborly love, should permeate all its efforts.[100]

German Catholics in the United States drew heavily from the activities of their coreligionists in Germany, who had earlier entered the field of social reform. Suggesting that Catholic women turn to their European sisters for models of organized charity, one writer maintained that if German Catholic women in the United States engaged in friendly visiting and related charity, "they would be building on good German custom." Another writer stated that German Catholic women in the United States had much to learn about social reform from their "elder sisters" in Europe, alluding to the work of two Catholic women's groups in Germany—the Elisabeth-Vereine and the Marianische Mädchenschutz-Vereine (St. Mary's Society for Protection of Girls), which Bavarian Catholics imported from France in 1895. The writer cautioned, however, that efforts must be tailored to American circumstances, because "[t]o transplant a foreign movement for social reform bodily, so to speak, into American soil, would be a serious mistake." Rohr emphasized in his article that "[t]he time, too, has come when we can no longer leave the field of settlement work to non-Catholic or purely humanitarian hands." The Central Verein provided a further catalyst for the establishment of a German American settlement house when, at its 1911 convention, its members passed a resolution indicating that German Catholics should cooperate with non-Catholic settlement houses and, more critically, create Catholic ones.[101]

In preparing to launch a social settlement in St. Louis, the Central Verein in 1915 surveyed an Italian neighborhood and, later, a largely Hungarian one, to discern the needs of poor Catholics in St. Louis. The settlement eventually was placed in the second neighborhood. One writer noted that "[o]ur first effort in our community work has been to place our families on their feet so that they could help themselves and thereafter be able to help others and assist in community endeavors." Echoing the principles articulated by the St. Vincent de Paul Society, a columnist discussing the settlement's activities stated that "[n]ot alone should they [Catholics] mechanically dole out alms, but give to this task at times their personal service."[102]

Like Mary Agnes Amberg at Madonna Center, those organizing the St. Louis settlement chose its name in order to appeal to those it served and to emphasize the common religious bonds between the workers and their clients. The organizers chose St. Elizabeth of Hungary as the settlement's patron saint, because of the large number of Hungarian speakers in the neighborhood, and they named St. Joseph, head of the holy family, its special protector. The day nursery further emphasized its association with the image of the holy family in its 1931 Christmas appeal pamphlet depicting the family visited by an angel, with the caption "Out of Love for the Child Born Poor." Lest readers miss the intended message, the pamphlet conveyed the hope that Catholics "will be moved by the charity taught by the Child of Bethlehem."[103]

The settlement initiative was strongly supported by Frederick P. Kenkel, Central Verein director and editor of *Central-Blatt* and *Amerika*, who later received the Laetare Medal from the University of Notre Dame for his lay efforts. Kenkel, whose parents had immigrated to the Midwest from Oldenburg, Germany, in 1848, was born in Chicago in 1863. When he was eighteen, he returned to Germany to further his education and married a German woman. Although the Kenkel family was nominally Catholic, they did not provide Frederick with a religious upbringing, and he married in the Lutheran Church. His wife's death in 1889 led him back to Catholicism. After his confirmation, he studied at the Franciscan monastery in Quincy, Illinois, where he developed a fascination with medieval society. By 1892, he had married again and entered the real estate business. He became involved in the German Catholic press, becoming editor of Chicago's *Katholisches Wochenblatt* in 1901, and then of St. Louis's *Die Amerika* in 1905. That work ultimately led him to become involved in the Central Verein social reform programs.[104]

While the Central Verein maintained conservative positions on many social issues, it was often critical of capitalism and materialist values. The group called for the laity to commit itself to improving conditions for workers and increase its role in charitable work. In fact, the New York branch of the Central Verein cited *Rerum Novarum*, the 1891 encyclical, as a major impetus for the branch's founding. A short history of the St. Elizabeth Settlement mentions, however, that the organizers encountered many initial objections to their plans. The reasons behind those objections are unclear, but it is likely that some members argued that day nurseries would encourage mothers to work full-time, to the detriment of their children's welfare.[105]

The major focus of the St. Elizabeth Settlement was its day nursery, which provided day care to the children of working mothers, widowed fathers, or ill parents. Married women in the middle-class CWU generally subscribed to the ideal of "Hausfrauen, nicht Ausfrauen" or "A woman's place is in the home."[106] Yet, in supporting the nursery program, the CWU and Central Verein recognized that while less than ideal, a day nursery was necessary because of the larger social and economic circumstances that led many poor mothers of young children to work. That proved especially true given the number of mothers who were widows or deserted wives, or who lacked adequate economic support from their husbands. In fact, the settlement workers recognized that in some cases nursery care allowed widowed and other impoverished mothers to avoid placing their children in orphanages. Moreover, a neighboring Presbyterian group had organized after-school play classes that attracted Catholic children, providing a strong impetus to organizing a Catholic alternative. The St. Elizabeth Day Nursery proved so successful that workers there claimed that women had told them they had moved into the neighborhood specifically in order to "enjoy the benefits it offers poor and deserving people."[107]

St. Elizabeth's staff emphasized that they employed modern methods of child care in attending to children's spiritual and material needs. By the 1930s the day nursery staff described their efforts in terms of socialization, as they sought to combine the roles of mother and teacher "in such a way as to counteract any unfavorable influences in the homes of the children, yet not alienating the affections [of the children] for their parents."[108] The settlement also offered lunches and after-school care to school-age children whose parents were not at home. A physician affiliated with the settlement provided routine medical care, and occasionally settlement workers brought children to a clinic or hospital. One newspaper reporter for the Catholic press noted approvingly that the infants were fed "scientifically," a reference to the prevailing child care methods of that era. As late as 1930, the day nursery boasted that it was the only facility of its kind in the city that cared for infants. Another attraction was the presence of a small playground that would allow children to play under supervised conditions. While some parents paid a nominal fee for care, others were not charged.[109]

St. Elizabeth's second major initiative was its home and hospital visits. Over the span of seven years, the settlement's "social visitor" made over a thousand visits to the homes of the poor to help families cope with illness, assist them with home management skills, mediate marital conflict, and provide them with food, clothing, shelter, and furniture. Using a typical Progressive-era analogy, one article in a German-language newspaper likened the role of the social visitor to that of a physician in a medical clinic. The writer further acknowledged the fact that while the settlement offered material and spiritual assistance to the poor, it simultaneously allowed those who ran it to gain insight into urban social conditions. Elizabeth Kuhlman, the second social visitor employed by the settlement, had graduated from the White Cross Social School, organized by Reverend Peter Dietz, a major proponent of social action among German American Catholics, an editor of the *Central-Blatt and Social Justice*, and a founder of the American Federation of Catholic Societies. The supporters of the settlement praised Kuhlman's training. One journalist visiting the settlement wrote that often family and marital

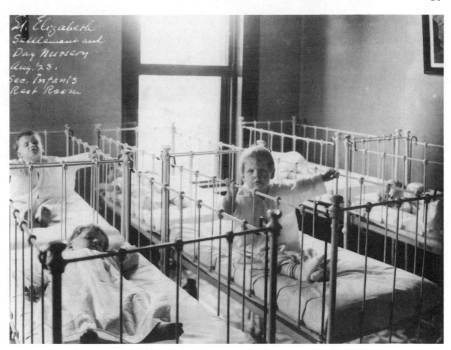

The day nursery at St. Elizabeth Settlement, St. Louis, 1925.
(Courtesy of Central Bureau, Catholic Central Union of America Archives, St. Louis)

problems "are not past remedying, if only there were someone interested enough and, [more important], tactful enough to undertake the task of re-adjustment. It is here that the social worker can be of highest service." The writer went on to praise Kuhlman's skills in the area of counseling a troubled family with the ultimate goal of family preservation: "It is not all who can, like the oyster, transform an injury into a thing of value."[110]

Because of its heavy emphasis on issues of economic and social justice and structural solutions to poverty, and because social work in Germany was widespread by the early twentieth century, the support of the Central Verein and cwu for professional social workers was far stronger at this time than that of many other American Catholic groups, who often looked upon the field with suspicion. Those involved in St. Elizabeth's modeled their efforts on those of German Catholics, who had made significant strides in the social work field by 1916; in that context, social work and reforms often associated with Progressives did not seem inconsistent with Catholic religious values.[111]

The Central Verein, and later the Catholic Women's Union, funded St. Elizabeth's through its branches throughout the United States. Volunteers from several Catholic women's societies in St. Louis, including the Missouri Frauenbund, the Young Ladies Sodality of Our Lady of Perpetual Help, and the Ladies of Laclede (the local women's auxiliary of the Knights of Columbus) also supported the institution. In 1925 the Catholic Women's Union contributed over $1,000 to the St. Elizabeth Settlement, while the Society of St. Vincent de Paul also supported it. Frederick Kenkel, director of the Central Verein, corresponded with Mother Petra, superior of the order, about the finances and administration of the settlement, once communicating the fact that one of the sisters seemed very unhappy with her work at the settlement and suggesting that she be replaced with another who "will bring to the work a genuine love for the poor children under her care." That concern does not seem to have been addressed immediately, however, because of a shortage of women religious in the community.[112]

A third aspect of St. Elizabeth's settlement work centered on the issue of desertion and nonsupport of families by men, which its workers viewed as a major cause of poverty among the Catholics they assisted. In several instances, settlement workers requested that the police or a government agency intervene to arrest and prosecute men who had failed to support their families, and elements of coercion were sometimes evident in the settlement worker's methods. In one instance, a woman was brought to court for deserting her husband and children and, as a result, returned to live with them. A regular column in the *Central-Blatt* detailing settlement activities noted: "The settlement always watches such cases closely—to prevent desertion, if possible, or to see that the husband is compelled to support the family if he does get away." Another activity in which the settlement engaged was securing paid positions for poor women in the city. These activities suggest the extent to which the settlement took literally the St. Vincent de Paul Society's goal of "preserving the family," even when parents clearly did not share it.[113]

Family preservation often involved assisting unmarried mothers. In undertaking the settlement's maternity work at the hospital, which often involved cases of unmarried Catholic mothers, the social visitor emphasized her intention of assisting mothers and children so that they were able to remain together. The social visitor took a "special interest" in unmarried women and often provided homes for them until they found employment and could support themselves and their children. Members of the CWU sometimes hosted these "unfortunate girls" and their babies in their homes for several weeks at a time. Such efforts allowed women to avoid placing their children in orphanages or giving them up for adoption, although some babies were placed out.[114]

The settlement's interest in infant and maternity issues emanated in part from the high infant mortality rates in Germany—which reached 20.7 percent in 1901. That exceptionally high rate brought the infant health and welfare issues to the fore among social reformers there, and coverage of such efforts in the German-language press influenced cwu members to direct their energies toward ameliorating poverty among poor mothers and their children in St. Louis. cwu members further viewed support for unmarried mothers as an important outgrowth of their political activism against birth control and abortion in this period. They viewed birth control initiatives as anti-Catholic and anti-immigrant, and as another attempt to interfere with Catholic parental autonomy. In 1917 the *Central-Blatt* column on St. Elizabeth's reported that its hospital work had been interrupted because "certain" people at the City Hospital had attempted to "force out the Catholic workers from certain parts of the hospital contrary to all ideas of justice."[115]

Other cases in which the settlement intervened to resolve conflict within families included a situation in which the parents of a twelve-year-old girl told officials that she was fourteen and "obstinately refused to allow her to go to school." Settlement workers contacted the Board of Education, which required her to attend school for an additional year. In that case, the workers intervened between parent and child, although on issues such as the Child Labor Amendment, many Catholics argued that the state should not intervene in similar decisions by parents. An additional case concerned alleged sexual abuse of a child by her father, in which settlement workers helped place the daughter in a house run by women religious and contacted the Legal Aid Bureau. Workers often referred parents to agencies to receive help for children with disabilities or illnesses. While conducting visits at the hospital, the social visitor also advised one man to consult lawyers rather than sign a settlement agreement with his employers after an industrial accident had left him hospitalized.[116]

The families who used the day nursery and other settlement programs were often immigrants. Yet, unlike the clients of Madonna Center, which operated in the midst of an Italian neighborhood, or of the Brownson House in Los Angeles, which served primarily Mexican immigrants, those who availed themselves of the services offered by St. Elizabeth's included immigrants with German, Hungarian, Spanish, and Polish backgrounds. To some extent, then, the settlement workers shared an ethnic background with those they served. Moreover, in stark contrast to the St. Vincent de Paul Society, the reports of the St. Elizabeth Settlement activities, published in *Central-Blatt*, often mentioned the ethnicities of the individuals who were assisted, although they did not discuss certain problems or behaviors as characteristic of particular groups.[117]

The settlement sought to improve the housing conditions within its neighborhood. Workers contacted the city's Health Department about hazardous conditions of apartments and encouraged many families to move out of poor housing. In at least one instance, workers contacted the Civic League, which had launched a campaign to improve housing regulations, after discovering that some families had been living in condemned housing.[118]

Unlike many other settlement houses, both Catholic and non-Catholic, no single major figure was associated with the St. Elizabeth Settlement or served as its catalyst. Moreover, laywomen's roles were much less prominent there than at other settlements. This is remarkable in light of the extended discussion of their growing importance in Catholic charity, including settlement work, in the *Central-Blatt and Social Justice* prior to the opening of the settlement house. This situation might have arisen because of reservations among those in the Central Verein about laywomen's organizing abilities, as well as from general sentiments about laywomen's capabilities held by others in the church.

By the late teens, St. Elizabeth's had outgrown its quarters, and the Central Verein raised the funds to build a new site for the settlement, which was occupied in December 1919. That new site also functioned as the meeting place for the Missouri branch of the Central Women's Union and the Ladies of Laclede, both of which supported the settlement's work.[119]

The Central Verein and the CWU portrayed the St. Elizabeth Settlement as a prototype for the development of settlement houses in other states by its male and female members. Because of its location in St. Louis, headquarters of the Central Verein, articles on the settlement's progress and activities appeared regularly in the publications of the Central Verein and the Catholic Women's Union. Yet by 1924 those organizations were still enjoining their members to initiate similar efforts in their home states. In the familiar lament of Catholic lay reformers, a writer in the CWU's *Official Bulletin* stated that the settlement was intended as a model, yet "no outsiders have approached the settlement and Day Nursery in all the years since 1915 with a view of systematically studying something of the methods employed."[120]

While St. Elizabeth's organized youth clubs for neighborhood children and provided civic and English classes on the premises, its limited space and resources led the settlement to focus on its day nursery and social visitation

Children and women religious outside St. Elizabeth Settlement, St. Louis.
(Courtesy of Central Bureau, Catholic Central Union of America Archives, St. Louis)

efforts. Therefore its ambitious goals of inspiring German Catholics throughout the United States to establish settlements in their own communities and
of launching more extensive neighborhood projects were not realized. After
1929 its clients were no longer predominantly the children of immigrants.
Instead, the Depression forced many native-born St. Louis residents to move
into poorer neighborhoods due to declining income or unemployment. St.
Elizabeth's, which operated in St. Louis into the 1980s, ultimately became a
Kenkel family project, as one of Frederick Kenkel's daughters, Eleanore,
worked as the settlement's social worker in the 1960s, while another, Sister
Mary Gertrudis, served as the superior in the 1940s.[121]

The strategies employed by the workers at St. Elizabeth, especially their
frequent requests for intervention by government agencies and the police,
parallel those used by the immigration agent employed by the Charitable
Irish Society and her cooperation with the Department of Immigration officials stationed at the port of Boston. In contrast, the Society of St. Vincent de
Paul, Madonna Center, and other Catholic lay groups proved far more reluctant to request assistance from government officials. Thus in the late nineteenth and early twentieth centuries there was no clear Catholic consensus on

the relationship between lay charity and social action and its relationship to the state.

German American Catholics tended to oppose state and federal legislation on issues such as Prohibition, the Child Labor Amendment, and several education issues, arguing that such legislation took important rights away from parents or unnecessarily intruded into personal decision making. Yet German Americans at St. Elizabeth's regularly sought government intervention in charitable cases.

Although the reasons for that difference in attitudes toward state intervention are not entirely clear, it seems that Catholics were more suspicious of federal power than of local government. As will be discussed in the following chapter, that suspicion, among Germans at least, arose in part because of anti-Catholic measures passed in Prussia in the 1870s, just prior to German unification under Bismarck. Some of those measures involved child welfare issues. Moreover, while the anti-Catholic Kulturkampf had occurred several decades earlier, it might have led German Catholics in the United States to harbor fears about the potential ramifications of federal power. Some of that difference might be attributed to gender—men taking on policy issues versus laywomen and women religious asking for state intervention on an informal, case-by-case basis—yet male members of the Central Verein who were involved with the St. Elizabeth Settlement did not seem to object to that type of government involvement. Therefore the disparity in attitudes can not be explained by gender differences alone.[122]

• • • • •

Like Mary Agnes Amberg, the laywomen leaders of other Catholic settlement houses tended to be middle class or wealthy, and some had postsecondary educations. Mary Workman, another Catholic laywoman, was instrumental in establishing Brownson House, a Catholic settlement in Los Angeles named for the famous Catholic convert of the nineteenth century, Orestes Brownson. That settlement provided programs that were targeted at Mexican American Catholics.

By 1918, Brownson House had turned its attention toward "Americanization" efforts, calling for "the united effort of all agencies public and private, which uphold and reinforce the ideals of liberty and justice which are the foundation of American institutions." As part of this effort, settlement workers persuaded Mexicans to register for, and respond to, the draft.[123] Mary Workman's leadership of the settlement was interrupted, however, by Bishop

John J. Cantwell's decision to merge Brownson House with the diocesan charity bureau, a shift that occurred with many lay activities throughout the United States in the post–World War I era. Workman resigned from the settlement in protest.[124]

Orestes Brownson's granddaughter, Josephine Van Dyke Brownson, served as a leader of the Weinman settlement in Detroit, although it remains unclear whether she or Father Ferdinand Weinman actually founded it in 1906 in an Italian and Syrian neighborhood. The major focus of Brownson's work involved the religious instruction of immigrants rather than the more general community programs that dominated other Catholic settlements' agendas. In New York, Grace O'Brien formed a settlement, St. Helen's, in Brooklyn in 1903, while Marion Guerney, a Catholic convert, began work in 1898 at St. Rose's settlement in New York under the direction of Father Clement Thuente, pastor of St. Catherine of Siena Church. Guerney resigned from St. Rose's in 1903 and, after several years of religious study, organized a community of women religious to undertake settlement work. In 1910 the community established Madonna House on Manhattan's Lower East Side.[125] Other Catholic settlement houses operated under women religious or diocesan auspices. On the whole, however, Catholic settlement houses suffered from a lack of financial and hierarchal support and did not flourish to the extent that their secular and Protestant counterparts did.

The skepticism that characterized many Catholics' perceptions of laywomen's roles in charity and settlement work also permeated their attitudes toward the female-dominated field of social work. As professional social work programs became increasingly popular from the mid-1910s to the 1930s and more laywomen were attracted to the field, many of those associated with charity questioned whether Catholics should embrace social work as a profession and, indeed, whether women were qualified to undertake the work. The fact that social workers would require salaries, which would shift the emphasis of lay charity from a voluntary endeavor to a remunerative one, also concerned Catholics, from both financial and spiritual perspectives.[126] German Catholics, however, had a more positive attitude toward social work, in part because they associated the field with German initiatives rather than viewing it as an outgrowth of American Protestant charity.

· · · · ·

Catholic charity and settlement work among the laity in the late nineteenth and early twentieth centuries occurred as part of a defensive strategy to counter proselytizing efforts by groups who sought to convert Catholic immigrants, especially Italians, to either Protestantism or secularism. Although the fear of socialism was pervasive in the Catholic Church in this era, it was not as widely articulated among the settlement house workers discussed here, nor among members of the St. Vincent de Paul Society, as were concerns over conversion to Protestantism. Catholics at the lay level expressed a proprietary responsibility for caring for their poorer coreligionists and implied that each religious group should do the same. Vincentians criticized Protestant, government, and professionalized charity for valuing efficiency and ostentatiousness over genuine concern for the poor; they also criticized some groups for their lack of compassion and inability to offer the poor more than material relief. In some ways, the Society's rhetoric was similar to that of the larger Progressive settlement movement. Yet the Society and members of the small Catholic settlement movement argued that the secularism of that movement would prove dangerous to the poor, because religion was central to family, society, and charity.

Catholics viewed charity through the lens of shared religion and, to a lesser extent, of ethnicity. They argued that their efforts differed from those of Protestants because of the common bonds of religion and recent European heritage shared by Catholic charity providers and the recipients. Those within the St. Vincent de Paul Society underscored the French origins of the Society, and its links to European conferences also remained important. But the Society in the United States had a more egalitarian composition than European conferences, and it modified some traditions, such as the sharing of beer and tobacco between Belgian members and those whom they assisted, in order to suit American circumstances. Furthermore, some of the rhetoric articulated by those involved in charity efforts often mirrored that expressed by proponents of Catholic colonization and total abstinence. Yet Vincentians did not emphasize ethnic issues to the same extent as those reformers, in part because of their interest in presenting charity as a universal undertaking. The Society was therefore able to adapt easily to the system of national parishes that flourished in nineteenth century America, rather than becoming the exclusive provenance of a particular ethnic group. Catholic lay reform also differed from Protestant initiatives in that Catholics were motivated by a desire to garner greater respect for their religion in an era in which anti-Catholicism had regained momentum. Moreover, Catholic activists countered the supposition that social work was a relatively recent product of the Progressive era by pointing to the long history of the St. Vincent de Paul Society, thereby suggesting that social work methods were not recent innovations. Catholic charitable efforts were not simply expressions of noblesse oblige—indeed, lay activists criticized wealthy Catholics for their indifference to charity—nor did Catholics view immigrants as inherently dangerous to urban society.

Catholic lay charity developed along distinct gender lines. Although women religious were renowned for their extensive administration of charitable agencies, laywomen had a very limited role in charity before the turn of the century. Even by the early twentieth century, Catholics only reluctantly ceded aspects of charitable activity to women. Although Catholics defined settlement work as an appropriate sphere for laywomen, they remained reluctant to encourage large numbers of women to enter this field. For example, writers in the Central Verein's journal repeatedly called on laywomen to expand their charitable endeavors, citing the need to counter Protestant settlements. Yet laywomen were given only a limited role compared to the women religious who administered St. Elizabeth Settlement.

Catholic women's roles in charity work differed greatly from those of women involved in Protestant and secular efforts at the time, and Catholic settlements never achieved the prominence of those counterparts. Instead, Catholic women's charity efforts remained confined largely to local groups, often at the parish level. Although many lay Catholics eschewed entering the political arena to the degree that Jane Addams and other Progressive reformers did, the St. Elizabeth Settlement in St. Louis did not hesitate to use government agencies and legal means to achieve change on an individual, local, and informal basis. Such cooperation with local government paralleled the Charitable Irish Society port agent's ties to immigration officials. At times, both relationships resulted in coercive actions against individuals whom they purported to protect. But case records at Madonna Center reveal that individuals sought assistance from the workers for legal and personal problems rather than contacting government agencies or the police directly, suggesting that some of the settlement's neighbors deemed the workers trustworthy.

Like other Progressive reformers, Catholic charity providers could not always meet their own goals of treating the poor without condescension—as friends and neighbors, and without harsh judgment. Yet, despite the failure to overcome elements of paternalism, many Catholics engaged in charity work remained less critical of poor urban immigrants than the wealthier men and women involved in COS and other Progressive efforts to alleviate poverty among the urban population. In fact, some of the attitudes toward the poor

held by the Catholic laity and others in this era remain extant today. Debates about the causes of homelessness and creating "cycles of dependency"
among those receiving government assistance have continued, most recently
giving rise to the welfare reform initiatives that culminated in the Welfare
Reform Act of 1996.

Promoting the Maternal over Material, Ideal over Idle

• • • • •

The Emergence of Catholic Women's Groups

American Catholic laywomen became involved in social reform efforts later than either Catholic men or Protestant women. Prior to the last two decades of the nineteenth century, laywomen's organized activities in the church generally remained confined to participation in parish-level groups, sodalities, or other devotional activities; more extensive and formalized charitable efforts were generally reserved for women religious, clergy, and laymen in the Society of St. Vincent de Paul. As the Catholic middle class grew substantially by the end of the nineteenth century, increasing numbers of laywomen began forming charitable and reform groups. Much of women's activism originated as auxiliary or supplemental efforts to those of men and tended to be more localized and of shorter duration. By 1910, larger and more influential groups emerged, and women's groups had gained a more significant role within the church by 1920, when the hierarchy created the National Council of Catholic Women.[1]

This chapter discusses the formation in the late nineteenth and early twentieth centuries of Catholic women's groups, including the Catholic Women's Union of the Central Verein and the League of Catholic Women, as well as several smaller groups that were organized for charitable and reform purposes. Many women's groups had a dual emphasis—to encourage women to become involved in reform and charitable efforts and, simultaneously, to articulate their views on the role of women in America at a time when modern values began to resonate more widely in society as a whole. Like many women's groups of the era, both in the United States and in Europe, Catholic women's groups often employed a maternalist perspective in order to expand their public roles. They justified their involvement in social reform, and, to a lesser extent, political activities, on the basis of the notion that women had essential qualities that should be directed to the care of others, outside of the home as well as in it.[2] Such maternalism could be directed in many ways— toward suffrage, protective labor legislation, and other social welfare laws, or toward more conservative ends. Women in Catholic groups in the United States generally followed the more conservative path.

Because of the lack of lay charitable and reform organizations among American Catholic women until the late nineteenth century, the male St. Vincent de Paul Society, the most extensive of all lay Catholic charitable groups, served as a model for many women's charitable activities. Groups with a regional or national focus began to develop only around 1910. The Frauen-bund, an organization comprised of local Catholic women's groups through-out Germany, inspired the creation of both the League of Catholic Women, based in Boston, and the Catholic Women's Union, which had branches throughout the United States. The Frauenbund had previously influenced a group of English Catholic women to form a League of Catholic Women. This group, in turn, served as a model for Catholic women in Boston, who formed an organization of the same name in 1910. The Catholic Women's Union, established in 1916, modeled itself closely on the German Frauenbund as a result of the organization's almost exclusively German American membership and its continued emphasis on ethnic issues. In fact, the Wisconsin chapter of the Catholic Women's Union called itself the D.R.K. Frauenbund in the Ger-man portion of its bilingual pamphlets, letters, and bulletins.[3] Boston's Arch-bishop William O'Connell closely supervised the activities of the League of Catholic Women (LCW), while the Catholic Women's Union remained under the jurisdiction of the all-male Central Verein. By the early 1920s these groups had affiliated with the National Council of Catholic Women, based in Wash-ington, as part of the larger trend toward centralizing lay groups.

Despite common origins and a shared conservatism on some issues, the CWU and the LCW diverged in their models of organization. The CWU followed an ethnically based model, drawing heavily from German reform influences. In contrast, the LCW patterned itself on an assimilationist, American Protes-tant organizational model. Both groups used a maternalist ideal to assist working women and the poor and opened their membership to working women, although they proved more successful in assisting than in including working women in their groups. The leadership of the CWU tended to be middle class, while LCW leaders tended to be upper class and often Catholic converts. In addition, LCW members proved more deferential in their attitudes toward the clergy and hierarchy than did members of the CWU, who challenged both the authority and the indifference of the church leadership.

By engaging in social reform programs, middle- and upper-class women in these organizations, most of whom were married, could to some extent quell criticism of their leisure and material wealth by extending their maternalism to the poor or working classes and by channeling their resources into more acceptable ends. They could, moreover, increase the visibility of Catholics in voluntary work without entering the more controversial arena of suffrage activism and other women's rights issues.

Although the orientation and goals of the women's groups remained removed from traditional politics, Catholic laywomen often became politically active on issues pertaining to morality or the family. In the early twentieth century, several groups took stances against a number of issues, including birth control measures, suffrage, the Child Labor Amendment, divorce, and immoral entertainment and dress. Women justified their activism on the basis of defending their homes and moral beliefs, in the same way that earlier generations of middle-class Protestant women had justified their involvement in temperance and other issues. Further, once the Nineteenth Amendment had passed, Catholic women urged others to exercise their right to vote by taking an active interest in politics in order to oppose the Child Labor Amendment, divorce, immoral entertainment, and other initiatives. Many Catholics opposed the Child Labor Amendment on the grounds that it interfered with parental authority, and because children's wages were often essential to poor Catholics' family economy. There were, however, notable exceptions to that opposition, most prominently Father John A. Ryan, the "labor priest" who later led the Social Action Department of the National Catholic Welfare Council.

Among Catholics, the home became a refuge from modern views and practices that threatened to undermine the importance of religion in much the same way that the mid-nineteenth-century home became a refuge for middle-class Protestants who feared the corrupting elements of urban life—which, in part, they viewed as resulting from the influx of poor, immigrant Catholics. Yet Catholic women drew many of their views on domesticity and separate spheres from European Catholic traditions rather than from their Protestant counterparts in the United States. In addition, non-Catholic women's groups, such as the Woman's Christian Temperance Union, proved blatantly anti-immigrant and anti-Catholic, thereby dissuading large numbers of

Catholic women, many of whom were immigrants or the daughters of immigrants, from joining them.

While the church took no official stance on women's suffrage—with some important exceptions, including Bishop John Lancaster Spalding and the usually conservative Bishop Bernard McQuaid of Rochester—most clergy and hierarchy opposed the measure, fearing that it would pose a threat to family stability and to morality. Some Catholic women, such as Leonora Barry Lake, ignored the widespread opposition to suffrage among the hierarchy and clergy. In fact, Lake worked simultaneously on behalf of women's suffrage and Catholic total abstinence. Several articles on *die Frauenfrage*, or the "woman question," in the Central Verein's publication criticized suffrage, citing arguments from attorneys, writers and anthropologists, bishops, and other authorities that suffrage was unnecessary and detrimental to relations between the sexes. The journal published other articles that offered mild endorsements of women's suffrage in Germany and in the United States, but this was primarily because the editors viewed it as inevitable and hoped to mobilize Catholic women in defense of the home and to counteract the influence of other women's groups.[4] After its 1916 founding, the cwu itself did not emphasize suffrage in its publications prior to the amendment's passage. Other women active in lay groups within the church, especially those in the lcw, would find it difficult to support suffrage publicly when members of the clergy and hierarchy who supervised those groups opposed it.[5]

Although Catholic women active in the social reform efforts discussed in this chapter subscribed to traditional notions of married women's roles as primarily domestic, several controversies erupted over women's roles that suggest the contested nature of laywomen's place within the church, even when the ideologies that the groups espoused were not in question.

Catholic women experienced a different dynamic in the development of a domestic ideology than did Protestant women. As discussed previously, in the late nineteenth century Catholic women and men began to develop the home as a middle-class institution at the same time that increasing numbers of Protestant women began to leave it for greater involvement in the public sphere. By the 1880s a distinct domestic ideology began to emerge in the popular Catholic press.[6] From the height of the immigration influx of the mid-nineteenth century into the twentieth century, most Irish women participated in the paid workforce until marriage. For many Catholics, the home grew in importance as a symbol of improved social status, in part because it signified a respite from the necessity of women's paid employment, which, for Irish and German women prior to marriage, often occurred in the homes of others.

The rhetoric surrounding Catholic women's roles, both within women's groups and outside of them, reflected an ambivalence about the values accompanying the rising economic and social status of many Catholics. Many critics in the church condemned the characteristics of "idleness" and "frivolity" among some women in the nascent Catholic middle and upper classes. They aimed their critiques particularly at those women who were viewed as emulating the materialist values and attributes associated with wealth and with Protestant society; such concerns were expressed routinely in articles, speeches, and other public forums beginning in the early 1880s. In particular, the LCW, a group that eschewed ethnic issues and sought to form alliances with non-Catholic groups, came under sharp attack by the hierarchy and others for becoming too "Protestant" or disloyal to both Catholicism and ethnic interests. To some extent, this criticism paralleled that directed toward Catholic total abstinence advocates. The two stereotypes about Protestants that Catholics maintained, however—the old-fashioned Puritan versus the modern, luxury-seeking woman—proved quite disparate.[7]

Married Catholic women served as symbols for class status in ways that men on the whole did not. Married men were not challenged for their materialistic values and consumption patterns to the same extent as women, because whether working class, middle class, or wealthy, they maintained a culturally approved role of providing for their families. In contrast, although most American Catholics concurred with the view that married women should not work outside the home except when it proved imperative to their family's economic survival, middle-class and upper-class women were nevertheless criticized both for their idleness and for engaging in excessive activity beyond their domestic duties.

These tensions over women's middle-class roles arose in part because of the differing roles prescribed for Catholic women before and after marriage, a phenomenon noted by several historians. Theologically, the church looked upon women's chastity more positively than did many other religions. Moreover, unmarried female immigrants who were Irish or German had traditionally worked in the American labor force in large numbers. Catholics in the hierarchy, in lay groups, and in the press portrayed unmarried women who participated in the workforce as noble, self-sacrificing, and pure because they fulfilled their filial obligations by contributing to their families as well as to society. That depiction arose in part to justify the economic necessity of immigrant women entering the workforce before marriage or when widowed. Moreover, many immigrant women, especially Irish ones, remained in the workforce permanently due to limited marriage prospects, and thus it was important that American Catholics viewed their circumstances as respectable. Irish Catholics further emphasized these women's purity to counter commonly held negative views of the reputation of working women, especially those in factories.[8]

The portrayal of single working women as selfless, pious, and virtuous helped Irish Catholics as a whole carve out an image of respectability in the face of negative stereotypes against them. Any slight against an Irish domestic symbolized prejudice against the entire group. Moreover, American support for the Land League in the early 1880s highlighted exploitation of Irish tenants by English landowners; the exploitation of servants by wealthy employers was a natural extension of that critique.

This characterization is illustrated dramatically in a sentimental and didactic short story, "Kathleen O'Neill: An Irish Girl's Fidelity," published in *Donohue's Magazine* and reprinted in *Catholic Citizen* in 1883. The story recounts the plight of Kathleen, an Irish servant working in the home of Mrs. Arnott, a demanding and anti-Irish lady. "Poor Kathleen" is homesick and ill-treated by both Mrs. Arnott and her children. When a painting of an Irish lake reminds her of home, her employer scoffs, "Your home! A shanty in a bog. It isn't likely that you ever saw such a spot as that." Although Mrs. Arnott provides Kathleen with only a closet-sized room with insufficient bedding, she had just redecorated the drawing room windows "with lace and brocatelle." She tells her husband that she intends to fire Kathleen, although he objects that it would be unduly harsh treatment. But when the Arnott children contract a fever, it is Kathleen and not the French nanny who nurses them back to health. Mrs. Arnott repents for her poor treatment and treats Kathleen as a friend and equal into her old age. In addition to extolling the selflessness of Irish working women, providing a model of single female behavior, and condemning nativism, the story sharply rebukes upper-class women who mistreat their servants and spend their resources on superficial endeavors and consumer goods. While the employer in the story is most likely Protestant, the message also applied to Catholic women with the means to hire servants.[9]

In contrast to the selfless working woman, middle- and upper-class married women who had attained leisure status did not conform to prescribed roles for laywomen, who were to work unceasingly, first for pay and then, if married, without pay, in order to support their families. This relatively new role as household employer further challenged the traditional division of roles among Irish American Catholic women, because by hiring unmarried women to work in their homes, the middle- and upper-class women abdicated part of their prescribed role, which was to care for their homes and families. A *Pilot* writer, most likely female, entreated Catholic women who employed household servants to set reasonable demands for them: "We have our maids and we expect them to be perfect. . . . When we break our china, it is an accident; when they do it is sheer carelessness." That remark suggested that wealthy Catholics should avoid perpetuating the "Biddy" stereotype of the hapless Irish maid and refrain from joining with other middle-class Americans in complaining about the servant problem.[10]

In an 1880 article, "A Mother's Mission," in Milwaukee's *Catholic Citizen*, "A Mother" bemoaned the frivolous nature of some mothers:

> It is unaccountable to me that there are mothers who seem to have their mental faculties highly cultivated, and yet can intrust almost the entire management and education to teachers and servants while they spend their time in dressing, visiting, and various other idle amusements. . . . How sad it is to see homes where the mother . . . inculcates into their young minds that fine appearance and good standing in so-called fashionable society, is the main object in life. Such children, with few exceptions, become vain frivolous worldlings, with no love for God, nor belief in His teachings.[11]

In 1891 a piece entitled "The Vulgarity of Social Pretense and Pushing" appeared in the "The Household," a column published regularly by the *Pilot*. The writer warned mothers that "[t]here [is] much tinsel and shallow gilt plating in this world," adding that mothers who sought the best for their children should avoid "pushing [themselves]; never compelling invitations, never 'cultivating' people with the sole shrewd and selfish thought of their stepping-stone value."[12]

Such critiques against idleness, superficiality, and frivolity were also voiced by many women's groups, who pointedly criticized middle-class married women who veered from their domestic and maternal duties in order to embrace material values. Among Catholics, issues of birth control and divorce were portrayed as inextricably linked to materialism, because a rejection of maternal or domestic responsibilities, or even their limitation, allowed women to devote more of their energies to social pursuits. Moreover, women came to symbolize growing patterns of American consumption at a time when modern department stores were emerging in urban centers.

Concurrently, however, Catholics increasingly viewed laywomen as having a natural ability to engage in charitable and reform efforts as a result of their inherent maternal qualities. Through the formation of local women's groups, married Catholic women in the late nineteenth century took on the responsibility of protecting young unmarried single women and poorer mothers in a maternal manner. One 1889 *Pilot* article called for Catholic women, presumably those of the middle class, to engage in work that could help poor women who "might have been saved by the kind and sympathetic ministrations of their own sex." The author continued by providing examples of cases in which Catholic women could assist hardworking but poor women who were victims of circumstances.[13] In 1909 the *Pilot* pronounced prematurely that "barriers . . . surrounding woman and her work" were fast giving way and that "[o]ur Mother Church has proclaimed woman's origin and destiny to be the same as man's . . . her dignity and mission are equal to man's."[14]

Therefore, Catholic middle- and upper-class married women risked appearing idle and frivolous by emulating aspects of Protestant middle-class behavior such as hiring servants and engaging in increasing amounts of leisure activities. Wealthy and middle-class Catholics were also viewed as susceptible to modern and materialist values in ways that men and working-class or poor women were not. By the late nineteenth and early twentieth centuries, those women could dispel such charges by engaging in voluntary religious work, which was portrayed as an appropriate extension of their domestic roles. Yet, as discussed below, some wealthy women, especially those with Protestant ties, were criticized for their activities and motives.

Lay Catholic Women's Early Reform Efforts

Prior to the formation of the LCW and CWU, laywomen had organized groups for reform and charitable projects on a smaller scale. The Catholic Young Women's Society was established in Worcester, Massachusetts, in 1888. Directed by Thomas Conaty, a promoter of total abstinence, the group sought to promote "the social, mental, and physical development of our young women" through sports, millinery and cooking classes, cultural events, and entertainment. It also sought to "enlist our young women in the Apostolate of Total Abstinence for the Home." In 1899 Catholic women joined together to form the Guild of St. Elizabeth to initiate programs for children in "those crowded

wards known as the *South End of Boston*." But, despite patronage from Archbishop Williams and Cardinal Gibbons, department store owners, publishers,
the Boston Elevated Railroad, and others, the guild's $2,400 annual budget
remained modest.[15]

In New York a group of Catholic women organized a Guild of the Infant
Saviour to "save the souls of the children" by taking babies that were to be
placed at Randall's Island and "boarding them out" to foster homes. These
women would make sure that the homes were suitable, watch the babies and
foster parents interact, and provide the foster parents with stipends. The *Pilot*
drew an analogy between the Guild of the Infant Saviour and the male St.
Vincent de Paul Society. In 1886 the Queen's Daughters established its headquarters in St. Louis to "improve the home life of the worthy poor" and to
work as a quasi-auxiliary group to the St. Vincent de Paul Society. By 1917,
the organization had sixty branches throughout the country.[16]

In 1888 a group of Boston Catholic women organized a Working-Girls
Home Friend Society to provide assistance to the Grey Nuns who ran a home
for young working women. Later this group changed its name to the Young
Ladies's Charitable Association (YLCA) to reflect the increasing diversification
of its activities. The name closely paralleled that of the Young Women's Christian Association, the Protestant organization founded in the mid-nineteenth
century. By 1895, the YLCA had became so successful in its efforts that a group
of men took the unusual step of forming their own society, which served as
"an auxiliary" to the women's group. In 1892 the YLCA launched an ambitious
fund-raising effort to build a Home for Consumptives in Dorchester for poor
tuberculosis patients. The group also ran a program in which its members visited the sick in their homes or in hospitals, brought them groceries, clothes,
and provisions, and finally, in the event of death, arranged for their burials.
The group achieved a great deal of success in its fund-raising efforts, in three
years raising $60,000 to benefit the 233 patients who had resided in the home
during that period. The YLCA earmarked an additional sum of $15,000 for
other services. In 1895 it boasted of 1,200 members. By 1902, its annual fund-
raising event, a garden party, attracted an estimated 10,000–15,000 people. In
1905 Father McCormack spoke highly of the YLCA, noting that its members
visited sick and poor people "quietly, *unostentatiously* and without praise.
They sought no earthy recompense; they looked beyond to the eternal reward."[17] Articles on the work of the YLCA published by the *Pilot* routinely
emphasized the fact that, in contrast to other church-sponsored homes for
those with tuberculosis, the Home for Consumptives admitted people of all

creeds, colors, and nationalities, and women volunteers did not discriminate against those they visited.[18]

Working Girls' Homes became popular in other Catholic communities during this period as well. In Providence, Rhode Island, a group led by Mrs. Joseph Bannigan opened a home for fifty girls in 1889 in order to "provide a good home in a healthy location." In Plainfield, New Jersey, St. Joseph's Parish opened a home for servants who were either unemployed or ill. Most of the domestics living in the area were Catholic, and a sizable proportion were Irish immigrants; the servants were "energetic and thrifty, and of sound moral character." Reverend James McKernan of St. Joseph's reassured the parish that men would not be allowed to visit the home, and that three married women would oversee its operation. An elderly woman, Mrs. Mary O'Reilly, took on the unpaid but full-time position of matron of the home, having agreed to give up employment as a domestic servant, a job she had held for many years. Parishioners donated furniture and other household goods to the home. Moreover, the *Pilot* noted, over 200 women expressed interest in helping to fund the home.[19]

By the last two decades of the nineteenth century, then, women had become involved at the local level in the type of charitable work and institution building that had previously been reserved for laymen active in the Society of St. Vincent de Paul and for women religious. Those efforts paved the way for larger Catholic women's groups to form and to affiliate with one another, as was the case for the cwu and the lcw. As the following sections illustrate, the cwu and lcw shared several characteristics, including a largely conservative view of gender relations and largely middle- and upper-class memberships. But the cwu members modeled their group on German Catholic women's organizations, while the lcw members portrayed themselves as offering a Catholic alternative to other American women's groups. By the 1920s the National Council of Catholic Women served as an umbrella organization for Catholic women's groups, part of the larger trend toward centralization and bureaucratization that occurred within the church and in American society as a whole.

Catholic Women's Union

German American Catholic women in the early twentieth century organized their reform efforts around the principle of home protection and chose St. Elizabeth of Thuringia as their patron saint. St. Elizabeth, who lived in the early thirteenth century, was the daughter of a king. After her early marriage, she devoted herself to charitable pursuits, including work with lepers and the poor, as well as relief efforts for flood and famine victims. She died a widow at age twenty-four, after having established a Franciscan Hospital in Marburg, and became widely known as the "Patroness of the Poor."[20]

In his discussion of St. Elizabeth in the *Catholic Charities Review*, Reverend John J. Lynch noted that she had long served as the model for Catholic women engaged in charity, adding: "Relieving the poor was for her not a privilege but a duty, not an interesting occupation or diversion but an organic part of her religious life." In addition, the Catholic Women's Union noted that St. Elizabeth had proved an excellent patron saint for the organization because she served as a model "for all the stations of a woman's life: maiden, wife, mother and widow, in private and public life, in prosperity and adversity." By adopting her as their symbol, the women of the CWU sought to emphasize the selflessness of their programs, their compassion toward the poor, the universality of charity among females, and the common ethnic bond between St. Elizabeth and the members of their organization.[21]

The CWU emerged in 1916 to complement the existing male Central Verein. As with the St. Elizabeth Settlement, the decision to create the CWU proved controversial. Key lay leaders and members of the hierarchy, including Milwaukee's Archbishop Sebastian Messmer and Chicago's Archbishop James Quigley, supported the creation of a woman's group. But the initiative also encountered resistance from some within the Central Verein, who believed that women should not have a public role. In recounting those early years, the CWU dismissed the objections of "these traditionalists" as old-fashioned, noting that as a result of technological advances women no longer needed to spend as much time managing their households as previously. By 1925 it had 50,000 members in branches in nineteen states and a national budget of $45,461. While the most active groups were concentrated in Wisconsin, Illinois, Texas, and Missouri, the CWU also boasted of branches in Arkansas, New Jersey, Connecticut, and several other states where the German American population was proportionately small.[22]

Although the domestic ideology of CWU members seems inspired by the middle-class Protestant separate-spheres ideology of mid-nineteenth-century America, their views on Catholic social reform drew extensively from central European influences. Because the German ethnic identity was a strong focus in both the male and female Vereins, these women appropriated models of social action that existed in Europe, as well as responding to secular, Protestant, and Catholic trends within the United States. In fact, as German historian Christof Sachße has discussed, many bourgeois women in late-nineteenth-century Germany articulated a similar view of "social motherhood" that emphasized the responsibility that middle- and upper-class women held for poorer women in their communities.[23]

In outlining their purpose, cwu members cited speeches by Archbishop Michael Faulhaber of Munich and Cardinal George Kopp of Breslau in 1908. According to Cardinal Kopp, the foundation of Catholic women's groups should be to "preserve our women from those many pitfalls threatening them and human society; it offers a firm base, on which women can co-operate for the welfare of their sex, guided by eternal truths." The *Central-Blatt and Social Justice*, the Central Verein journal, regularly reported on women's social reform activities in Europe in its column, "Das Soziale Frauenaposto-lat." One column discussed a 1918 meeting of fifty Catholic women in Vienna active in charitable and reform efforts, which "encompasses women of the most varied social classes and of every age," and reported on their efforts at homes for working women, for "fallen girls willing to improve themselves," and for the elderly. Bishop Wilhelm von Ketteler of Mainz, a major opponent of the Kulturkampf, spearheaded Catholic involvement in German social reform efforts and was quoted in cwu and Central Verein publications in support of greater social activism among Catholics in the United States.[24]

Despite their emphasis on domesticity, members of the cwu simultaneously acknowledged that many mothers had no choice but to remain in the workforce. They advocated the expansion of day care facilities for children, such as those of the St. Elizabeth Settlement in St. Louis, and promoted the establishment of a mothers' pension program. Although, like Leo XIII, they condemned socialism, the cwu and Central Verein were also quite critical of modern capitalism and its effects on the working class and poor. In countering those critics who opposed women's involvement in social causes, a writer in the cwu *Bulletin* stated that those critics "cannot be so blind as not to see how powerless the individual is, indeed entire groups are, in the face of the economic necessity that tears the woman from her home." The writer then summarized for *Bulletin* readers *The Women's Movement: Its Problems and Organization*, a book by Liane Becker, a woman active in German Catholic women's issues. Becker's book traced the historical role of women artisans in Europe since the thirteenth century and discussed their membership and leadership in craft guilds alongside men. The writer concluded that through an understanding of such a history "one can more easily see that the ethical

factors that in earlier times provided support and protection to female workers are absent today, and set about trying to replace them." Although that
account clearly romanticized an earlier age, it justified women's greater involvement in social reform efforts directed at the problems of modern industrial society.[25]

The CWU emphasized the principle of *Kleinarbeit*, or "preparatory work"—
basic tasks performed by women within the household—which should also be
extended to the "larger spheres of social welfare."[26] CWU members compared
their mission to that of the Society of St. Vincent de Paul. "Why," they asked
rhetorically, "should work like that of the venerable pioneer, the St. Vincent
de Paul Society be restricted to men?" In fact, much of the rhetoric in the
CWU emphasized the unique prerogative that women, as mothers and wives,
held for extending their influence throughout society, except in ways that
involved traditional political activities.[27]

For German American Catholic women active in social reform through
church-sponsored organizations, the family served as the "original model for
society," in which "the social virtues are only subvarieties of the domestic
virtues, for the wide circles of social relationships are nothing but concentric
extensions of the narrow and small family circle." An article in the women's
column of *Central-Blatt and Social Justice* criticized the current climate of
"modern shallowness" for failing to recognize the "importance of domestic
life for cultural progress."[28]

German Catholic women believed that as females they were uniquely able
to influence society while remaining within the domestic sphere. This sphere
was not limited, however, to the private home. "Men might indeed have
greater influence than women on the outer trappings of culture; but this
means nothing. Women have as much influence as men on the inner structure, the actual heartbeat of cultural life." Another article in the *Central-Blatt
and Social Justice* discussed the views of F. W. Foerster as an important
basis for social interaction. Foerster believed that the relationship between
employer and employee should be changed and that "[l]ordly behavior and
slave mentality must be removed from modern culture," as all types of work
are socially valued and respected. He believed in abolishing rigid class divisions, and in the dignity of the working class. Women also called for an end to
the rigid class divisions and stressed the need to value all types of work—
including that of the domestic servant, who had been made to feel ashamed
of her livelihood. "It is easy to see that women's more delicate tact will lead
the way to the rebirth of ossified social divisions." The journal further quoted

Professor Franz Hitze, a German Catholic proponent of activism on labor issues, as stating that "the upper classes should become conscious of their responsibility[;] they should consider means of protecting the daughters of the common people."[29]

A lecture by Elizabeth Lenz in 1918 in Appleton, Wisconsin, suggested the role that members of German Catholic women's leagues should play. Lenz, an officer of the CWU and briefly the editor of its *Bulletin*, said, "The beginning must naturally be made with one's self and the family, the foundation of society. . . . But Catholic women must not confine their activities within their four walls." As examples of such outside activities, she indicated that "[n]urseries and kindergartens must be established for the care of children whose mothers are forced by circumstances to help supplement their families." Moreover, she added, "[P]oor mothers with their babies should be provided for." Lenz also urged the women in her audience to monitor "libraries, theatres, movies, [etc.]" to guard against immoral forms of entertainment. She added that "the work must be done intelligently, which requires study."[30] This remark suggests that Lenz believed that the CWU should implement some elements of social work. In addition to supporting mother's pensions, the group emphasized the need to reduce infant mortality rates among poor women.

Clergy who advised and presided over the CWU's activities reinforced this view, which I would label "activist domesticity." For example, following Lenz's speech, the Wisconsin chapter's spiritual advisor, Reverend Raphael Wittig, asked the women to "remember that we are not Idle but trying to be Ideal women, according to the heart of God."[31] Father A. B. Salick, speaking about the group, stated that its members "should be veritable Guardian Angels for their sex."[32]

Unlike other Catholic women's groups in the United States, German American women readily acknowledged the existence of class differences within society; although other Catholic lay groups implicitly recognized divisions between its members and those they sought to assist, they did not refer to them in class terms. Yet while the Catholic Women's Union stated that it sought "to unite the Catholic women of all classes into one large organization," it was clear from the activities undertaken by the group that poorer women were viewed as primarily the beneficiaries of the society's work rather than as equal participants in it. Although the CWU's members emphasized women's domestic and maternal roles, their actions illustrate that they remained assertive in promoting the interests of their organization among the clergy and the Central Verein leadership.[33]

One of the CWU's four goals, articulated in the Missouri branch's constitution, was the "promotion of religiosity and class consciousness of the members." The term "class consciousness" seems to refer to a sense of middle-class responsibility, or a form of noblesse oblige, toward poorer Catholics, who were referred to as *Geschlechtsgenossinnen*, or "fellow women." These goals were to be carried out by "creating class groups," such as servants' associations, commercial societies, and "working women's societies," similar to those initiated by Catholic women in central Europe.[34]

Many of the initiatives undertaken by the CWU in the early twentieth century were patterned on those of Catholic women's organizations in Germany, particularly the Katholischer deutscher Frauenbund (KDF). Elisabeth Gnauck-Kühne, a recent convert to Catholicism, began the KDF in 1903 at age fifty-three. Previously, she had been active in a variety of labor and social reform activities and in 1890 had spoken before the Protestant-Social Congress on the social situation of women. After taking a job at a box factory in order to investigate women's working conditions and then supporting a strike there, she encountered criticism from middle-class women and was denounced as being "worse than a socialist" in the Reichstag. During the course of her social activism, she became acquainted with Father Augustin Rösler, a supporter of women's rights, and converted to Catholicism in 1900. Gnauck-Kühne found that German Catholics generally opposed women's rights, and her efforts to gain widespread support for such issues were unsuccessful.[35]

Despite some early setbacks, Gnauck-Kühne successfully launched the KDF, whose goals were both to elevate women morally, economically, and spiritually and to combat the "rising tide of materialism." The group also planned to work on behalf of labor issues. Once she established the KDF, Gnauck-Kühne decided not to serve as head of the organization because of poor health and the heated controversy she expected to encounter. As the KDF was forming, debates emerged in Germany over the relationship between the Catholic Church and the labor movement. Because many of the socialist-oriented unions in Germany were neutral toward, or opposed to, religion, many laity and members of the hierarchy opposed labor activism within the church, while others viewed the issue as central to the church and supported its involvement in unions. The KDF ultimately supported the creation of

Christian unions. The organization also encountered opposition from male labor leaders, who believed that women should not become involved in the sphere of economic and political activism but rather attend to spiritual affairs alone. The fact that the KDF members were largely upper middle class also caused tension between them and the labor leaders. Nevertheless, the KDF chose to work primarily on behalf of women workers. Therefore, while the KDF did not initiate the ambitious program of labor activism and women's rights advocacy that Gnauck-Kühne had first envisioned, the group did become active on a number of social issues. Like some other Catholic social reforms initiated by converts, the programs of the KDF meshed Protestant-originated objectives with Catholic ideals.[36]

Members of the KDF and CWU forged relationships between their two groups, shared many of the same views on social issues, and launched similar charitable efforts. The CWU referred to the German organization's members as "our sister members across the sea," and several KDF members visited CWU leagues throughout the United States. Frau Professor Wilhelmine Keppler, the sister-in-law of Bishop Paul von Keppler of Rothenburg, Germany, and another leader in the KDF, spoke to CWU members in 1921. An educator, Keppler had been born in South Carolina, where she had organized a kindergarten association while her husband taught at a military academy there. She later established a Froebel Academy in Jacksonville, Florida. The academy was named for Friedrich Froebel, who, like Maria Montessori, was a pioneer in the early education movement. Froebel, the founder of kindergarten, advocated that children should learn through play and promoted an active rather than didactic approach to education. Yet Froebel's methods came under criticism by the Prussian government as potentially subversive in the years following the 1848 uprisings. In 1851 the government forbade kindergartens, deeming them anti-Christian and antisocial, despite Froebel's strong Christian beliefs inculcated by his father, a Lutheran minister. By the late nineteenth century, Froebel academies arose in several European countries, including several in England, as well as in the United States. After the Florida academy was destroyed by fire, Keppler and her husband moved to Germany, where she became active in Catholic women's reform issues.[37]

Keppler came to the United States as a designated representative of the Rothenburg diocese to encourage the CWU and others to support assistance programs for children and women enduring the economic devastation in Germany following World War I.[38] In her speeches, including those to CWU branches in Effingham and Teutopolis, Illinois, Keppler gave advice on running a successful organization. Stressing the issue of class, Keppler, who by almost any measure numbered among the elite, counseled CWU members to encourage working-class women to join their group because "[w]e found our most earnest and effective workers in the ranks of house wives—the women of the middle and working classes," adding that wealthy women did "nothing in proportion to their wealth and position." She also claimed that by recruiting such women, "we have won thousands of Catholic men from socialistic groups." Yet, despite the links between the two groups, the CWU, unlike the KDF, never became active in labor issues, nor were its leaders drawn primarily from the elite.[39]

In 1923 the KDF president, Hedwig Dransfeld of Berlin, also visited the United States to speak to German Catholic women who had organized charitable efforts on behalf of German Catholics who had suffered economically following World War I. While in the United States, she criticized the American reparations policy as unduly harsh, although in light of strong anti-German sentiment in the United States, the CWU's *Bulletin* did not report on that aspect of her lectures. In this period, the KDF had grown immensely, claiming 240,000 members in 1927, compared to just 36,000 prior to the war. Dransfeld accomplished that feat by establishing a League of Catholic Social Workers, encouraging the formation of local women's groups, and creating a youth division of the organization. Dransfeld, born in 1871 and raised in a Catholic orphanage, had hoped to became a writer or poet but eventually worked as a teacher. At a 1912 meeting in Strasbourg, Dransfeld emphasized the KDF's need to commit itself to social reform on behalf of poor women, based on a shared national identity, rather than simply functioning as an upper-class women's group focused on intellectual and spiritual matters. She had been elected as KDF's president after gaining prominence through her editorship of the Catholic magazine *Die christliche Frau (Christian Woman)* and a successful public-speaking career. She had also protested on behalf of women workers during World War I, who were paid less than men for factory work and, because some women worked as the supervisors of male workers, also encountered a backlash against women's rights. Dransfeld had became seriously ill prior to her trip to the United States and died in 1925. Another KDF leader, Helene Weber, also toured the United States after the war. Weber had worked with Dransfeld to establish a school for female Catholic social workers (die soziale Frauenschule) and the League of Catholic Social Workers of Germany and was later elected to the Reichstag.[40]

One difference between the leaders of the German organization and the

American CWU leaders was the more modest economic position of those in the United States. For example, the leadership of the Wisconsin German Catholic Women's League, which belonged to the CWU, was comprised mostly of wives and daughters of businessmen. Most were not wealthy—instead, these women were drawn primarily from families with small to medium-sized enterprises. The president of the Wisconsin league during the late teens, Minnie Springob, was married to the owner of a German newspaper advertising agency in Milwaukee. Her husband also served as a national officer for the Central Verein. Anna Birck, on the state league's executive committee, lived above a Milwaukee saloon owned by her husband. Catherine Drolshagen, the recording secretary, served as treasurer of her family-owned business, Milwaukee Pattern and Manufacturing, while Elizabeth Bergs worked as the secretary of the Bergs Realty Company in Milwaukee. Both Drolshagen and Bergs were unmarried. The finance secretary lived in Racine and had been widowed for at least a decade. Another Racine member, Mrs. J. Welfl, served as treasurer and was married to the owner of a shoe store.[41]

The CWU's major work, directly influenced by German Catholic women, involved the development of a traveler's aid network. This work was to be undertaken in the name of "Christian Solidarism." The program targeted rural German Catholic women who had left their homes for work in cities such as Milwaukee and Chicago; CWU reformers sought to create a network of affiliated traveler's aid societies. This particular emphasis of the CWU also proved similar to that of Catholic women's organizations in Germany. There, women's groups claimed to have benefited 2 million working women and had launched a network to protect young women at railroad stations and ports, like others developed for Catholic immigrants in the United States and elsewhere.[42]

A Catholic group, L'Oeuvre de la Protection de la Jeune Fille, was founded in Fribourg, Switzerland, at the turn of the century by Madame la Baroness de Montenach and quickly spread to other European cities. Members of the group sought to protect young Catholic women materially and morally and, like Charlotte O'Brien and other reformers, to insure that these young women did not fall prey to white slavery. One of their boardinghouse programs, in Liege, Belgium, assisted 2,000 women from 1919 to 1923. The organization emphasized the need to create a Catholic network of working girls' homes and traveler's aid societies. The initiative was quite similar in its concerns to those of Charlotte O'Brien and the Boston port assistance program.[43]

In 1920 CWU members, many of whom were engaged in similar work in their state branches, affiliated with the Fribourg-based organization, which they called the International Railroad Mission, and they also sought to coordinate their efforts with the cwu's counterpart in Chicago. Depot guides, or contact women, volunteered to receive telephone calls from female travelers and to provide them with temporary lodgings. They also directed women to employment possibilities and to approved agencies. The guides' names and addresses were printed on cards for distribution throughout the states, and the same information was posted in railway stations. This program was important because "many country girls working in the cities return home to assist in the farm work." Again, as the white slavery issue became an international concern, unmarried Catholic women were portrayed as virtuous due to their industriousness, selflessness, and loyalty in their continued support of their families.[44]

The Wisconsin league's "Bulletin" routinely quoted its members or advisors as emphasizing "certain dangers that threaten girls from 12 to 16 years of age in large cities" and "the great lack of proper lodging-places for office and factory girls that come to the city." Ultimately, by 1920, the Wisconsin branch of the cwu had established a working-girls home in Milwaukee, Our Lady of Good Counsel, and employed a matron to run it. The group had raised an initial $5,000 toward the building's $18,000 purchase price and subsequently organized fund-raisers to pay off the balance. While many of the women residents, who paid $6–8 for room and board per week, were of German descent, the home also welcomed women of various ethnic backgrounds. By 1919, the Wisconsin league stated that it had assisted 114 women in obtaining lodging or employment. The league's 1922 report stated, without further comment, that in addition to assisting women with employment, lodging, and travel advice, members had rescued six girls from white slavery. In New York, the cwu branch established St. Elizabeth House in 1929 as a home for immigrant and working girls and supported the efforts of Leo House, whose director, Reverend C. Spohr, also served as their spiritual director.[45]

Although the cwu did not establish port programs similar to those initiated by Charlotte O'Brien or the Charitable Irish Society, members did intervene in at least one immigration case. That case, which occurred in the mid-1920s, involved two German sisters, ages twenty and twenty-three, who had immigrated to St. Louis to live with an uncle and aunt in their boarding-house, in a neighborhood "whose respectability was open to question." The girls repaid the debts owed to their uncle for their passage from Germany and then moved from his house to a better neighborhood. According to a cwu report: "This act angered the uncle who made false statements regarding the character of the girls also stating that the girls were likely to become public charges and should be deported." An attorney took on their case pro bono, and then a German-speaking priest, the Central Verein, and the CWU also became involved. The immigrants had a week-long hearing at the Bureau of Immigration, posted bond, and were ordered to live under supervision. During a CWU meeting, one member offered to host the young women in her home. The National Board of Immigration reviewed the case, placed the girls on parole for a year, under supervision of the Central Verein, and ordered them to report monthly to the Bureau of Immigration. When the elder sister married, her younger sister moved in with her.[46]

The account suggests the distinct possibility that the women might have been involved in prostitution or that their uncle had exerted pressure on them to become involved in it. But, more definitively, it illustrates that the threat of deportation was sometimes used by relatives or others to intimidate or retaliate against the actions of young immigrants. In this case, however, the uncle used provisions of the immigration law as a blunt weapon to coerce vulnerable immigrants into acting illegally, whereas the CIS port agent in Boston used the threat of deportation to discourage or punish questionable activities.

Anti-German sentiment permeated American society during World War I, leading the New York branch of the Central Verein to suspend its conventions in 1917 and 1918. Yet the CWU did not discuss the issue of divided loyalties in their publications. The Wisconsin branch of the CWU referred only obliquely to the issue in their statewide publication by stating: "Christian Prudence suggests that our next Bulletin appear in the English language only: we must bring sacrifices to serve the good cause." In that same issue, the group announced that it had changed its name from D.R.K. Frauenbund von Wisconsin/G.R.C. Women's League, to the less ethnic-sounding Catholic Women's League of Wisconsin. It also reported on the success of Liberty Bond drives, underscoring the CWU's loyalty to the United States.[47]

Ethnic concerns returned to the fore following the war, largely as a result of the severe economic depression plaguing Germany and Austria. Hedwig Dransfeld and others emphasized in their correspondence with the CWU that members of the middle class suffered alongside the poor. The chairwoman of a Catholic woman's group in Austria, Clementine Metternich, wrote to the CWU requesting that members send sewing materials so that Austrian women could produce garments for export to the United States.[48] In fact, a significant percentage of the CWU's annual budget was allocated for relief efforts in

Germany. Of the New York union's annual expenditures of $1,266 in 1925, almost half went to Catholic institutions in Germany. The other state unions did not specify to which countries they sent relief, but the Central Illinois District directed $1,820 of its $4,897 budget to "Foreign Relief" and an additional $300 to "Foreign Missions."[49]

Despite their conservatism on many issues and an emphasis on domestic roles for women, CWU members proved quite outspoken about the direction of their organization and expressed opinions on some national political issues. Many of them asserted that the lack of interest taken in the organization among the clergy and hierarchy served as a major inhibitor to its continued growth. This indifference was readily acknowledged by clergy who were involved in the local CWU chapters. At the union's 1925 meeting, a male delegate from Arkansas recounted the problems faced by the group. "In Father Hoffman's time, an open rupture occurred. The Bishop prohibited the women to belong to this Union. Father Hoffman met the Bishop, and patched up the difficulty." The speaker noted that the union then received the bishop's approval. Mrs. Kellenberger, a delegate from Hudson County, New Jersey, recounted the problems faced there. Members of the union "have not the backing of the priests or the Bishop. The ladies take no interest in it." The national spiritual advisor, Father Albert Mayer, concurred with these views, lamenting, "Although we do not want it to go out that there is any animosity against the Catholic Council of Women [CWU], still it is there." But he added, "Even the sections that are working and making fine progress are laboring under the spirit of opposition from sides where we should find no opposition." In 1922 the CWU sent a letter to the clergy of the United States that strongly urged them to support the organization, noting that they had failed to do so in the past. The writers strayed from an otherwise deferential tone when they stated: "No wonder if we cannot compete with others, who have enthusiastic and energetic leaders! . . . Are we not told that the priest is taken from out the people and constituted mediators for the people? Are we women not part and parcel of the people?"[50]

In their letter to clergy, CWU members also criticized commercialism and modern women's concern for material goods, especially as expressed in recent fashions: "[W]e bow so easily to flattery and the lure of fineries!" In a pamphlet urging middle- and upper-class women to become active in social welfare efforts, they contrasted the plight of poor Catholic women in tenements with those "at ease in their beautiful, peaceful homes, idling away their precious time with a poodle dog—instead of a child—on their lap, while their care-worn sisters in the city stare at their starving children in their arms!" This remark served as both a critique of modern values and a call for middle-class Catholic involvement in charity on the basis of maternalism. As part of their objection to modern influences cwu members actively opposed birth control laws and the Child Labor Amendment and wrote letters to their political representatives to express their views on those topics. The cwu and Central Verein advocated the creation of mothers' pension programs, health insurance, and other maternal assistance programs. The programs that they advocated would have had a far greater impact than those created under the Sheppard-Towner Act of 1921, which provided federal matching funds to states for the provision of prenatal and infant care, child care clinics, and visiting nurses. Yet the Wisconsin members sent at least one petition opposing the Sheppard-Towner bill to a Wisconsin congressman, arguing that it would allow the federal government to take away power from local and state agencies. The fear that it would remove the stigma against unmarried motherhood might have influenced their decision. cwu members also viewed the Child Labor Amendment as a potential infringement of parental authority and distributed pamphlets urging Catholics to oppose it.[51]

German American Catholics in particular had opposed laws on the grounds that they intruded into parental decision making or into their cultural practices. For example, they vigorously opposed the Prohibition Amendment and Wisconsin's Bennett law, which required that instruction be conducted in English in private and parochial as well as public schools. Opposition to federal initiatives such as the Sheppard-Towner Act and the Child Labor Amendment had their counterparts in German debates over welfare policies. In the midst of Bismarck's Kulturkampf, Catholics in Prussia objected to an 1876 law that addressed juvenile delinquency by placing offenders in institutions or in Protestant foster care rather than with their parents. Indeed, German Catholics viewed the measure as a "serious assault on the rights of the parents," using rhetoric that was similar to that later used by German Americans. Catholics also objected to Germany's policy of public legal guardianship of children from around 1905 to 1912, because Catholic children were routinely placed with Protestants, thus threatening their religious training.[52]

While German Americans in the cwu did not refer specifically to Kulturkampf policies in their opposition to Sheppard-Towner and the Child Labor Amendment, their concern about the impact of federal power on religion and the family arose in the context of German events. German Catholics associated with St. Elizabeth Settlement did not hesitate to involve local authorities in certain cases. Therefore German Catholic objections to such federal initiatives in the United States, while rooted in conservative social views, had a more complex history than has been acknowledged.

The role of women leaders also became a heated issue within the CWU. Sophia Wavering, the CWU's president throughout much of the 1920s, became embroiled in controversies with the hierarchy and with Central Verein leaders when she challenged their authority. The first case concerned Bishop James A. Griffen's refusal to award her the Cross Pro Ecclesia et Pontiface for her work on behalf of the CWU in 1927. According to Wavering, "Quincy [Illinois] people have made complaint that I am not worthy." She continued by delineating the charges against her, which included submitting a bill for a meal, giving just $15 to the St. Mary's Hospital Drive, writing an "impertinent letter to the Provincial," and disagreeing with the bishop over what action to take on the Child Labor Amendment. She further asserted that people charged that her husband was "not, as usually given out by me, a sickly man, but a drunkard." She concluded, "It would seem that a woman without means, in my station in life has no business in a prominent position. Almost I could regret that I ever accepted the responsibility, but not quite. . . . Quincy is just the right size for jealousy to flourish."[53]

Bishop Griffen had jurisdiction over Wavering's diocese in Illinois. In the meantime, however, Reverend Raphael Wittig, then on the CWU's executive committee, had asked Archbishop Sebastian Messmer of Milwaukee to confer the cross on Wavering. Messmer agreed to do so, apparently unaware that her own bishop had refused. Frederick Kenkel, director of the Central Verein, replied that Griffen had jurisdiction in the matter and that Wavering should not attempt to receive the cross in Milwaukee. He closed his letter by stating, "It is highly regrettable that what was intended to be an honor and a reward for your efforts now turns out not merely a disappointment, but worse, a humiliating experience."[54]

Charles Korz, Kenkel's successor as Central Verein director, was not nearly as diplomatic in his response to Wavering. He wrote to Kenkel in 1930, asking rhetorically: "When will we ever get rid of that woman. Or better, is there anybody with courage enough to say 'halt'[?] I am convinced more than ever that the object of the woman is to gradually create an independent body of women which at the proper moment will separate from the Central Verein. She does not care for F[ather] Mayer and is not *afraid* of him. In my opinion, the only solution for the Frauenbund is to select another President, *one who knows her place* and does not intend to use the organization as a stepping-stone for future financial security."[55] These charges, however, did not end Wavering's career as a Catholic women's leader. Ultimately, she received the award, and Pope Pius XI granted her a private audience in 1927. As late as 1935, Wavering served as president of the CWU.[56]

Whether or not Wavering was guilty of the rather minor charges against her, Korz's and Griffen's responses suggest that her true transgressions lay in her refusal to "know her place" and in her nondeferential leadership of the CWU, including her challenging its status as an auxiliary to the men's group. Wavering also implied that fellow members of the union, as well as the clergy and hierarchy, held negative views of her because she was neither wealthy nor perhaps even solidly middle class.

Another major controversy arose among CWU leaders in the early 1920s, with the emergence of the National Catholic Welfare Council (NCWC) and National Council of Catholic Women (NCCW), the national lay groups sponsored by the hierarchy after World War I. The CWU members viewed those organizations suspiciously as a threat to the identity, agenda, and vitality of their own group. As a national group with a larger constituency, the NCCW had the potential to overshadow the CWU and to divert resources and support from the organization. Although ultimately the CWU did affiliate with the NCWC and NCCW, CWU members voiced their resentment of the fact that the new organizations sought to engage in the pioneering work of the CWU. In early 1921 the CWU suggested that members refrain from affiliating with the two groups. Leaders deemed the issue of affiliation a "grave problem" for the CWU. "If they are faithful members and not only dead ones, they are doing what the N.C.W.C. wants them to do. . . . We don't believe in joining half dozen associations and then not doing anything in any one of them." By May, Father Hoffman had replied to Agnes Regan, head of the NCWC, about her group's plan to affiliate with the Association des Oeuvres de Protection de la Jeune Fille, with which the CWU had previously affiliated. Stating dryly, "[W]e are not at a loss for guidance," Hoffman defended the CWU by emphasizing the fact that the CWU was a pioneer in Catholic social reform, having advocated "the very issues now undertaken" by the NCWC. At their annual convention in August, however, CWU members passed a resolution expressing their support for the aims of the NCWC, and the *Bulletin* made no reference to the heated controversy that had occurred earlier in the year. Later the CWU rebutted the NCCW's claim that it was the only national Catholic group that had lobbied against birth control legislation. While such resentment eased over time, the tension did not completely disappear. As late as 1966, in its golden jubilee publication, the cwu reminded its members that it had been founded in 1916, adding pointedly, "This was four years before the National Council of Catholic Women was organized by the Bishops in May 1920."[57]

During the 1920s a significant proportion of cwu members were second-generation German Catholics, a situation reflected in the group's activities and methods. Yet debates arose about the importance of maintaining a distinct ethnic identity. At the 1925 annual convention of the union in Cleveland, members debated whether or not to allow Catholic women who were not of German origin to join. Father Mayer, the spiritual advisor, replied that it was preferable to refrain from organizing in non-German parishes, because "[i]f we go into their circle, they have a right to go into ours." He implied that the cwu should organize among German women prior to establishing groups among other Catholic women. Reverend Raphael Wittig of Wisconsin held a different view. He advocated that all Catholic women be admitted into the cwu, regardless of their ethnic background. He conceded, though, that the time might not yet have come in the United States for this to occur.

Ultimately, in the wake of anti-German sentiment resulting from World War I, and following the creation of the NCCW in 1920, the cwu gradually moved away from a strong ethnic identification and toward greater uniformity with other Catholic women. In 1923, responding to the popular initiatives aimed at assisting German Catholics to rebuild their lives and institutions after the war, the cwu *Bulletin* stated, "The C.W.U. is not a European, but a genuinely American organization." It continued by suggesting that the union should concentrate on American projects rather than expending so much effort on providing charity to assisting Catholics in Germany. A year later, at its annual meeting in Allentown, Pennsylvania, the cwu replaced its patron saint, St. Elizabeth, an ethnic as well as religious symbol, with Mary, Our Lady of Good Counsel, a universal Catholic saint, stating that they were doing so because Pope Pius XI "expressed the wish that Catholic women's groups place themselves under her protection."[58]

The special link between German groups and the cwu increasingly gave way to the idea that Catholic women's groups throughout the world were involved in a common endeavor. In 1925 cwu publications began to emphasize the emergence of Catholic women's organizations in a variety of countries—including New Zealand, Denmark, and Norway—as well as the International Congress of Catholic Women's Leagues, held in Rome. Finally, when the cwu revised its constitution in 1936, the new document reflected the fact that the group did not "limit membership, as some had thought, to

Roman Catholics of German ancestry." And, while the influence of *Rerum Novarum* had always been implicit in the work of the CWU, the group's revised constitution mentioned explicitly Leo XIII's encyclical as an influence on its program of social action.[59]

The CWU, and its local affiliates, represented an ethnically based women's group that, like its male counterpart, modeled itself on German Catholic organizations and appropriated many of their philosophies about charity and women's roles. Like other Catholic groups, it criticized "idle women" of the middle class, many of whom were viewed as adopting modern values that were incompatible with Catholicism. Despite the overall conservative nature of the group, its members openly criticized their bishops and clergy for failing to promote and support the organization. Although the CWU and the LCW shared some of the same values, positions, and activities, the emphases and the models of the two groups proved quite different, largely because of their differing attitudes toward ethnicity and their relationship to the majority culture.

League of Catholic Women

A group of Boston Catholic women formed the League of Catholic Women in 1910, with support and encouragement from Archbishop O'Connell (soon to be Cardinal O'Connell), to "unite Catholic women for the promotion of religious, intellectual, and charitable work." A year later it affiliated with the International Federation of Leagues of Catholic Women, as one of twenty-one such leagues. It operated under the close supervision and control of two of the cardinal's assistants, Monsignor Michael Splaine, the archdiocese's chancellor, and Reverend Richard Haberlin. Indeed, Splaine, who became the league's spiritual director, drafted its constitution, while Cardinal O'Connell approved its officers.[60]

The LCW differed from the CWU in part because of O'Connell's conservative and powerful position in the church, as well as a result of the unique ethnic and religious circumstances in Boston. Moreover, unlike the CWU, which was a national group, the LCW was regional. Therefore O'Connell's tight control on the activities of the league and his opposition to suffrage, feminism, and other reforms had a significant impact on the issues in which the LCW became involved.[61]

Though, like the vast majority of middle-class Catholics in early-twentieth-century Boston, most LCW members were Irish American, they eschewed ethnic issues. Unlike members of the CWU, they did not strongly identify their work with a patron saint. In fact, through many of their activities they sought to emulate existing Protestant-oriented women's groups in Boston. Thus the LCW's goals differed dramatically from those of the CWU. The LCW eventually became more ethnically diverse; Lithuanian and Polish groups affiliated with the league as it expanded its base from Boston to other areas. By 1919, such affiliates included one in Lowell. By 1920, the LCW claimed 6,000 members.[62]

Although the LCW was founded with the intention of including women from all classes, the group remained largely in the hands of upper-class Catholics. In an essay introducing the concept and purpose of the LCW to Boston Catholics, its leader stated: "There is a large number of working women who must not be left out. Many of them are thoughtful and serious-minded and their ideas and suggestions gained from the more practical experiences of life are of great value to those whose lives are less busy."[63] This sentiment seemed to support the positive view that the American church maintained on single working women. Yet women who sought to join the LCW had to secure the signature of two members before submitting an application and then needed to be elected by the league's executive committee. Because the founding members tended to be wealthy, that requirement restricted the ability of working women to become involved until parish and local church groups in Lowell and other areas began affiliating with the league.[64]

The LCW proved very successful in its fund-raising efforts. In 1914 the league had a modest budget and apologetically requested $500 from Cardinal O'Connell to help fund its programs "among the Italians." By 1920, its fund-raising capabilities had improved considerably; by holding bazaars and other events, the LCW raised over $173,000 to donate to the Diocesan Central. Later Cardinal O'Connell requested that the league lend $50,000 from the proceeds of its bazaar to the Boston School for the Deaf.[65]

In the early 1920s, after a successful fund-raising campaign in which the members earned $200,000, the LCW moved to new headquarters—a "magnificent" five-story townhouse "on one of the best corners in Boston." The building served as an important physical symbol of the Catholic group members' upper-class status in the midst of a Protestant upper-class neighborhood. The house contained the league's offices but also functioned as a club where members could eat breakfast and take afternoon tea, as well as furnishing other "conveniences to be found in the best clubs." Although men were prohibited, female guests could accompany LCW members there. In order to operate the club, league members employed domestic help, a house man, and paid a salary to a nun who oversaw its operations. Members of the LCW believed that the building represented a turning point in their organization, stating, "[W]e expect to see the influence of the League spread everywhere, a force that is best in the civic and religious life and a means of uplift for all in the community."[66]

In keeping with its goal of providing a "means of uplift" for Boston's Catholics, the LCW established a lecture series on particular issues of interest to Catholics. The series was well attended and featured priests and laity who "were experts in their field" speaking on subjects pertaining to social reform and charity issues, literature, the arts, and education. One lecture, given at the Boston Public Library, drew 800 members. "The result," the writer of an LCW report asserted confidently, "is that our organization is recognized as the leading moral force in the community." This in turn, the writer added, led the governor and mayor to seek out the league's president to serve on state and city committees.[67]

The LCW engaged in a variety of charitable efforts. As with the CWU, the work included activities directed toward the "protection of young girls." For the league, this type of work entailed "Probation Work," or taking over juvenile court cases involving young girls. The service had been previously undertaken by the Society of St. Vincent de Paul, which requested that the LCW assume the responsibility. Its members hired a woman to serve as "probation officer," having raised the money to pay her salary and expenses through a card party and other fund-raising efforts. The writer of the league's 1914 report urged more members to engage in probation work, asserting, "Some may be victims of temptations more subtle than we know, or of home conditions that we could not endure,—and, with the right guidance may develop stronger and finer characters than those that have not known the struggle." The report's author enjoined members to develop a "special interest in one girl, to win her friendship and confidence," to contribute to the program, or to refer the committee to "good families" who might provide foster care.[68]

In 1915 May Burke, the LCW's probation officer, noted that the majority of cases involved larceny charges, "due partly to poor home conditions and defective delinquency." She noted that in several cases "[p]lacement in homes has worked a marked change in the girls." Yet the fear that young urban Catholic women were in physical and moral danger was much less pronounced in the league's reports than in those of the CWU and served as only one emphasis in its overall program of reform and charity. During its first year, the program took on fifty-two cases in which girls had been brought into court, usually due to truancy and shoplifting. But the reports also reveal that several girls were brought into court as a result of "immorality," or for being "Idle and Disorderly; Wayward; Stubborn." Two girls had been brought in because their families had neglected them, rather than as a result of their own behavior.[69]

An information bureau, or clearinghouse for voluntary work, constituted a third element of the LCW's work. The league kept a registry of Catholic groups involved in various charities throughout Boston. Through the service, Catholics could find out how to place relatives or others who were ill, aged, or destitute in appropriate Catholic institutions. It also aimed to provide employment information for "educated women" after they had obtained high school or college degrees.[70]

Soon after its formation, LCW members formed two committees for charitable work. The first undertook a modest effort to engage in friendly visiting for lapsed Catholics. League members would visit "those who have drifted away from the Faith." The second entailed social work among Italian immigrants, including the hiring of a sewing teacher.

The LCW, along with the Catholic Charities Bureau, also became involved in efforts to regulate immoral entertainment. A league representative served on the State Committee on Motion Pictures. In 1923 the LCW protested against the production of "The Lullaby" at Boston's Colonial Theatre, a play featuring Florence Reed and produced by Erlanger, Dillingham, and Ziegfield. The theater's manager wrote to Mayor James Curley's office indicating that the parts found objectionable by a censor, whom the mayor's office had sent to see the play, had been deleted. The manager added contritely that the producers would follow the mayor's wishes in the future because they sought "always to have splendidly clean and wholesome productions." The previous year, however, O'Connell had informed league president Lillian Slattery that, for the time being at least, he did not want her to become involved in film censorship.[71]

The LCW's activities came under the strict supervision of Cardinal O'Connell, who held strong ideas regarding appropriate behavior for the leaders of the league. The cardinal required the LCW officers to obtain his approval for proposed lectures and for all "other matters of importance" through his assistants, Haberlin and Splaine. One example of that control occurred in 1918, when Mrs. Mahony, of Medford, Massachusetts, sought to establish a Medford branch of the league. After meeting with Splaine, she agreed to abandon the effort "in the quietest and most tactful manner possible." Splaine commented approvingly, "I found her most docile and anxious to obey in everything where the church was concerned."[72]

Despite the growing membership and influence of the league, it remained separate from secular and Protestant organizations performing similar work. In 1916 the LCW envisioned cooperating with various charities throughout the city: "[B]y cooperating with societies in these many charities where the work is non-sectarian, we can do infinite good for our Catholic people and our Catholic children." Yet the league's level of cooperation remained limited. For example, during the First World War, Cardinal O'Connell vetoed a proposal allowing Catholic women's groups to join the Special Aid Society for American Preparedness, proposing instead that "it would be better to organize a Special Aid Society of our own." O'Connell also prohibited the LCW from participating in a national traveler's aid society because of its Protestant orientation.[73]

In 1916 Cardinal O'Connell concluded that some members of the LCW had moved away from appropriate activities of the group by becoming too closely associated with Protestant and secular charities. O'Connell sent a strong message to Richard Haberlin through Splaine about the behavior of Elizabeth Dwight, the league's president, and a few other members who, O'Connell believed, "seem to have forgotten that it was organized to assist in carrying on the work of the Catholic charities and [he believed] that some of their activities are far from being in accord with the purpose for which the LCW was organized." They had veered from their aim, O'Connell contended, "by catering to Protestant Social Service movements, and by making the League a sort of subsidiary to the various organizations directing non-Catholic activities." He concluded his letter with a severe rebuke: "If Catholic women of means can not be loyal to interests of their organization it is time for them to disband and to leave the work entirely in the hands of the working-girls." Later, through Haberlin, Cardinal O'Connell reminded Michael Scanlan, director of the Catholic Charitable Bureau, that the women in question "must be constantly reminded of the purpose of the organization to which they belong." O'Connell undoubtedly viewed working-class women as less likely to challenge authority within the church, while concluding that married women of the upper class saw themselves as entitled to greater status and autonomy as a result of their family's wealth.[74]

The controversy extended to Scanlan, who felt compelled to rebut several charges against him in a sixteen-page letter to Cardinal O'Connell. In addition to an overall indictment of the way in which he directed the CCB, the charges, from unnamed sources, were that he gave Miss Lally, a CCB employee, too much authority, that he had neglected the Guild of the Infant Saviour, a lay group under his direction, and that he took "both sides of every question which comes up for my consideration rather than to take the side which is known to be the side for which Your Eminence stands." Scanlan also directly refuted all charges related to the LCW, stating that he had had virtually no contact with the organization for nearly two years. In discussing the charges about "the false influence which some persons are said to be trying to exert on our charitable organizations," he asserted that the women's groups seemed safe from such tendencies but added, "Of course, the richer ones or those whose associations are more or less among non-Catholics do sooner or later develop a spirit of independence or a desire for what is commonly called cooperation, this cooperation referring to non-Catholics particularly. The cure for this seems to be to choose for leaders those who have no such leanings or who are not half Protestant in origin or by alliances."[75]

Elizabeth Dwight and her circle again became objects of suspicion a few years later. Martha Moore Avery, a former socialist who had renounced her political beliefs and become a Catholic, wrote to O'Connell about a report she had heard from another Boston Catholic woman. The woman told Avery she had visited the CCB accompanied by Dwight and heard Miss Cunniff, who worked there, state that she routinely removed files from her office to prevent others from discovering that she disobeyed orders because she disagreed with O'Connell's policy on unmarried mothers and their babies.[76] Scanlan investigated the matter and reported that Cunniff had denied these actions but admitted that she had spoken publicly on the issue on one occasion.[77]

In 1920 Cardinal O'Connell sent Lillian Slattery, the league's president, a list of recommendations for Lent, which he requested that she read at the league's next meeting. He made seven points, most of which addressed the need to resist or to campaign against modern values. Moreover, O'Connell spoke forcefully against perceived idleness and frivolity among women. He entreated the women, "Let us protect against this unchristian decadence by frugal living and cheerful work. . . . Against the rampant squandering of money for senseless extravagance let us practice rigid economy accompanied by a greater generosity toward God, the Church and the poor." He urged the women to boycott immoral plays and indecent dances and clothing and to replace "idle waste of time, harmful gossip and unprofitable chatter" with worship and reflection. It is not clear whether he directed his comments toward particular women in the LCW or whether they were general remarks intended to dissuade Catholic women from imitating the "new woman." It was probably not coincidental that his message came just after the Nineteenth Amendment had been ratified.[78]

O'Connell's Lenten pronouncement revealed his ambivalence about the rising social and economic status of Catholics in Boston. Although the recommendations highlighted the importance of charity toward the poor, and of valuing spirituality over consumption, they also contained an implicit criticism of middle-class and upper-class women who had the means to buy fine wardrobes and attend the theater—and who, unlike men, had time in which to be "idle." Simultaneously, however, the cardinal had worked hard to cultivate an image of respectability for Boston Catholics by demonstrating their increasing significance to the city's political, economic, educational, and social institutions, while insuring that they retained the distinctiveness of their Catholicism.

In addition to being the target of criticism from Cardinal O'Connell and his assistants, the LCW became the object of controversy among the laity in the Irish Catholic community. In 1919 the league received a vitriolic attack from a Boston laywoman, Margaret Ryan, for its failure to advance Irish nationalist and other ethnically based issues, despite the predominance of Irish Catholics in the league. Ryan claimed that she had helped to organize the Irish National Bureau with Hanna Sheehy-Skeffington, the widow of an Irish political activist killed by the British during the 1916 Easter Rising. Sheehy-Skeffington had arrived in the United States later that year to promote the cause of Irish independence among those in the U.S. government. She created the Irish National Bureau in Washington as part of that effort and also spoke publicly on behalf of suffrage.[79]

Ryan's most immediate criticism emanated from the LCW's refusal to become involved in efforts on behalf of Irish nationalist issues, despite the fact that, as she claimed, "at least ninety percent of the members were of Irish ancestry." Yet, Ryan noted, league members were enthusiastic about entertaining the visiting Belgian cardinal on his trip to Boston. She claimed that a member had told her that the LCW had not become involved in the Irish cause because "Ireland is a political organization. The work of the League is spiritual." The same member had conceded that LCW members had attended a mass meeting on the Irish political situation because Cardinal O'Connell had advised them to, and not because they were interested in the issue. Ryan responded that such an admission would confirm accusations among Americans that the Irish were "priest-ridden." She attacked LCW members as "the daughters and grand-daughters of the curse of our race in America, the rum-sellers and [ward] politicians," and charged that "[b]ut for [their] spirituality they would not today be in a Catholic League." Instead, she continued, they would be "smug '[M]enace' readers. They are of the same type of mind!" She further accused league members of needing the approval of "Back-Bay's Anglo-Saxondom" and asserted that convent schools trained Catholic girls to be "snobs and social climbers." Although one might be inclined to dismiss Ryan's criticisms as an isolated diatribe based on her ardent nationalism, her remarks echoed Cardinal O'Connell's criticism of LCW leaders as being too Protestant-oriented, and as being less interested in religious issues than in gaining acceptance among Boston's elite. Coming from an Irish nationalist, Ryan's rebuke against the LCW went further than those of Cardinal O'Connell against Dwight because it contained an added implication—that the league's leaders had denied their ethnic heritage in the name of social advancement in Boston society.[80]

The LCW exemplified a group that emulated many aspects of Protestant-oriented women's organizations in order to gain societal acceptance. In part, this was the result of the cultural and economic dominance of a small number of Boston families and the intense antagonism toward Catholic immigrants there, dating from the mid-nineteenth century. Unlike many members of the CWU who confronted individual members of the clergy and hierarchy, LCW members chose to accept Cardinal O'Connell's tight control of their activities and their positions on social issues. While controversies over the role of the LCW occurred, they rarely were as public as those that emerged within the CWU.

The National Council of Catholic Women

The National Council of Catholic Women served as an extension of localized or ethnically exclusive Catholic women's groups active in the early twentieth century. Many of the organization's programs, and the principles behind them, remained conservative. Existing women's groups, such as the CWU, looked upon the larger national group with trepidation because of its perceived threat to those groups' activities, membership base, and ethnic identity. Yet, as a national group, the NCCW was also freed from some of the constraints imposed upon local women's groups by local ecclesiastical and clerical leaders. Father John Ryan's leadership also influenced its stand on a number of issues.

The NCCW grew out of the Committee on Women's Activities of the National Catholic War Board, which was first created in 1917. Once the war had ended, the National Catholic Welfare Council succeeded the War Board. The NCCW emerged as part of the NCWC's Department of Lay Activities. In 1920, 123 women, appointed as delegates by their bishops or local societies, arrived in Washington to establish the NCCW and to formulate its procedures. A similar group for laymen was also formed within the Department of Lay Activities.[81] The creation of the NCCW signaled a move toward centralized authority with significantly more hierarchical control, and the NCCW encountered opposition from existing Catholic women's groups.

Some of the programs launched by the NCCW were expansions of those that had been put in place at the local, regional, and national levels by women's lay groups. For example, the executive board established a bureau for girls' welfare that unified the activities of existing laywomen's groups in this area. Yet, while the *Catholic Charities Review* noted that each group "would maintain its own identity," the NCCW sought to employ "experienced and trained workers" to implement the new work, rather than to continue relying on volunteer labor.[82]

The creation of the NCCW inspired its affiliated groups to interact with one another in ways they had not done previously, but it also threatened to undermine their purpose. For example, in 1921 the LCW's president, Lillian Slattery, who had served as an original delegate to the NCCW, wrote to Mrs. Hackett, of Milwaukee: "When we hear of our sisters in the great Middle West doing the same thing, there can be no doubt in my mind but that this national organization is the greatest step taken by the Catholic women of America." Yet the NCCW also took some of the impetus away from the activities and growth of local groups. Mrs. Kellenberger of the New Jersey branch of the CWU lamented that the NCCW "is holding us back. . . . [T]hey eventually will absorb this organization." She arrived at that conclusion because the bishop and priests in the area had questioned the need for organizing local groups "when the National Catholic [Welfare] Council is doing practically the same thing."[83]

In promoting "Circles of Study" within its Educational Department, the NCCW maintained that Catholic women in both Europe and America had successfully avoided the general tendency toward "material valuation" of life. The council suggested that women in its affiliated organizations form groups to apply religious principles to existing social problems. It also echoed the views of the CWU when it declared in a pamphlet, "The family is the social unit of Christian civilization, and, therefore, government as an institution rests on the home." Another activity heavily promoted by the NCCW was the formation of community houses, in which Catholic women would consolidate community service–based activities. Support for Catholic traveler's aid programs, a CWU hallmark, was also mentioned as a priority. In 1921 the NCCW emphasized that only "two percent of our children are in high schools" and urged that local Catholic women's organizations set up scholarship programs.[84]

Throughout the 1920s, a debate arose over the issue of child labor legislation within the Catholic Church, and within Catholic women's organizations in particular. Many in the church opposed the Child Labor Amendment because, they argued, it would have a detrimental effect on parental control. In 1923 Agnes Regan, executive secretary of the NCCW, stated in congressional judiciary committee hearings that the NCCW had passed a resolution in support of a Child Labor Amendment that would prohibit the employment of those under sixteen years of age; she indicated that NCCW members had agreed to "lend active support to the passage of such legislation against child labor." Regan, a teacher, school administrator, and board of education member from San Francisco, was the central lay leader in the newly formed NCCW and was crucial to the formation of the National Catholic School of Social Work. In 1920, when she was in her early fifties, Regan had moved to Washington, where she led the NCCW for twenty years, until shortly before her death in 1943. She shared two characteristics with many other lay reformers: she was not a college graduate, and several members of her family had joined religious orders. Two of Regan's sisters and four of her nieces had become nuns, while two of her nephews were priests. Father Ryan, codirector of the Social Action Department of the National Catholic Welfare Conference, and the most vocal Catholic supporter of the Child Labor Amendment and later of the New Deal, also spoke before the same committee. Ryan had influenced NCCW leaders on this subject, and it was he who submitted the resolution in favor of the amendment at the NCCW's annual meeting.[85]

The NCCW's position encountered opposition from some of its affiliates, however. Lillian Slattery, the LCW's president, wrote to Regan denouncing the NCCW's position; the letter came at the behest of Cardinal O'Connell, who had vociferously opposed child labor legislation in Massachusetts. Finally, O'Connell sent his assistant, Michael Splaine, to Washington to confront the amendment's supporters. Splaine lobbied Regan, requesting that the NCCW overturn its endorsement of the amendment, but his efforts proved unsuccessful. In 1929 the LCW continued to oppose a Child Labor Amendment as well as the Sheppard-Towner Act, which would fund maternal and infant care, condemning the two initiatives as socialist. Lillian Slattery claimed that the Child Labor Amendment was "aimed at the destruction of our country, our religion and our homes." The NCCW also supported efforts to use the vote "for safeguarding religion and morality" and advocated minimum wage laws, workers' compensation, and mothers' pensions. Despite its close association with the hierarchy, the NCCW was in a much better position than were local groups to take controversial stands on such issues, because of its independence from strict archdiocesan control.[86]

Americanization efforts were also a critical component of the NCCW's program proposals. The council suggested that Catholic women form civic clubs to teach English, American history, and other subjects. It encouraged them to recruit other women of various nationalities and to help them to form their own Catholic clubs, which would then federate with the NCCW. The women targeted for participation included Italians, Poles, and Slovaks. One pamphlet suggests that the NCCW assumed that new immigrants would naturally assemble into ethnically homogeneous groups, which might then be affiliated with a citywide federation of Catholic women's clubs.[87]

In describing proposed work among foreigners, the NCCW assumed that the Catholic women to whom it was speaking were fully assimilated, demonstrating that by the early 1920s many Catholic women had assumed a sense of responsibility toward newly arriving immigrants. But unlike other groups, who supported immigration restriction because of the danger immigrants posed to the stability of American society, the NCCW advocated a cultural pluralist approach to immigrants. A council publication quoted an author who urged Americans to show more sensitivity to the cultural needs of immigrants rather than forcing them to abandon their language and cultural practices once in the United States. "We quite rightly ask them to abandon their old loyalties; but we shall be incredibly foolish if we ask them to forget the culture they have inherited. We blame our foreigners for their clannishness. We resent the fact that they sequester themselves among people of their own race, and do not take the trouble to understand our language, or our history and institutions; but we are guilty of an exactly analogous piece of provincialism when we betray our unwillingness to learn from them, while expecting them to learn from us."[88]

Another major focus of the NCCW was the establishment of a social work school for women under its direction. Within a year of its formation, the council bought the National Catholic Service School for $353,000. The director, Charles P. Neill, estimated that the cost of operating the school would be approximately $600,000 per year. Following a speech by O'Neill at the first convention of the NCCW, delegates had pledged $50,000 toward the school's costs.[89]

* * * * *

In the late nineteenth century women in the emerging Catholic middle class began to organize lay groups beyond the parish level for charitable and reform purposes. Although the groups often emphasized the need to encourage working-class Catholic women to join their efforts, those women tended to serve as the beneficiaries of the organizations' programs rather than as their members. Gradually, by the second decade of the twentieth century, these groups had expanded to include regional and national Catholic women's groups. Moreover, many women's groups expanded the scope of their activities beyond charitable efforts intended to ameliorate the effects of poverty and illness in order to engage in a variety of reforms, such as those pertaining to the Child Labor Amendment, entertainment standards, and Americanization programs. Yet, despite the political nature of such activism, most women's groups maintained that they avoided involvement in political issues; instead, they defined their efforts as emanating from a concern over morality, which proved compatible with their domestic roles.

Both the CWU and the LCW expressed concern over the popularity of modern values that ushered in birth control, divorce, and other trends that the groups feared would subjugate traditional maternal and domestic interests to material ones. These views, in turn, were influenced by a broader critique of middle- and upper-class Catholic women who demonstrated tendencies of emulating elite Protestant women by being idle or frivolous—traits that were cast as specifically female.

Yet in several ways the concerns and interests of the LCW and the CWU and its affiliates diverged. The latter group focused extensively on ethnic issues and drew inspiration from European views on Catholic social reform as well as from the actual activities of Catholic women's groups there. Although the organization's ethnic interests were challenged briefly during the First World War, the group resumed many actual and figurative ties to Germany in the 1920s, although members retained their use of English. Members of the CWU criticized members of the clergy and hierarchy, challenging their indifference or hostility toward women's organizations. They reluctantly moved toward a more universal Catholic women's movement and away from emphasizing the particularly German features of their work by joining the NCCW.

In contrast, members of Boston's LCW chose not to incorporate ethnic issues into their group's identity, despite the fact that they were predominantly Irish American. Instead, they sought to establish a parallel group to those of Protestant women in Boston. The LCW accepted the stringent controls over its choice of activities and its administration imposed by Cardinal O'Connell. Nevertheless, it came under scrutiny for emulating too closely non-Catholic groups, and for seeking to identify with the established Boston elite at the expense of its members' religious and ethnic heritage.

By the early 1920s these groups had affiliated with the NCCW, whose activities were less accountable to particular bishops, and which sometimes acted against the wishes of its member groups, including the CWU and LCW. CWU members saw the NCCW as usurping its agenda and its membership base, and affiliation with it threatened their ethnic identity as German Americans. The LCW, and Cardinal O'Connell, objected to several of the NCCW's national campaigns. The NCCW, a centralized body under the direction of the national hierarchy, enjoyed a higher national profile and larger funding than previous Catholic women's groups. Yet women's initiatives, leadership roles, and community concerns on the local level were often overshadowed by the programs of the NCCW.

Catholic women who joined church-based groups in the late nineteenth and early twentieth century tended to view their participation as an extension of their maternal and domestic roles, which in some ways proved similar to the ways in which Protestant women viewed their organizations in the mid-nineteenth century. Yet Catholic women formed a domestic ideology that often incorporated European Catholic traditions, that emanated from a critique of materialist values, and that reflected an ambivalence about the newly created Catholic middle class, given the continued necessity of workforce participation by many Catholic women. Several controversies that developed around women's organized activities and their leaders further suggest that laywomen's changing roles within the church in this era remained contested. Because women often symbolized Catholic upward mobility, their behavior reflected both an expanding sense of noblesse oblige among Catholics and a deep ambivalence about the implications of improved economic status among some American Catholics.

Conclusion

This study has analyzed the ways in which Catholic lay group participation in social reform efforts revealed a sharp tension between the expression of European reform traditions and the need to demonstrate the basic compatibility of Catholicism with American values and institutions. That tension distinguished Catholic lay reforms and goals from concurrent efforts by Protestant-oriented reformers in the late nineteenth and early twentieth centuries, even when the two groups undertook similar activities. Catholic reformers operated from an international perspective when they addressed problems facing Catholics in the United States, creating a reform network in conjunction with Catholics in Europe. In reclaiming the Catholic reform tradition, they cast European reform traditions and methods as older and often superior to those emerging in the United States, just as they had challenged the definition of the historical legacy of the United States as Protestant at the 1893 Columbian Catholic Congress.

Ethnic traditions and nationalism became integral to the efforts of reformers in the Catholic temperance movement, in the rural colonization movement, and in the formation of urban port programs. They further influenced the efforts of the Catholic Women's Union and the founders of St. Elizabeth Settlement House. Reformers often placed Catholic reform in an ethnic context. Temperance reformers thus debated whether the Irish had a unique proclivity toward alcohol abuse, while some advocates of immigration assistance programs argued that the tendency of the Irish to congregate in urban enclaves was an outgrowth of Irish gregariousness and the need to re-create a sense of community. In contrast, German Americans opposed to temperance reform argued that banning alcohol would erode their unique cultural traditions and that Germans did not need limitations imposed on their drinking. The highlighting of ethnic issues in reform led to an emphasis on self-help as a way to improve social and economic conditions for American Catholics.

Distinctions between Catholic and Protestant reform were further expressed through Catholic stereotypes of Protestant reformers. The first stereotype was that of the Protestant-oriented temperance activist as a "Puritan fanatic" who eschewed sociability along with alcohol. Emphasis on masculine sociability was a crucial component of the Catholic temperance movement, because unlike Protestant-oriented efforts in the late nineteenth century, it relied heavily on men as agents of the crusade. That drinking led to negative stereotypes of Irish males, but not females, was partly responsible for the strategy, but so too was the movement's reliance on moral suasion rather than on prohibition.

A second stereotype was that of the charity provider as either a superficial and ineffectual philanthropist or a cold and dispassionate recordkeeper, more concerned with statistics than with truly meeting the needs of the poor. The stereotype of the Protestant charity giver as aloof was based on the Charity Organization Society and its members, who believed that providing alms to the poor would lead to dependency. Catholics also criticized those involved in Protestant-based charity programs for concentrating on the material welfare of the poor, without concerning themselves with the spiritual needs of the recipients.

Catholics pointed to the ideals articulated by Frederic Ozanam, whom they regarded as the founder of the modern field of social work because of his emphasis on the reciprocal nature of charity and the need to develop personal relationships between charity providers and recipients. Catholics argued that they were uniquely qualified to care for their coreligionists, and that principle underlay the work of the Society of St. Vincent de Paul. A similar view motivated Mary Agnes Amberg's vision of a shared community of Italian Catholic immigrants and Catholic workers at Madonna Center based on their common religion and recent European heritage, even though that ideal reflected a romanticized notion of peasant life. Moreover, many lay reformers, including members of the Catholic Women's Union, the New York branch of the Central Verein, and Mary Agnes Amberg specifically cited *Rerum Novarum*, Pope Leo XIII's encyclical on social reform, as a catalyst for their activities.

Despite their frequent laments that too many Catholics remained disinclined toward involvement in charity, many lay leaders, both well-known and obscure, embarked on national social reform efforts despite modest financial resources. The percentage of Catholics in the middle and upper classes was lower than it was for many urban-based Protestant denominations. In light of that situation, the church needed to devote a significant amount of its budget to building new churches, schools, and charitable institutions to accommodate new immigrants, and many of its members had neither the time nor the money to contribute to Catholic lay reform. It is not surprising that the laity felt that its initiatives required greater support than they received.

Catholic lay activism also reflected the extent to which the church and its members were experiencing Americanization. As Catholics increasingly entered the middle class toward the end of the nineteenth century, they not only continued to share the concerns of other middle-class Americans but were also eager to disprove prevailing anti-Catholic attitudes. As part of that effort, the role of socially prominent converts to Catholicism became increasingly important. While some Catholic reform leaders took a defensive posture, the liberals among them advocated an accommodationist stance that involved a willingness to forsake ethnic traditions in favor of greater acceptance among Americans as a whole.

At the same time that descendants of mid-nineteenth-century Irish and German immigrants were creating an Americanized Catholic middle class, a new wave of immigrants from Southern and Eastern Europe threatened to reinforce the larger society's impression of the church as an alien and menacing institution. Though the large number of Catholic immigrants offered promise for the future, Catholics sought to encourage the newcomers to maintain or strengthen their faith at the same time that they were urged to adopt many of the values of the dominant culture. During the late nineteenth century, the laity became increasingly involved in developing urban-based charitable institutions and programs, including social settlements. Those programs sought to assist immigrants and other poor Catholics to adjust to American society and to provide them with the means to improve their economic status. While Catholic efforts often emphasized a more pluralist approach to immigrant cultures than some of their Protestant-oriented counterparts, Catholic reforms could also prove punitive at times. This was most clearly illustrated in the joint port program of the Charitable Irish Society/St. Vincent de Paul Society in Boston.

The tension between emphasizing European traditions and encouraging Americanization was perhaps expressed most vividly in the changing roles of

women in Catholic reform. Women's activism also revealed tensions surrounding the improved economic status of Catholics at the turn of the century. The members of the German-based Catholic Women's Union, who organized as a means to maintain their ethnically based traditions, looked largely
to Germany for models of social reform. They joined the move to a more
universal and Americanized National Council of Catholic Women with great
reluctance. In contrast, the women involved in Boston's League of Catholic Women patterned their activities on an American Protestant mode and
thereby came under criticism for disloyalty to their faith and to their ethnic
identity.

The period immediately following that of this study brought a resurgence
in lay-based social reform movements. In 1933 Dorothy Day and Peter Maurin
established the Catholic Worker Movement, one of the best-known Catholic
lay movements in the United States. Day was an unlikely Catholic activist.
She had been active in communist circles, was a single woman raising a child,
and acknowledged having had an abortion prior to her conversion to Catholicism. The Catholic Worker Movement blended pacifism, support for labor,
leftist politics, and voluntary poverty with Catholic teachings. Its leaders criticized capitalism and materialism as antithetical to the practice of Catholicism
and relied on lay initiative and direction rather than on hierarchical or clerical direction. By 1940 the movement's members had established thirty "hospitality houses" in cities throughout the United States, where they lived and
provided food and shelter to workers and the unemployed. Though aspects of
the hospitality houses seemed similar to Catholic settlement houses, and the
movement's emphasis on treating the poor without condescension echoed
the precepts of the Society of St. Vincent de Paul, the Catholic Worker Movement was far more radical than either of these movements. Its adherents
believed that social reform or providing charity alone were inadequate to
address the problems facing modern society and hewed to a particularly
Franciscan notion of humility and devotion to the poor.[1]

Yet, despite her radical stance, Day was not as distant from the tradition of
previous lay reformers as it would first appear. As a Protestant convert to
Catholicism, Day, like many converts before her, enjoyed a special and high-
profile role in the church. In fact, female converts were especially active in
literary and journalistic endeavors within the American church, and Day, as a
college-educated journalist, fit squarely into that mold. While the Catholic
Worker Movement was American, it drew upon European lay movements for
inspiration, as Day worked in tandem with Peter Maurin, a French Catho-

Dorothy Day reading to her daughter, Tamar.
(Courtesy of Marquette University Archives)

lic who had been active in lay movements before his arrival in the United States. In order to pursue her work, Day chose to become celibate, much like women religious and laywomen reformers such as Mary Agnes Amberg and Rose Hawthorne Lathrop before her. Finally, like Leonora Barry Lake and other Catholic women discussed in this study, she professed discomfort with aspects of women's rights while acting independently, challenging gender norms and defying social convention. Like Sophia Wavering of the Catholic Women's Union and other female lay leaders, Day clashed with the hierarchy, most famously with Cardinal Spellman in 1949, when she supported a grave-digger's strike against the Archdiocese of New York.[2]

During the interwar years, Catholic social reform and charity became further centralized and concentrated at the archdiocesan, regional, and national levels, relying on strong leadership by clergy members and bishops. That pattern sometimes led to the eclipsing of more localized lay initiatives. The National Catholic Welfare Council, the group organized by the American hierarchy immediately after the First World War, undertook several social reform efforts under the direction of Father John Ryan, who served as co-director of its lay-based Social Action Department. The National Council of Catholic Women, the women's organization within that department, embarked on an ambitious and centralized program of charity and educational activities, while the NCWC's Immigration Bureau began establishing its own port assistance programs. A decade later, Ryan became an important figure in Catholic support for the New Deal, and he served on several advisory boards within the Roosevelt administration. By the Depression era, with the church's continued centralized approach to social problems, the tension between Americanization and ethnic issues that had been integral to Catholic social reform from 1880 to 1925 had become increasingly muted.

Notes

ABBREVIATIONS

In addition to the abbreviations used in the text,
the following abbreviations occur in the notes.

AABo
Archives, Archdiocese of Boston, Boston, Mass.

AAC
Joseph Cardinal Bernadin Archives and Records Center,
Archdiocese of Chicago, Chicago, Ill.

CVA
Central Verein Archives, Central Bureau,
Catholic Central Union of America, St. Louis, Mo.

MHS
Massachusetts Historical Society, Boston, Mass.

UNDA
Archives, University of Notre Dame, Notre Dame, Ind.

INTRODUCTION

1. Rodgers, *Atlantic Crossings*.

2. Ryan, *Cradle of the Middle Class*; Blumin, *Emergence of the Middle Class*; Mc-Dannell, *Christian Home in Victorian America*. Stuart Blumin notes that middle-class culture or way of life encompasses patterns of "work, consumption, residential location, formal and informal voluntary association, and family organization and strategy" (11). My study focuses particularly on how middle-class culture is expressed through participation in formal voluntary associations and gender roles.

3. Allen Davis, *Spearheads for Reform*, 33.

4. Addams, *Twenty Years at Hull-House*, 388–89.

5. Brown and McKeown, *The Poor Belong to Us*, 62–65. Other historians have also suggested that the Progressive era was longer than often recognized. See, for example, Connolly, *Triumph of Ethnic Progressivism*, 161–62.

6. Walch, "New Tools for American Historical Research," 201. Leslie Woodcock Tentler makes a similar argument in "On the Margins."

7. O'Brien, *American Catholics and Social Reform*; Abell, *American Catholicism and Social Action*; Brown and McKeown, *The Poor Belong to Us*; Halsey, *Survival of American Innocence*.

8. Kane, *Separation and Subculture*; Gleason, *Conservative Reformers*; Kauffman, *Faith and Fraternalism*.

CHAPTER ONE

1. Schlereth, "Columbia, Columbus, and Columbianism"; *The Christopher Columbus Encyclopedia* (1991), s.v. "Celebrations"; Rydell, *All the World's a Fair*. Schlereth and Rydell discuss controversies over the prevailing theme of industrial progress and over the lack of representation of African American perspectives at the fair.

2. Doenecke, "Myths, Machines, and Markets"; Badger, *Great Fair*; Seager, *Dawn of Religious Pluralism*.

3. "Judge O'Brien's Address as Chairman," in *World's Columbian Catholic Congresses and Educational Exhibit*, 1:17 (hereafter cited as *Columbian Catholic Congresses*). Sister M. Adele Francis [Gorman], "Lay Activity of the Catholic Congresses"; Cleary, "Catholic Participation in the World's Parliament of Religions."

4. Kauffman, *Faith and Fraternalism*; Vecoli, "Contadini in Chicago."

5. John Bodnar defines the concept of public memory as "a body of beliefs about the past that help a public or society understand both its past, present, and by implication, its future. It is fashioned ideally in a public sphere in which various parts of the social structure exchange views." Bodnar, *Remaking America*, 15.

6. Hennesey, *American Catholics*, 179.

7. Hughes, *Souvenir Volume*, 16.

8. Ibid., 17–18.

9. Higham, *Strangers in the Land*, 62, 80; Kinzer, *Episode in Anti-Catholicism*.

10. Gleason, "New Americanism in Catholic Historiography"; Fogarty, "Catholic Hierarchy"; Wangler, "Americanist Beliefs and Papal Orthodoxy"; and Janus, "Bishop Bernard McQuaid." The entire issue of *U.S. Catholic Historian* 11, no. 3 (Summer 1993) centers on the Americanist controversy.

11. Cross, *Emergence of Liberal Catholicism*, 199–201; Gleason, *Keeping the Faith*.

12. O'Brien, *Isaac Hecker*, ix, 14, 383–87; Gallagher, "Americanist Hierarchy," 130.

13. O'Connell, *John Ireland*; Gleason, "New Americanism."

14. See Cross, *Emergence of Liberal Catholicism*; Hennesey, *American Catholics*, 195–203; Leckie, *American and Catholic*; Downey, "Tradition and Acceptance"; Gleason, *Conservative Reformers*, 29–51.

15. Cross, *Emergence of Liberal Catholicism*, 92–93; Gleason, *Conservative Reformers*, 34; Hennesey, *American Catholics*, 196; Barry, *Catholic Church and German Americans*, chapter 4.

16. Robert Douglas to William Onahan, August 2, 1893, Correspondence, IX-1-e, William Onahan Papers, UNDA. The letter from Douglas, a lawyer from Greensboro,

North Carolina, suggested that Powderly originally was expected to speak at the congress.

17. *Pilot*, July 16, 1887; Hennesey, *American Catholics*, 166–67, 189. Hennesey notes that Elizabeth Gurley Flynn, the socialist and labor activist, claimed that her family broke with the church over the McGlynn controversy (215). Also see Curran, "McGlynn Affair," *Michael Augustine Corrigan*, and "Prelude to 'Americanism.'"

18. Earlier in the nineteenth century, Catholics had been the targets of a more violent series of attacks, including the 1836 burning of an Ursuline convent in Massachusetts. Moreover, a series of books had been published by authors claiming to be former women religious and detailing lurid accounts of convent life. See Franchot, *Roads to Rome*. In midcentury, the Know-Nothing Party grew in response to increased Catholic immigration.

19. Gladden, "Anti-Catholic Crusade," 789–790; Higham, *Strangers in the Land*, 81, 85.

20. Gallery, *Life of William J. Onahan*, 6–7. Gallery was Onahan's daughter and a presenter at the 1893 congress. Bennett, *Father Nugent of Liverpool*, 102.

21. Gallery, *Life of William J. Onahan*, 1–5, 16–17, 32, 40; Pahorezki, "Social and Political Activities of William James Onahan."

22. The Congress of Representative Women featured speakers from around the world on topics including women's involvement in religious, civic, and other reform efforts. The women's building was designed by a female architect. Doenecke, "Myths, Machines and Markets," 542; Sewall, *Congress of Representative Women*, 2.

23. See Kane, "The Pulpit and the Hearthstone." The Boston *Pilot*, a source used throughout this study, first began operating under that name when Patrick Donahue took over its editorship in 1836. Bishop Fenwick of Boston had established a newspaper in the diocese in 1829, the first Catholic newspaper in the United States, changing its name several times before selling it to Donahue. For much of its history the *Pilot* was owned and edited by the laity, but it became the official newspaper of the Boston archdiocese in 1908. Other editors included Thomas D'Arcy McGee (see Chapter 3) and John Boyle O'Reilly, an ardent Irish nationalist who had escaped from an Australian penal colony and settled in Boston. A poet and novelist, O'Reilly edited the *Pilot* from 1870 until his death in 1890. He published literary works, including those by Mary Anne Sadlier, supported the Democratic Party, and advocated the view that Celtic culture was superior to British culture. In 1890 Donohue resumed ownership and appointed James Jeffrey Roche, the *Pilot*'s assistant editor, as O'Reilly's replacement. Roche greatly admired O'Reilly, but under his editorship the paper published more popular writing, was more critical of Democratic Party politics, and viewed Boston's new Catholic immigrants in a more positive light. Its estimated circulation rose from 500 in 1836 to over 100,000 in 1872, before declining in the 1890s. For much of the nineteenth century, the *Pilot* appealed primarily to working-class immigrant readers, but by the late nineteenth century it increasingly focused on attracting Irish Catholic middle-class readers. Francis Walsh, "Who Speaks for Boston's Irish?"; Lane, "James Jeffrey Roche and the Boston *Pilot*"; O'Toole, *From Generation to Generation*, 40–41.

24. Katherine Conway to William Onahan, February 12, 1893, Correspondence, IX-1-d, Onahan Papers.

25. Ibid.

26. Ibid.; Katherine Conway to William Onahan, February 19, 1893, and July 7, 1893, ibid. On January 20, 1894, the *Pilot* reprinted a highly critical article by John Ingalls of *Cosmopolitan Magazine*, "Women at the Fair."

27. Katherine Conway to William Onahan, May 10, 1893, Correspondence, IX-1-d, Onahan Papers.

28. *Columbian Catholic Congresses*, 1:78. Italics mine. The source does not contain the full transcripts of speeches or introductions.

29. *Columbian Catholic Congresses*, 1:29.

30. "Discourse of Most Reverend John Ireland. Inauguration of the Work of the Congress Auxiliary of the World's Columbian Exposition," Columbian Catholic Congress, Speeches, IX-1-m, Onahan Papers.

31. *Columbian Catholic Congresses*, 83. For more on Lathrop, see Culberson, *Rose Hawthorne Lathrop*.

32. Cyprian Davis, *History of Black Catholics*, 163–64, 168, 28, 77. David Spalding, "Negro Catholic Congresses."

33. Cyprian Davis, *History of Black Catholics*, 175.

34. For a detailed discussion of these tensions, see Bernstein, *New York City Draft Riots*.

35. Roediger, *Wages of Whiteness*. Roediger also argues that Irish Americans projected their own pre-industrial traditions onto African Americans when they targeted them for violence. On cartoons, see Curtis, *Apes and Angels*; Ignatiev, *How the Irish Became White*; and Jacobson, *Whiteness of a Different Color*.

36. This argument is related to that of Edmund S. Morgan in *American Slavery, American Freedom*, in which he claims that in colonial Virginia the white elite forged a common racial bond with poorer whites in order to subvert potential class alliances between blacks and poor whites.

37. Cyprian Davis, *History of Black Catholics*, 175, 182.

38. See Woodward, *Strange Career of Jim Crow*.

39. William S. Lofton to William Onahan, June 2, 1893, Correspondence, IX-1-d, Onahan Papers.

40. John R. Slattery to William Onahan, June 10, 1893, ibid.

41. Cyprian Davis, *History of Black Catholics*, 183.

42. David Spalding, "Negro Catholic Congresses," 350–57.

43. Cyprian Davis, *History of Black Catholics*, 189–90.

44. Likewise, another woman speaker at the Columbian Catholic Congress, Eliza Allen Starr, came from an old Boston Protestant family. Starr's niece, Ellen Gates Starr, was a Hull-House reformer and later converted to Catholicism as well. *Notable American Women*, s.v. "Starr, Ellen." See also Allitt, *Catholic Converts*, and, for several individual converts, the Sources of American Spirituality series from the Paulist Press.

45. Their son, Francis, died in 1881 at age three. After her husband's death in 1898,

Rose Hawthorne Lathrop founded the Dominican Congregation of St. Rose of Lima in New York, taking the name of Mother Mary Alphonsa, and opened an institution to care for cancer patients. *Notable American Women*, s.v. "Lathrop, Rose Hawthorne"; Culberson, *Rose Hawthorne Lathrop*.

46. Katherine Conway to William Onahan, July 13, 1893, Correspondence, IX-1-d, Onahan Papers.

47. J. M. Rozan to William Onahan, August 17, 1893, Correspondence, IX-1-f, ibid.

48. Walter Elliott to William Onahan, February 17, 1893, Correspondence, IX-1-d, ibid.

49. M. J. Elder to William Onahan, June 6, 1893, Correspondence, IX-1-e, ibid.

50. William Onahan to John Carroll, October 28, 1889, 1889 Congress, IX-1-a, ibid.

51. John Hyde to William Onahan, October 20, 1889, ibid. O'Connell, *John Ireland*, 275–78. O'Connell suggests that this decision, which Bishop Foley of Detroit carried out, came partly in response to the controversy in Rome over papal sovereignty. Anticlericalism had been heating up since 1870 and reached a high point in 1889. Gibbons and Ireland felt that to emphasize the issue at the congress would incite anti-Catholic sentiment, but Pope Leo XIII wanted a paper to be presented in support of papal independence.

52. Organizing Committee to "Right Reverend Bishop" [form letter], July 31, 1889, 1889 Congress, IX-1-a, Onahan Papers.

53. Support for the Land League is discussed in Chapter 3.

54. Reverend Joseph Andreis, "Essay on Italian Immigration and Colonization," Speeches, IX-1-n, Onahan Papers.

55. Larkin, "Devotional Revolution in Ireland"; Dolan, *Immigrant Church*, chapters 4 and 5.

56. The term "new" immigrants is one used by immigration historians to identify the second wave of immigrants arriving in the United States from Italy, Poland, Lithuania, and elsewhere in eastern Europe. It is a convenient shorthand intended to distinguish that population both chronologically and geographically from the earlier wave of immigrants from Ireland and Germany that began in the 1840s. There is considerable variation in the English spelling of many eastern European names.

57. Dolan, *American Catholics*, 173; Archdeacon, *Becoming American*, 116–19. Significant numbers of Italians repatriated to Italy.

58. Buczek, "Polish-Americans," 39–40; Bodnar, *The Transplanted*, 153; Vecoli, "Prelates and Peasants."

59. Juliani, "Parish as an Urban Institution"; Greene, "For God and Country"; Wolkovich-Valkavičius, "Lithuanian Immigrants."

60. Dolan, *Immigrant Church*, 72.

61. Buczek, "Polish-Americans," 49; Wolkovich-Valkavičius, "Lithuanian Immigrants," 24–27.

62. Wolkovich-Valkavičius, *Lithuanian Religious Life*, 53–55. Cada, "Pioneers," 26.

63. Palmieri, "Contribution of the Italian Clergy," 129–30.

64. Wolkovich-Valkavičius, "Lithuanian Immigrants," 44–49.

65. Tentler, *Seasons of Grace*, 220–22.

66. Dolan, *Immigrant Church*, 72–73, 164.

67. Tentler, *Seasons of Grace*, 30–33.

68. See, for example, ibid., 307; Liptak, *Immigrants and Their Church*, 145–46.

69. Orsi, *Madonna of 115th Street*, 51–52.

70. Palmieri, "Contribution of the Italian Clergy," 145–47.

71. Catholic Central Union, Souvenir Program, 36th General Convention, File: Catholic Central Union (Czech Organization), CVA. The society's name was similar to that of the Central Verein after it was Americanized in the 1940s. Also see Society of St. Vincent de Paul, "Ten Decades of Charity," Pamphlet, 1945; Reports of Catholic Charities, St. Louis, 1919–1920, Pamphlet, both in Microfilm Collection, CVA.

72. *Harvard Guide to American Ethnic Groups*, s.v. "Lithuanians." Audyaitis, "Catholic Action of the Lithuanians," 12–13, 23, 37.

73. Audyaitis, "Catholic Action of the Lithuanians," 42, 48, 52–58, 88–90.

74. Parot, *Polish Catholics in Chicago*, 51–53.

75. Downey, "Tradition and Acceptance," 90–91; Fogarty, "Catholic Hierarchy," 30.

CHAPTER TWO

1. Much scholarship on the Protestant-oriented temperance movement focuses on the antebellum era. See Faler, "Cultural Aspects of the Industrial Revolution"; Johnson, *Shopkeeper's Millennium*; Dannenbaum, *Drink and Disorder*; Bordin, *Woman and Temperance*; Clark, *Deliver Us from Evil*; Gusfield, *Symbolic Crusade*.

2. Exceptions include Bland, *Hibernian Crusade*; Rosenzweig, *Eight Hours*; Dinneen, *Catholic Total Abstinence Movement*; Stivers, *Hair of the Dog*; Towey and Sullivan, "Knights of Father Mathew"; and Meagher, " 'The Lord Is Not Dead.' "

3. See Malcolm, *"Ireland Sober, Ireland Free"* and "Irish Temperance Movement"; Kerrigan, "Social Impact" and "Father Mathew and Teetotalism"; Quinn, "Vagabond Friar"; Kearney, "Fr. Mathew."

4. Maguire, *Father Mathew*. "Temperance" denotes abstaining from alcoholic beverages completely. Catholics often used the terms "total abstinence" and "temperance" interchangeably. Although Mathew's followers claimed that upward of 4 to 5 million Irish and "hundreds of thousands" of Americans took the pledge from him, it is unlikely that the majority of the Irish population had embraced total abstinence. *Pilot*, October 11, 1890; Malcolm, *"Ireland Sober, Ireland Free,"* 124–25.

5. Kearney, "Fr. Mathew," 168–69, 174.

6. O'Connell joined a temperance parade at the height of his popularity and kept the pledge for a period, but historians have suggested that Father Mathew was never entirely at ease with their relationship. See Malcolm, *"Ireland Sober, Ireland Free,"* 127–33; Kearney, "Fr. Mathew," 173–75; Kerrigan, "Social Impact," 38. Larkin, "Devotional Revolution in Ireland," 636.

7. Maguire, *Father Mathew*, 177–82, 189–208.

8. Clark, *Deliver Us from Evil*; Gusfield, *Symbolic Crusade*; Billington, *Protestant Crusade*; Higham, *Strangers in the Land*. On anti-immigrant and anti-Catholic senti-

ment, see Bordin, *Woman and Temperance*, 57, 86–88, 122–23, 155, 162. On Catholic women in the movement, see Campbell, "Reformers and Activists."

9. Dannenbaum, *Drink and Disorder*, 122.

10. Patrick O'Brien to Reverend John Mullen, March 2, 1904, Folder 2; Reverend Peter McLean to Reverend John Mullen, June 28, 1904, Folder 4, PTAL Records, AABo. In his June letter, McLean discusses the difficulty of "enlist[ing] our brother priests in a temperance society." This record group contains mostly correspondence between Reverend John T. Mullen, secretary-treasurer of the PTAL, and members of diocesan branches of the league throughout the country from 1900 to 1906, along with some temperance pamphlets and a sermon. Secondary references to the group are scant.

11. Reverend Ferdinand Kittel to Reverend John Mullen, July 28, 1904, Folder 4, PTAL Records.

12. In addition to the 90,000 Catholics affiliated with the CTAU, others belonged to independent groups; in 1876 an estimated 100,000 Catholics belonged to total abstinence groups. *Pilot*, September 11, 1880. On "Whisky's Work," see *Catholic Citizen*, October 7, 1882; on the Phelan column, see *Pilot*, February 3, 1894, and February 2, 1895.

13. High license laws involved increasing the fees required for a local liquor permit in an attempt to reduce the number of establishments that served alcohol.

14. *Pilot*, April 20, 1889; *Catholic Citizen*, December 1, 1883.

15. *Pilot*, September 11, 1880.

16. In his *Pilot* column, Edmund Phelan cited a lecture by T. J. Nichols in Glasgow, who "exposed the not uncommon fallacy that total abstinence was the outcome of the fanaticism of Puritan times." *Pilot*, February 3, 1894. The term "Puritan" was itself a stereotype, of course.

17. *Pilot*, February 21, 1880, January 12, 1889.

18. The temperance advocate actually spelled her first name "Carry." *Central-Blatt and Social Justice*, January 1910, 11. The article appeared originally in *The Western Watchman*. Historians have noted that many German Americans were suspicious of any efforts to regulate alcohol and its consumption. The *Pilot* noted that the Turner Bund opposed "the mediaeval system" of lawmaking "which destroys the rights and curtails the liberties of the many on account of the immoderation and the vices of the few." *Pilot*, October 11, 1884.

19. Barry, *Catholic Church and German Americans*, 16–18.

20. *Monatsbote* 22, no. 7 (April 1921): 11–15, AABo.

21. On Conaty, see *Pilot*, August 3, 1889. On Crowley, see *Pilot*, September 10, 1887, and August 3, 1889; Dinneen, *Catholic Total Abstinence Movement*, 33–34. On Lake, see Diner, *Erin's Daughters in America*, 100. On Cooney, see Finding Aid, Peter Cooney Papers, UNDA.

22. See *Pilot*, May 10, 1890, for Spillane, and May 17, 1902, for Carbery. For additional examples of those who took the pledge in Ireland, see *Pilot*, April 26, 1902, and August 16, 1902, and Dinneen, *Catholic Total Abstinence Movement*, 26, 36, 61. On veneration of veterans, see Bodnar, *Remaking America*, 84–85.

23. Historians have suggested that during the mid-nineteenth century, rates of alcohol consumption in Ireland were lower than those of other countries, including England and Scotland. See Stivers, *Hair of the Dog*. However, Irish immigrants in both England and the United States had higher rates of alcohol consumption than those Irish remaining in Ireland. See Malcolm, *"Ireland Sober, Ireland Free,"* 332–33.

24. Reverend Thomas Conaty and Daniel O'Connell also supported this view. See *Pilot*, August 17, 1889, and Maguire, *Father Mathew*, 102.

25. On Reverend William Dollard, see *Pilot*, April 9, 1904. See also Reverend Peter Cooney, Sermon, Folder 7, Box 3, Peter Cooney Papers.

26. *Pilot*, August 12, 1882.

27. *Pilot*, August 3, 1889. Italics mine. Note that the word "tyrant" connotes the popular analogy between alcoholism and either colonialism or slavery discussed below.

28. *Pilot*, August 13, 1898.

29. *Pilot*, July 26, 1902.

30. *Catholic Citizen*, September 8, 1883; *Pilot*, August 12, 1882. This analogy had been imported from Ireland. Hugh Kearney noted that Irish workingmen in the mid-nineteenth century had used this battle to symbolize the political implications of temperance. Kearney, "Fr. Mathew," 174.

31. Although the terms "alcoholism" and "alcoholic" were not used at the time, they are now accepted usage.

32. CTAU, "Bulletin," no. 7, quoted in *Pilot*, March 12, 1881. *Pilot*, August 15, 1885.

33. In Ireland this view took shape in the 1880s and 1890s in the slogan "Ireland Sober, Ireland Free." That slogan opened the New Temperance Hall, where "garlands and banners of a *religious* and *patriotic* character were hung." *Pilot*, February 14, 1891. Another *Pilot* article noted approvingly that in a picture in many Irish homes called "Illustrious Sons of Ireland," Father Mathew appeared with Wolfe Tone, Robert Emmet, and other patriots. *Pilot*, April 18, 1896. Some Irish nationalists withheld support for temperance, fearing it would detract attention from their major goals and alienate the publicans who formed a significant bloc of Parnell and Land League supporters. See Malcolm, *"Ireland Sober, Ireland Free,"* 265.

34. *Pilot*, September 22, 1883.

35. Powderly, *The Path I Trod*, 180. *Pilot*, August 6, 1881; *Catholic Citizen*, February 21, 1890, and June 10, 1882. James J. Kenneally discusses this incident in "Sexism, the Church, Irish Women," 8–10.

36. *Pilot*, July 23, 1892.

37. *Pilot*, April 16, 1887.

38. Reverend James A. Walsh Diary, James Anthony Walsh Papers, RG VII 13.1, AABo. On the Murphy family, see entries dated December 22, 1898, and June 1, 1899. James Walsh later became a founder of the Catholic Foreign Mission Society, often referred to as the Maryknoll Fathers. Linda Gordon explores the relationship of alcohol to family violence in immigrant families in *Heroes of Their Own Lives*.

39. Attempts to analyze an 1887 membership list from Sacred Heart Parish's Father Mathew Society (East Cambridge) at the archives of the Archdiocese of Boston to

determine the age and occupational status of its members were largely unsuccessful. The city directory listed just a third of the men, while the federal census manuscript for 1890 does not exist. The 1880 federal census listed only a few members, suggesting their high mobility rates and modest economic circumstances. For discussion of the economic position of Catholic temperance advocates in Worcester, Massachusetts, see Rosenzweig, *Eight Hours*, 107–8.

40. *Pilot*, August 14, 1886.

41. *Pilot*, August 13, 1887; Powderly, *The Path I Trod*, 4–8; Weir, *Beyond Labor's Veil*, 47.

42. *Pilot*, August 13, 1887, and June 17, 1887.

43. *Pilot*, June 17, 1887; Powderly, *The Path I Trod*, 190, 292, 344. Laborers had earlier supported Father Mathew during his travels in the United States; see Dinneen, *Catholic Total Abstinence Movement*, 25.

44. Powderly, *The Path I Trod*, 190.

45. *Pilot*, August 19, 1905. Also see Gluck, *John Mitchell*, 140, 197, 208; Finley, *Corrupt Kingdom*, 24; and Phelan, *Divided Loyalties*.

46. "In his zeal for making 'converts,' neither age, nor sex, nor condition, was a protection against his seductive arts." See Maguire, *Father Mathew*, 79, 41, 48, 69, and 80. Philadelphia's societies did not emphasize sex segregation.

47. Malcolm, *"Ireland Sober, Ireland Free,"* 146.

48. See Stivers, *Hair of the Dog*, 75–100. Stivers discusses the distrust many drinking males held for total abstainers.

49. Dinneen, *Catholic Total Abstinence Movement*, 32–33. For a Wisconsin example, see *Catholic Citizen*, February 10, 1883.

50. *Pilot*, December 24, 1910, and July 18, 1914. For additional examples of ethnic celebrations, see Bodnar, *Remaking America*, chapter 3; Schultz, " 'The Pride of the Race' "; Jacobson, *Special Sorrows*.

51. Father Mathew Total Abstinence Society, Minutes, 1924–28, Sacred Heart Parish Records, AABo. The Catholic Church and the Ancient Order of Hibernians had an often tense relationship. Miller, *Emigrants and Exiles*, 532.

52. Father Mathew Total Abstinence Society, Minutes, 1924–28, Sacred Heart Parish Records; *Pilot*, March 17, 1888; *Catholic Citizen*, July 7, 1883.

53. Maguire, *Father Mathew*, 39.

54. *Pilot*, July 20, 1889, September 16, 1899, November 17, 1883; *Catholic Citizen*, February 16, 1884.

55. *Catholic Citizen*, February 9, 1884; *Pilot*, October 15, 1887. I wish to thank Philip Gleason for information on the Fairmount Park fountain.

56. Conaty quoted in *Pilot*, May 14, 1892. Maurice Dinneen notes that as early as 1871 women participated in temperance events, but they never established their own societies in large numbers. On women, see Dinneen, *Catholic Total Abstinence Movement*, esp. 234, 82, 88–89, 129–37.

57. *Pilot*, August 20, 1898.

58. See Bordin, *Woman and Temperance*, 4–5. Bordin notes that Protestant women had gained a greater public role in the temperance movement by the 1850s.

59. Reverend James A. Walsh Diary, James Anthony Walsh Papers, RG VII 13.1, AABo. See entries for December 16 and 23, 1898, January 2 and 22, 1899, and March 15, 1900. Phelan column, *Pilot*, July 21, 1894.

60. Dinneen, *Catholic Total Abstinence Movement*, 168.

61. See *Notable American Women* (1971), s.v. "Barry, Leonora," 101–2. Weir, *Beyond Labor's Veil*, 186–88.

62. Bland, *Hibernian Crusade*, 215, 219.

63. Ibid., 209; Leonora Barry Lake to John Mullen, November 9, 1900, PTAL Records. On Lake's effect on membership of the St. Veronica Society, see Dinneen, *Catholic Total Abstinence Movement*, 131. On Glennon, see Bland, *Hibernian Crusade*, 233–34. Weir, *Beyond Labor's Veil*, 186–89.

64. Dinneen, *Catholic Total Abstinence Movement*, esp. 129–37.

65. *Pilot*, November 14, 1891.

66. On non-Catholics speaking to total abstinence conventions, see *Pilot*, February 26, 1881. On Roosevelt's speech, see *Pilot*, August 24, 1895. On the success of Protestant temperance groups, see Patrick Callahan to Peter Gannon, September 11, 1933, Folder 1, Correspondence 1923–38, Patrick Callahan Papers, UNDA; *Pilot*, March 10, 1894, and August 14, 1896. On Protestants joining local total abstinence societies, see *Pilot*, August 15, 1896.

67. Bordin, *Woman and Temperance*, 87; *Pilot*, November 28, 1891. The Committee of One-Hundred was a Boston-based nativist organization. Bordin does not mention Lake in *Woman and Temperance*.

68. Malcolm, *"Ireland Sober, Ireland Free,"* 317.

CHAPTER THREE

1. The Young Ireland movement consisted of a group of intellectuals and others who had organized in 1842 and split from Daniel O'Connell's Repeal movement. For more on the movement, see Richard Davis, *The Young Ireland Movement*.

2. Ireland was bishop of St. Paul from 1884 until 1888, when he was named archbishop.

3. Beck, *English Catholics*, 575; Bennett, *Father Nugent of Liverpool*, 11–12, passim; Irish Catholic Colonization Association, Report, 1880–1881–1882, Madaj Collection, AAC (hereafter cited as ICCA Report).

4. For more on the Land League's reception in the United States, and its links to temperance, see Foner, "Class, Ethnicity, and Radicalism." For a discussion of Jewish charitable efforts in this era, see Soyer, *Jewish Immigrant Associations*.

5. Kelly, *Catholic Immigration Colonization Projects*, 15–18, 42, 119, 143–46; Schrembs, "Catholic German Immigrant," 68; Barry, *Catholic Church and German Americans*, 15.

6. Kelly, *Catholic Immigration Colonization Projects*, 214–17.

7. Ibid., 213.

8. Ibid., 217–20, 251–52.

9. Browne, "Archbishop Hughes." Browne argues that Hughes's verbal comments objecting to colonization are stronger than his more measured written comments.

10. Ibid., 267–68, 277–78; John Lancaster Spalding, *Religious Mission*, 147.

11. ICCA Report, 2.

12. John Lancaster Spalding, *Religious Mission*, 73.

13. Ibid., 85.

14. For a discussion of the importance of the yeoman class in an earlier era, see Morgan, *Inventing the People*, 153–73.

15. Foner, *Free Soil, Free Labor, Free Men*, 11–24, 232.

16. *Pilot*, December 9, 1893.

17. Italians, whose migration flow began in 1880, also came predominately from rural backgrounds and overwhelmingly settled in urban areas.

18. *Catholic Citizen*, July 25, 1885; September 22, 1883.

19. Crèvecoeur, *Letters from an American Farmer*, 60–61.

20. *Catholic Citizen*, July 25, 1885; September 22, 1883. Crèvecoeur quote in Schrembs, "Catholic German Immigrant," 66. Conzen, *Immigrant Milwaukee*, 27–31.

21. Barry, *Catholic Church and German Americans*, 20.

22. Schrembs, "Catholic German Immigrant," 68; Smith, *German Nationalism and Religious Conflict*, 19, 40–44; Ross, *Failure of Bismarck's Kulturkampf*; Barry, *Catholic Church and German Americans*, 5–6; Blackbourn, *Long Nineteenth Century*, 262.

23. Ross, *Failure of Bismarck's Kulturkampf*, chapters 5 and 6; Herwig, *Hammer or Anvil?*, 136–38.

24. On the relative prosperity of German and Swedish immigrants (as compared with famine-era Irish immigrants), see, for example, Archdeacon, *Becoming American*, 50, 104.

25. John Lancaster Spalding, *Religious Mission*, 106. See also "Advice to Immigrants," *Catholic Citizen*, April 10, 1880.

26. *Pilot*, July 16, 1891.

27. John Lancaster Spalding, *Religious Mission*, 175. On Nugent, see Henthorne, "John Lancaster Spalding," 105; Beck, *English Catholics*, 282–83, 561; *Catholic Citizen*, June 24, 1882.

28. On Parnell and the development of the Land League, see Lyons, *Ireland since the Famine*, 151–66; Kee, *The Laurel and the Ivy*, esp. 199–224; and Thomas Brown, *Irish-American Nationalism*, chapters 4, 5, and 6.

29. Kissane, *Irish Famine*, 171–73; Thomas Brown, *Irish-American Nationalism*, 101; Miller, *Emigrants and Exiles*, 399, 573.

30. Lyons, *Ireland since the Famine*, 138–43, 148–50, and 151–69.

31. Ibid., 170–80.

32. Ibid., 188–95.

33. *Pilot*, August 13, 1881.

34. *Catholic Citizen*, September 23, 1882; ICCA Report, 8; *Pilot*, August 13, 1881.

35. Of course, the view of English colonization in North America as a benign process has been substantially revised by scholars in recent decades.

36. ICCA Report, 10–11.

37. *Catholic Citizen*, July 25, 1885.

38. There are three full-length studies concerning the history of Catholic colonization efforts: Shannon, *Catholic Colonization*; Henthorne, "John Lancaster Spalding"; and Kelly, *Catholic Immigration Colonization Projects*.

39. Henthorne, "John Lancaster Spalding," 121, 126.

40. ICCA Report, 1–5.

41. McDermott, *Pioneer History of Greeley County*, 33–35, 43–45, 184; ICCA Report, 8.

42. *Pilot*, April 14, 1883.

43. John Lancaster Spalding, *Religious Mission*, 194.

44. Diner, *Erin's Daughters in America*, 52.

45. *Pilot*, December 23, 1882.

46. ICCA Report, 5; McDermott, *Pioneer History of Greeley County*, 45.

47. *Pilot*, July 16, 1891.

48. *Pilot*, April 14, 1883.

49. *Catholic Citizen*, March 20, 1880; Henthorne, "John Lancaster Spalding," 110, 113. James Shannon discusses the Connemara immigration controversy in *Catholic Colonization*. See also Moran, "'In Search of the Promised Land.'"

50. Catholic Colonization Bureau of Minnesota, "Catholic Colonization in Minnesota," 32; *Pilot*, July 3, 1880.

51. *Pilot*, July 7, 1883; *Catholic Citizen*, May 19, 1883.

52. On Irish women's immigration patterns, see Diner, *Erin's Daughters in America*, esp. chapter 2.

53. See also Meyerowitz, *Women Adrift*; Odem, *Delinquent Daughters*.

54. The British government had tried O'Brien for high treason for his role in the failed Irish revolution in 1848. Gwynn, *Charlotte Grace O'Brien*, 8–9 (hereafter cited as *Memoir*). Stephen Gwynn was Charlotte O'Brien's nephew. See also Touhill, *William Smith O'Brien*.

55. *Pilot*, February 5, 1890. *Memoir*, 4–5, 8–9, 37–38, 44–50, 103, 108, 111; quote, 37. The Irish presidency was created in 1937.

56. *Memoir*, 50.

57. Ibid., 66–67; *Pall Mall Gazette*, May 6, 1881. Single men had separate quarters.

58. The controversy is covered in the *Pall Mall Gazette*, May 6, 9, 10, and 12, 1881; *Memoir*, 60. Joseph Chamberlain was the father of the future prime minister, Neville Chamberlain.

59. On the increased physical vulnerability of female migrants to urban areas, see Hellerstein, Hume, and Offen, *Victorian Women*, 121. Ruth Rosen takes issue with historians who have concluded that the fear of white slavery was "merely a myth that expressed certain tensions, fears, and conflicts in American society." She estimates that perhaps 10 percent of all prostitutes became victims of white slavery. Rosen, *Lost Sisterhood*, 113. Joanne Meyerowitz discusses the role of unmarried women workers in *Women Adrift*.

60. Diner, *Erin's Daughters in America*, 21–22. Diner contrasts this confidence in internal constraints with the use of chaperones in other cultures in which women's chastity was valued highly.

61. For more on this issue, see Chapter 5.

62. Luddy, *Women and Philanthropy*, esp. chapter 4; Fitzgerald, "Irish-Catholic Nuns."

63. See Gabaccia, *From the Other Side*, esp. chapter 3.

64. *Memoir*, 61–66. *Pilot*, April 7, 1883.

65. On the Onahan-Nugent acquaintance, see Pahorezski, "Social and Political Activities of William James Onahan," 2, and Bennett, *Father Nugent of Liverpool*, 102.

66. Relatively few sources exist on O'Brien's views.

67. *Pilot*, April 7, 1883. Mona Hearn's book on domestic service in Dublin illuminates the conditions of work. She argues that parents often encouraged their daughters to enter domestic service because they believed that it would provide them with a good substitute for parental supervision. Hearn, *Below Stairs*, esp. 1, 3, 15. For an English example, see Gillis, "Servants, Sexual Relations."

68. *Memoir*, 82–83. *Pilot*, November 18, 1882. While in Chicago, O'Brien stayed with the Onahan family.

69. *Memoir*, 83.

70. Ibid., 63–64.

71. *Pilot*, May 23, 1885; January 30, 1892. On the prostitution incident, see *Pilot*, January 30, 1892.

72. O'Brien was probably referring to the activities of the Friendly Sons of St. Patrick in Philadelphia.

73. For more on Carey, see Kenneally, *History of American Catholic Women*, 64. *Memoir*, 78.

74. *Pilot*, April 7, 1883; December 23, 1882. *Memoir*, 84; *Pall Mall Gazette*, May 6, 1881.

75. *Memoir*, 77. Lord Derby, speaking of the "assisted immigration" policy, said: "Personally I believe that some millions spent in promoting Irish immigration, if Parliament and the Cabinet saw their way to it, would pay us well." Ibid., 76.

76. Ibid., 76–79, 81–82, 85, 105–6, 127. Several sources on Irish American and Catholic history mention O'Brien or her work briefly, but few discuss her programs in detail. They include Miller, *Emigrants and Exiles*, 426, 506, and Diner, *Erin's Daughters in America*, 120, 123. Maureen Murphy discusses O'Brien's work in Ireland and New York in "A Mission Remembered" and "Charlotte Grace O'Brien."

77. Barry, *Catholic Church and German Americans*, 5, 21–26, 262.

78. Ibid., 25–28, 106–7, 262–74.

79. Ibid., 40–43, 89–93. This was a controversial change, and Kölble claimed he had never been properly informed of the decision.

80. St. Raphael Society of America, "Golden Jubilee of the Leo House." Barry, *Catholic Church and German Americans*, 27–28, 86–93, 262–74.

81. Barry, *Catholic Church and German Americans*, 35.

82. "Program for 175th Anniversary of Charitable Irish Society, Preamble," March 18, 1912, Business Papers, CIS Records, MHS. Earlier efforts on a smaller scale existed elsewhere.

83. ICCA Report, 7.

84. *Pilot*, November 18, 1882, and February 1, 1896; "Program for 175th Anniversary of Charitable Irish Society, Preamble," March 18, 1912, Business Papers, CIS Records.

85. Julia Hayes briefly resigned from her position in 1911, "due to overwork and nervous strain," and visited friends "in the old country" (most likely Ireland), but she returned as the CIS agent shortly afterward. Charles Dasey to P. O. O'Loughlin, October 6, 1911, Business Papers, CIS Records; *The Boston Directory* (1911).

86. [ ] to Charles O'Malley, May 27, 1922, Business Papers, CIS Records. The president of the CIS in 1911 boasted that its membership included "judges, lawyers, doctors and businessman. . . . while the large majority of its seven hundred members are Catholic, we have yet as members, some excellent Protestant gentlemen." Patrick O'Loughlin to Reverend Bernard Vaughn, November 7, 1911, ibid. See also Bernard Kelley to Bartholomew Brickley, December 2, 1913, copy appended to letter of John Keenan to Patrick Conley, December 6, 1913, ibid.

87. The Jewish groups were the Council of Jewish Women and the Hebrew Immigrant Aid Society; the Scandinavian groups were the Swedish Congregational Society, the Lutheran Swedish Society, the Norwegian Congregational Church, the Danish Lutheran Society, and the Women's Home Missionary Society, which is identified as Scandinavian. Lulu [Julia] Hayes to John Keenan, December 22, 1913, ibid.

88. On the North American Civic League, see Higham, *Strangers in the Land*, 241. Julia Hayes mentioned this figure of one-quarter in several of her reports. See, for example, "Report for the Three Months Ending December 31, 1913," Business Papers, CIS Records.

89. As Hayes observed in one of her reports: "The friendless girl is the exception rather than the rule and the number of girls who have to be placed even temporarily, to await the arrival of friends from points near Boston, is gradually falling off. Ireland has contributed so generously in the past to the population of America that no girl comes, who has not been preceded by a relative, friend or neighbor, so that she is at least provided for temporarily." "Report of the Immigration Work from October 1, 1912, to March 1, 1913," Business Papers, CIS Records.

90. "Immigration Report for the Six Months Ending March 30, 1912"; "Report of the Immigration Work from October 1, 1912, to March 1, 1913," ibid.

91. "Immigration Report for the Six Months Ending September 30, 1912"; Michael Scanlan to John Keenan, October 7, 1918; Katharine McDermott to [John Keenan], May 1, 1916; Anna Cassidy to John Keenan, June 28, 1916, Business Papers, CIS Records. For more on remigration, see Wyman, *Round-Trip to America*.

92. "Immigration Report for the Six Months Ending September 30, 1913," Business Papers, CIS Records.

93. Julia Hayes to John Keenan, March 23 and 20, 1916; undated note, signed "An Irishman," attached to a newspaper clipping from the *Boston Post*, March 16, 1916,

ibid. It is unclear whether the people offering Delia Burke positions in their households were Irish Catholics. The story was first reported on the front page of the *Boston Post* on February 27, 1916.

94. Julia Hayes to John Keenan, March 23 and 20, 1916; Julia Hayes to John Keenan, April 14, 1916; "Immigration Report for the Six Months Ending March 31, 1910," Business Papers, CIS Records.

95. "Report on Immigration Work for the Month Ending November 30, 1914," ibid.

96. Ibid.

97. "Immigration Report for the Six Months Ending September 30, 1910," ibid.

98. In addition, the law allowed for the deportation of immigrants "likely to become public charges, persons suffering from a loathsome or contagious disease, persons who have been convicted of a felony or other infamous crime or misdemeanor, involving moral turpitude, polygamists, and also any person whose ticket or passage has been paid for with the money of another." Shenton, "Ethnicity and Immigration," 263.

99. John Trant to John Keenan, January 24, 1917, Business Papers, CIS Records. Also see Mary Tinney, "A Shelter for Unmarried Mothers," *Catholic Charities Review* 5, no. 4 (April 1921): 113–15. Tinney notes: "There is again, the easily acceptable doctrine that all who do wrong, and especially the immoral girls, are feeble-minded, or at least bordering on the mentally deficient line. Much as we might like to believe this, we are forced to acknowledge that we know it is not true." See also Alexander, *"Girl Problem,"* 64–65.

100. Lulu [Julia] Hayes to John Keenan, December 22, 1913, Business Papers, CIS Records.

101. George Creel to John Keenan, April 2, 1918; Memo from Charles O'Malley to "Chairmen and Gentlemen," December 18, 1922; Memo, n.d. [January 1922]; Julia Hayes to John Keenan, October 3, 1918, Business Papers, CIS Records.

102. There was considerable tension between the IWD and D'Alfonso. In a 1921 letter, Scanlan remarked about the San Raffaele Society for Italians that "practically this society does not function because it is not supported by the Italians." Richard Haberlin to Michael Scanlan, March 14, 1921, and Scanlan to Haberlin, March 15, 1921, Folder 1, Box 2, CCB Records, AABo.

103. Male workers "represented" only two nationalities, Syrians and French. The French-speaking worker had apparently been chosen to replace his wife in the position. "Special Works. Immigrant Welfare Department. Annual Report, 1921," Folder 11, Box 8, CCB Records.

104. Despite Cardinal O'Connell's legendary opposition to the establishment of the NCWC, this attitude was not apparent in the correspondence from his secretary, Richard Haberlin, to the IWD.

105. Annual Report, NCWC, Bureau of Immigration, July 1, 1922–July 30, 1923, 1–3, 4, 18–22, Chancery Records, AAC. Filipinos were neither aliens nor citizens. In 1934 they were effectively excluded from the United States by a clause in the Tydings-McDuffie Act that limited Filipino immigration to fifty people per year. Chan, *Asian America*, 55–56.

106. Annual Report, NCWC, Bureau of Immigration, July 1, 1922–July 30, 1923, 1–3, 4, 26, Chancery Records, AAC.

107. Ibid., 2–6. The family reunification bill, H.J. Resolution 464, was never introduced before the close of the congressional session. The NCWC supported this initiative for humanitarian and moral reasons. The immigration restriction bill, or Reed-Johnson bill, is referred to as the "Three Percent Restriction Law" in the NCWC report. On Mohler's unsuccessful opposition to immigration restriction efforts in Congress, see Slawson, *National Catholic Welfare Council*, 237.

108. Annual Report, NCWC, Bureau of Immigration, July 1, 1922–July 30, 1923, 13–14.

109. Ibid., 8–9, 15.

110. Ibid., 26–28.

111. Ibid., 237; Wiebe, *Search for Order*.

CHAPTER FOUR

1. I define charity as the activities undertaken by individuals or groups to ameliorate poverty through the donation of food, clothing, money, medical care, and sometimes lodging. It sometimes encompasses the creation of free programs for the poor. Charity usually extends beyond the amelioration of poverty to include efforts to reform individuals, social institutions, or structures, but this does not necessarily occur. Two recent works that also discuss charity initiatives in the American Catholic Church are Brown and McKeown, *The Poor Belong to Us*, and Oates, *Catholic Philanthropic Tradition*.

2. Society of St. Vincent de Paul, *Proceedings of the National Conference*, 1911, 200 (hereafter cited as *Proceedings*, 1911); *St. Vincent de Paul Quarterly* 3, no. 4 (November 1898): 271. For additional examples of Catholic praise for Jewish charitable efforts, see *Central-Blatt and Social Justice*, August 1914, 137.

3. On the St. Vincent de Paul Society's nondiscrimination policy, see, for example, "Report of the Conference of the Holy Name," [n.d.], 3, Box 3244, Society of St. Vincent de Paul Collection, AAC: "No distinction as to creed, color or nationality is made in giving relief, but all are alike the recipients of the charity of the Society, in fact less vigilance is used when the applicant differs from us in religion." See also *Pilot*, May 12, 1883. That article lists many charitable agencies in Boston charged with discriminating against Catholics. In addition to those that refused Catholics, other charities stipulated that recipients were to have been born in the United States, or have lived in the town for ten years.

4. For more on the COS, see Boyer, *Urban Masses and Moral Order*; Lubove, *Professional Altruist*; Trattner, *From Poor Law to Welfare State*; Huggins, *Protestants against Poverty*.

5. On World War I and its impact on German and Irish Americans, see Higham, *Strangers in the Land*, esp. 198–99.

6. As Ruth Crocker Hutchinson discusses, many lesser-known settlement houses

existed in smaller cities, in addition to those discussed most frequently by historians. Hutchinson, *Social Work and Social Order*. Radicals generally criticized the movement. Emma Goldman, for example, dismissed settlements as "teaching the poor to eat with forks." Nevertheless, some of the more well-known settlements came under criticism as a result of their workers' ties to radicals and socialists. Also see Carson, *Settlement Folk*, 161–63, and Trolanger, *Professionalism and Social Change*.

7. See, for example, Rose, "From Sponge Cake to *Hamentashen*."

8. Amberg, *Madonna Center*, 46.

9. For more on Italian immigrant Catholics, see Tomasi, *Piety and Power*; Vecoli, "Prelates and Peasants"; Orsi, *Madonna of 115th Street* and *Thank You, St. Jude*.

10. *Messenger of the Sacred Heart* (New York), as quoted in *St. Vincent de Paul Quarterly* 1, no. 2 (February 1896): 137.

11. On Protestant efforts to convert through settlements, see Carson, *Settlement Folk*, 63, and Hutchinson, *Social Work and Social Order*, 165. On Protestant evangelical attitudes toward Italian immigrants, see Tomasi, *Piety and Power*, 47–50. Carson and others discuss the tension between parents and settlement house workers.

12. Notes on Y.M.C.A. by Reverend Monsignor Thomas Bona, St. Mary's of Perpetual Help, [1927]; Bishop James Griffen to Cardinal Mundelein, January 14, 1927, Chancery Correspondence, AAC.

13. See Kerby, *Social Mission of Charity*; Brown and McKeown, *The Poor Belong to Us*; Lescher, "William J. Kerby"; and Lavey, "William J. Kerby, John A. Ryan." Charles Patrick Neill, another Catholic University professor, was also active in Catholic social work. See Neill, "Training for Social Work."

14. Braunagel-Brown, "Pineapple of Philanthropy," 118; McColgan, *A Century of Charity*, 26–44. I will refer to the Society of St. Vincent de Paul as simply "the Society."

15. Society of St. Vincent de Paul, *Proceedings of the International Convention*, 1904, 96–97 (hereafter cited as *Proceedings*, 1904); *Proceedings*, 1911, xiii, 12; *Report of the Superior Council of New York*, 1909, 4 (hereafter cited as *Report*, 1909). Conferences in several cities with active societies, including those in Milwaukee, Chicago, and St. Louis, failed to report their progress. For more on the Society, see McColgan, *A Century of Charity*, 36–38, 11, 14, 16–17.

16. Society of St. Vincent de Paul, "Ten Decades of Charity," Pamphlet, 1945, Microfilm Collection, CVA.

17. Ibid. See also Cochran, "Saga of an Irish Immigrant Family," 3–47, 53, 67, 98–100. In *A Century of Charity*, Daniel McColgan suggests that a meeting between Mullanphy and Ozanam was unlikely (65, 68–70).

18. Society of St. Vincent de Paul, "Ten Decades of Charity"; McColgan, *A Century of Charity*, 61.

19. Society of St. Vincent de Paul, *Report of Proceedings at the Fourth General Assembly*, 1886, 21 (hereafter cited as *Report*, 1886); *Report*, 1909, 32.

20. *Report*, 1909, 49.

21. See Fitzgerald, "Irish-Catholic Nuns."

22. *St. Vincent de Paul Quarterly* 1, no. 2 (February 1896): 115.

23. Superior Council of New York, Report, May 1865, Folder 1, Box 3244, Society of St. Vincent de Paul Collection. Many members of the Society expressed concern that the membership tended to be comprised of middle-aged and older men. See *Proceedings*, 1904, 101. An 1858 membership list for St. Gall's Conference in Milwaukee indicates that most members were skilled workers, with merchants and a few laborers also listed. Schimberg, *Humble Harvest*, 24.

24. *Proceedings*, 1911, 3; Joseph A. Kernan, Jr., "The Work of the St. Vincent de Paul Society," in *World's Columbian Catholic Congresses and Educational Exhibit*, 1:90–91. On Onahan, see "Report of the Conference of the Holy Name," Box 3244, Society of St. Vincent de Paul Collection. On Dwight, see entries in *Who's Who in America, 1899–1900* and *Dictionary of American Biography*, and also *St. Vincent de Paul Quarterly* 1, no. 1 (November 1895): 16–18. On Boston's Vincentians, see Walton, *To Preserve the Faith*. Walton and I reach differing conclusions about the socio-economic background of most Vincentians.

25. *Report*, 1886, 20, 34–35; *Proceedings*, 1911, 266.

26. Golden Jubilee Address in Society of St. Vincent de Paul, "Annual Report of the Upper Council of St. Louis, 1883."

27. *St. Vincent de Paul Quarterly* 1, no. 1 (November 1895): 33. On pages 7–8 of that journal a speaker asserted, "I say of the non-Catholic portion of New York . . . whatever prejudices our dissenting brethren may, from lack of knowledge of us and of our practices, entertain towards Catholic works and devotions, there is one work, one society for which they have nothing but the utmost veneration and respect, and that is the Society of St. Vincent de Paul." *Report*, 1909, 5. See also Walton, *To Preserve the Faith*, on this point.

28. *St. Vincent de Paul Quarterly* 1, no. 1 (November 1895): 18–20; *Report*, 1886, 61.

29. *Report*, 1886, 19, 38, 61; *Proceedings*, 1911, x; *St. Vincent de Paul Quarterly* 1, no. 2 (February 1896): 123.

30. Schimberg, *Humble Harvest*, 46–48, 85–86.

31. Kernan, "St. Vincent de Paul Society," 90; *Report*, 1886, 78.

32. At the 1904 annual convention of the Society, Georges Blondel of the Committee General of Paris gave a paper that alluded to this principle. He asserted that those in the Society "can powerfully aid Catholics, whatever may be their political opinion, to seek that which unites instead of that which so often divides, and thus loyally extend to each other the hand on the basis of Charity—Union in Charity. It is thought that this can and should be realized not only between individuals of the same country, but also between nation and nation." This suggests that within a country where Catholics were ethnically diverse, universality rather than ethnicity should be emphasized. *Proceedings*, 1904, 32. Society of St. Vincent de Paul, "Sixth Annual Report, 1919," 4.

33. *Proceedings*, 1904, 32.

34. *Report*, 1886, 30, 33, 36, 39, 48–49.

35. *St. Vincent de Paul Quarterly* 1, no. 2 (February 1896): 90–91; McColgan, *A Century of Charity*, 37.

36. *St. Vincent de Paul Quarterly* 1, no. 2 (February 1896): 95, 97; *Proceedings*, 1911, 145; "The Society's Founding, Work and Activities During Its 75 Years in Chicago, Centenary Celebration, May 30, 1933," Folder 2, Box 3207, Society of St. Vincent de Paul Collection.

37. Quote from Kathleen O'Meara, *Life and Works of Frederick Ozanam* (New York, n.p., n.d.), 84, published in Souvay, "Society of St. Vincent de Paul," 447. Another metaphor about charity proved very similar to that expressed by Ozanam. On page 238 of its November 1915 issue, *Central-Blatt and Social Justice* reprinted an article that appeared originally in the *Philadelphia Bulletin*, quoting Bishop Penhurst's parody of charitable events: "'Some charities,' he said, 'remind me of a cold, proud, beautiful lady who, glittering with diamonds, swept forth from a charity ball at dawn, crossed the frosty sidewalk, and entered her huge limousine. A beggar woman whined at the window 'Could you give me a trifle for a cup of coffee, lady?' The lady looked at the beggar reproachfully. 'Good gracious!' she said, 'Here you have the nerve to ask me for money when I've been tangoing for you the whole night through.'" In the September 1910 issue of *Central-Blatt and Social Justice* a writer suggested that U.S. Catholic women become more active in charity, but "not the card-party, charity-ball type of Christianity will cure the many evils of our day, but active charity like that of a St. Vincent de Paul."

38. *Pilot*, September 1, 1903; McCarthy, *Noblesse Oblige*.

39. In "Society of St. Vincent de Paul," Souvay maintains that while 100 percent of the Society's money was distributed to the poor, 50 percent or more of public or semipublic charities' funds was needed for administration costs. See page 448. *Proceedings*, 1911, 5.

40. *Proceedings*, 1911, 9, 75; *Central-Blatt and Social Justice*, April 1913, 12–15; Helmes, "Thomas Mulry"; Meehan, *Thomas Maurice Mulry*.

41. Lubove, *Professional Altruist*, 3–7; Trattner, *From Poor Law to Welfare State*, 88. Also see Fitzgerald, "Irish-Catholic Nuns."

42. Lubove, *Professional Altruist*, 3–5.

43. Trattner, *From Poor Law to Welfare State*, 86–88; Lubove, *Professional Altruist*.

44. Huggins, *Protestants against Poverty*, 65–67. On page 69 Huggins provides a quote that illustrates the difference between the Provident Society (or "old" charity) and the Associated Charities (or "new" charity). "'The Old Charity sees a woman begging, having in her arms a child with diseased eyes, distorted legs, festering sores'; it gives her what she asks for, money or food. It 'thereby puts a premium on diseased, distorted children; and so such children were made to order by the thousands, while the Old Charity goes away hugging itself over the tenderness of heart.' The 'New Charity,' on the other hand, treated the child, sent the woman to jail, and removed 'all inducement for the production and exhibition of distorted children.'" For differences among charities in Boston, see Traverso, "Politics of Welfare."

45. Trattner, *From Poor Law to Welfare State*, 90–91.

46. *Report*, 1886, 78.

47. Society of St. Vincent de Paul, "Special Works of the Conferences in Belgium," in *Proceedings*, 1904, 112; *Proceedings*, 1911, 260.

48. *Catholic Citizen*, January 24, 1880; Society of St. Vincent de Paul, *Rules of the Society*, 153; *St. Vincent de Paul Quarterly* 1, no. 2 (February 1896): 93. Quote: Louis Fusz of St. Louis, in *Proceedings*, 1911, 86.

49. *Pilot*, September 1, 1903.

50. *Proceedings*, 1911, 119, 164, 257–58, 268.

51. Ibid., xxi, 22.

52. Kerby, *Social Mission of Charity*, 52.

53. *Central-Blatt and Social Justice*, October 1916, 203–4. On Budenz's later activities, see Allitt, *Catholic Intellectuals*, 26–28; Budenz, *This Is My Story*, esp. 21 and 35; and Schrecker, *Many Are the Crimes*.

54. *Proceedings*, 1911, 81, 50; Kerby, *Social Mission of Charity*, 8.

55. On settlement house philosophy, see Carson, *Settlement Folk*, 51, 65–67.

56. Society of St. Vincent de Paul, *Rules of the Society*, 24, 37, 152.

57. *Proceedings*, 1911, 103; *Proceedings*, 1904, 177.

58. McColgan, *A Century of Charity*, 27.

59. Ibid., 39.

60. The term "friendly visiting" had been used by non-Catholic groups to describe visits to poor immigrants by their women volunteers. Souvay, "Society of St. Vincent de Paul," 455.

61. *Proceedings*, 1904, 94–95.

62. Schimberg, *Humble Harvest*, 122, 125, 151; *Proceedings*, 1911, 170.

63. *Report*, 1909, 22; *Proceedings*, 1911, 165.

64. *St. Vincent de Paul Quarterly* 1, no. 2 (February 1896): 100; *Report*, 1886, 51; *Proceedings*, 1911, 53, 146–47.

65. Margaret Tucker, "Catholic Settlement Work—An Analysis," *Catholic Charities Review* 2, no. 10 (December 1918): 304–8; 3, no. 1 (January 1919): 18–20. There is a debate about the number of Catholic settlement houses established in the United States. Aaron Abell, in *American Catholicism and Social Action*, his standard monograph on Catholic social reform, claims that at least 2,500 existed. Margaret McGuinness justifiably takes issue with Abell's estimate, believing it to be greatly overstated. See McGuinness, "Response to Reform," 20. Amberg, *Madonna Center*, 45.

66. Tucker, "Catholic Settlement Work," 305. There was at least one exception to this pattern, however. The Margaret House Association in New Orleans had a male board of directors and was run by Sisters of Charity. *Central-Blatt and Social Justice*, July 1916, 106.

67. Tucker, "Catholic Settlement Work," 18–19.

68. Amberg, *Madonna Center*, 72.

69. Bennett, *Father Nugent of Liverpool*, 127–28; Luddy, "Women and Charitable Organizations," 304.

70. Sharkey, *New Jersey Sisters of Charity*, 76. For background on women religious and their changing relationship to ecclesiastical authority, see, for example, McNamara, *Sisters in Arms*.

71. Sister Marie Walsh, *Sisters of Charity of New York*, 34.

72. Amberg, *Madonna Center*, 7, 14. Allen F. Davis concludes that nearly 90 percent of Protestant-oriented settlement house workers had received a college education, and over 50 percent had attended graduate school. Davis, *Spearheads for Reform*, 33.

73. Amberg, *Madonna Center*, 69, 89, 124; December 1915 fund-raising letter written by Frederic Siedenberg, Box 1, Folder 1, Series 3, Madonna Center Records, Archives of Marquette University, Milwaukee, Wis.

74. Mary Agnes Amberg to Miss Montegriffo, n.d. [1913?], Folder 1, Box 1, Series 3, Madonna Center Records.

75. Amberg, *Madonna Center*, 27. The Ambergs received assistance in their work from Father Edward Dunne.

76. Ibid., 113. Amberg's father was born in the United States but shortly after his birth remigrated with his family to their native Germany; he returned to Wisconsin during his youth (ibid., 5).

77. Ibid., 59, 78-79; on *Rerum Novarum*, see 78.

78. Ibid., 75; quote, 73.

79. Ibid., 72-73, 40. Prior to Mary Agnes Amberg's decision to run the mission, her mother had contacted a religious order of women in Paris, called the Little Helpers of the Holy Souls, to ask whether they would assist in the running of Guardian Angels in Chicago. They were not available, however. Ibid., 73-74. Vineyard quote: Fund-raising letter [no addressee], from the teachers of the Italian Mission Sunday School, January 1903, Folder 1, Box 1, Series 3, Madonna Center Records.

80. Amberg, *Madonna Center*, 59, 85.

81. Ibid., 63-64, 47, 128, 133, 142, 135-37, 174-76.

82. Ibid., 140-42, 168-70.

83. Ibid., 157.

84. Fund-raising letter [no addressee], from the teachers of the Italian Mission Sunday School, January 1903, Folder 1, Box 1, Series 3, Madonna Center Records; Lissak, "Myth and Reality," 36, and *Pluralism and Progressives*.

85. Amberg, *Madonna Center*, 42-44.

86. Ibid., 163, 158, 157.

87. Ibid., 38-39.

88. Ibid., 133, 36.

89. Ibid., 177.

90. Amberg, *Madonna Center*, 133. Letter to People's Gas Light Co., October 24, 1912, File 1, Box 1, Series 3, Madonna Center Records. On page 22 of her article "Myth and Reality," Rivka Lissak notes that while some historians have described Jane Addams as a cultural pluralist, others disagree with that assessment.

91. Amberg, *Madonna Center*, 170-71.

92. During World War II, Italians had particular difficulty obtaining American citizenship because they had been classified as citizens of an Axis nation. Ibid., 170.

93. It is possible that Amberg's silence on socialism derived from the fact that she wrote her memoir in 1940, after the first Red Scare and prior to the Cold War.

94. Amberg, *Madonna Center*, 190, 39. The Pucciarellis were a composite family that Amberg used to illustrate conditions among the Italians in the settlement's neighborhood.

95. Ibid., 65, 190–91. Ellen Gates Starr was the niece of Catholic convert Eliza Allen Starr, who presented a paper at the 1893 Columbian Catholic Congress.

96. Ibid., 134.

97. Ibid., 190–94, 188, 184.

98. *Central-Blatt and Social Justice*, October 1916, 221. Giess sometimes appears in records as Giesz.

99. On social welfare policy, see Lee and Rosenhaft, *State and Social Change*, xi, 32; Blackbourn, *Long Nineteenth Century*, 177–81, 346–47.

100. Edward Ross Dickinson terms as "Progressive" the movement for child welfare reform that existed in Germany in the late nineteenth and early twentieth centuries, emphasizing parallels to the American one. Dickinson, *Politics of German Child Welfare*, 30–31. Newspaper clipping, *Aurora und Christliche Woche*, January 6, 1922, File: St. Elizabeth Settlement: early clippings and items, Central Verein Records, CVA; *Central-Blatt and Social Justice*, September 1910.

101. *Central-Blatt and Social Justice*, January 1914, September 1910, July 1911, November 1911, October 1911.

102. Ibid., August 1915, August 1916.

103. Ibid., November 1911, August 1915, July 1916, 124, August 1916. St. Elizabeth Day Nursery, 50th Anniversary Pamphlet, File: St. Elizabeth Settlement; Christmas Pamphlet, [1930], File: St. Elizabeth's Pictures, Central Verein Records.

104. Gleason, *Conservative Reformers*, 91–110.

105. "Twenty-Fifth Annual Convention of the Catholic State League of New York," 1922, File: NCWU 1922; typed manuscript draft of the St. Elizabeth Jubilee Celebration [1949?], File: St. Elizabeth Settlement, Central Verein Records.

106. CWU, *Official Bulletin*, May 15, 1925. Literally: "House-wives, not out-wives."

107. *Central-Blatt and Social Justice*, October 1916, June 1919.

108. Ibid., October 1916, 221. Sister Mary Hortence Crabtree, S.S.N.D., "St. Elizabeth Settlement and Day Nursery," June 1949, File: St. Elizabeth Settlement; newspaper clipping, *Aurora und Christliche Woche*, January 6, 1922; newspaper clipping, *Catholic News*, April 8, 1934, File: St. Elizabeth Settlement: early clippings and items, Central Verein Records. In the 1922 article, the term "social visitor" appears in English, suggesting that it was a recently coined term and thus relatively unfamiliar to readers.

109. "Activities of the *Central Verein* Day Nursery at St. Louis" [Christmas 1930], Pamphlet, File: St. Elizabeth's Pictures; *The Sunday Watchman*, August 11, 1918, File: St. Elizabeth Settlement: early clippings and items, Central Verein Records.

110. Newspaper clipping, *Sunday Watchman*, August 11, 1918, File: St. Elizabeth Settlement: early clippings and items, Central Verein Records.

111. Dickinson, *Politics of German Child Welfare*, 93. As discussed in the following chapter, in 1916 Catholic women in Germany had established a school for Catholic

social workers, die Soziale Frauenschule, and the League of Catholic Social Workers of Germany. See Wilhelm Spael, *Das katholische Deutschland*, 97.

112. "Ninth Annual Convention of the Catholic Women's Union, Held at Cleveland, Ohio, August 22 to 26, 1925," 4, CCCV 9/04, Catholic Central Verein Collection, UNDA (hereafter cited as CCV Collection). *Central-Blatt and Social Justice*, October 1917, 218; August 1919, 161. F. P. Kenkel to Mother Petra, June 24, 1920, File: St. Elizabeth Settlement: early clippings and items, Central Verein Records.

113. *Central-Blatt and Social Justice*, February 1917; July 1918; October 1917, 218; July 1916.

114. "Endeavors of the Settlement and Day Nursery, Christmas 1927," File: St. Elizabeth Settlement, early clippings and items, Central Verein Records.

115. Dickinson, *Politics of German Child Welfare*, 52–56. Also see *Central-Blatt and Social Justice*, April 1917, for discussion of infant mortality in Germany, and February 1917, on the hospital incident.

116. *Central-Blatt and Social Justice*, August 1916, November 1916.

117. Ibid., February 1917, July 1918. It is unclear whether "Spanish" referred to the nationality or to Spanish speakers from Mexico.

118. Ibid., October 1916, 221; August 1916, 156; September 1916, 187; April 1917, 16.

119. Ibid., November 1918; October 1917; January 1920; February 1917.

120. CWU, *Official Bulletin*, May 15, 1924.

121. Typed manuscript draft of the St. Elizabeth Center Jubilee Celebration [1949?]; St. Elizabeth Day Nursery, 50th Anniversary Pamphlet; Sister Mary Hortence Crabtree, S.S.N.D., "St. Elizabeth Settlement and Day Nursery," 1949, File: St. Elizabeth Settlement; newspaper clipping, *Catholic News*, April 8, 1934, File: St. Elizabeth Settlement: early clippings and items, Central Verein Records.

122. On German child welfare issues, see Dickinson, *Politics of German Child Welfare*.

123. Workman, "Brownson House," 212–13.

124. For more on Brownson House, see McGuinness, "Body and Soul."

125. McGuinness, "A Puzzle with Missing Pieces," 6–16, and "Body and Soul," 69–71; Tentler, *Seasons of Grace*, 226–27. Secondary literature on these efforts remains modest.

126. Brown and McKeown, *The Poor Belong to Us*, 72–85.

CHAPTER FIVE

1. On the charitable activities of women religious in the urban United States, see, for example, Fitzgerald, "Perils of 'Passion and Poverty,'" and Hoy, "Caring for Chicago's Women and Girls," as well as the discussion in Chapter 4.

2. For more on the concept of maternalism as the foundation of women's social reform movements, see Koven and Michel, "Introduction: 'Mother Worlds.'"

3. D.R.K. was an abbreviation of Deutscher Römisch-Katholischer, or German Roman Catholic (abbreviated G.R.C.). The national organization was generally re-

ferred to as the Central Women's Union but was also known as the Frauenbund or the Women's Section of the Central Verein. The state affiliates were usually referred to as leagues or branches. In 1924 the group began referring to itself and its state branches as the National Catholic Women's Union, perhaps to emphasize that it had existed on a national scale prior to the National Council of Catholic Women.

4. An early historian of the Central Verein, Sister Mary L. Brophy, suggests that the Verein provided a mild endorsement of suffrage, but my evidence suggests that most articles opposed it. *Central-Blatt and Social Justice*, August 1912, 102–3; September 1912, 120–21; November 1912, 166; September 1913, 244 n. Brophy, "Social Thought of the German Roman Catholic Central *Verein*," 26–27.

5. Kenneally, "Question of Equality," 130. For an informative discussion of Catholic gender ideologies, including the Eve/Mary dichotomy and the LCW, see Kane, *Separation and Subculture*.

6. McDannell, "Catholic Domesticity," 52–53. McDannell dates the development of a domestic ideology to 1880.

7. Colleen McDannell, Timothy Meagher, and Paula Kane have all mentioned the admonition against idleness. This concern was an important departure from, and indeed a critique of, the upper- and middle-class Protestant values and an indication of the ambivalence of Catholics toward their new prosperity, contrasting with the positive view of single women workers, especially domestics. The attitude was prevalent among German Catholic women as well as among Irish Catholics. See McDannell, *Christian Home in Victorian America*, 50, 61–62; Meagher, " 'Sweet Good Mothers,' " 342; Kane, *Separation and Subculture*, 151–52.

8. On the virtuousness of Irish women, see Diner, *Erin's Daughters in America*, 22. Also see comments by Bishop Spalding in Chapter 3, above. Other examples include *Pilot*, November 6, 1880, and "Why Catholic Girls Are Pure," *Catholic Citizen*, January 21, 1882. The generally negative perception of female factory workers in the nineteenth century was critical to the decision of the Lowell mill owners to build supervised living quarters for "ladies"; see, for example, Dublin, *Women at Work*.

9. *Catholic Citizen*, May 26, 1883.

10. The authors of these articles did not usually have a byline. Paula Kane suggests that Katherine Conway, discussed in Chapter 1, might have written one column in the *Pilot*, "In the Family Sitting Room," that covered domestic issues. Kane, "The Pulpit and the Hearthstone," 363–64.

11. *Catholic Citizen*, February 14, 1880.

12. *Pilot*, March 28, 1891. The *Pilot* reprinted an article from the *New York Ledger*: "Girls who grow up to luxuries of this sort usually make fretful, discontented women, uncomfortable and capricious wives and injudicious, unreliable mothers. Early accustomed to the best of everything, they soon get weary of that, and pine with unsatiable longings for something finer and more costly and rare." *Pilot*, June 11, 1892. Another example appears in John Lancaster Spalding, *Religious Mission*, 92–93: "A fashionable woman can hardly create a happy home or be the mother of true men. The woman of wealth may, indeed resist this temptation and find her happiness in the

fulfillment of duty, but she cannot change the conditions of city life which make the club-house, the theatre, and the ball-room the enemies of the home."

13. *Pilot*, January 26, 1889.

14. *Pilot*, January 23, 1909. For a discussion of middle- and upper-class Protestant charitable work, see Ginzberg, *Women and the Work of Benevolence*.

15. Guild of St. Elizabeth, "Second Annual Report." On the Catholic Young Woman's Society, see *Pilot*, November 4, 1893. See also Wilson, *Young Women's Christian Association*, 1.

16. *Pilot*, January 2, 1904. Toomey, "Queen's Daughters' Society."

17. *Pilot*, February 13, 1892, April 23, 1892; for other examples, see issues of March 16, 1895, May 12, 1900, July 5, 1902, June 10, 1905. Italics mine.

18. On the YLCA commending the work of "the Jewish people" in the area of charity, see *Pilot*, November 25, 1893. On the home's racially and religiously inclusive policy, see *Pilot*, February 1, 1896, March 14, 1896, February 26, 1898, May 29, 1898, May 27, 1899.

19. *Pilot*, March 16, 1889, and March 11, 1893. As if to underscore the qualities of thrift and hard work that characterized Irish Catholic domestic servants, the *Pilot* noted that "Mother" O'Reilly, probably a widow, was able to leave her service position and take on a volunteer job because "by saving she has accumulated some money."

20. *Catholic Charities Review* 2, no. 1 (February 1918): 41–42; see also Count de Montalembert, *Life of Saint Elizabeth*. St. Elizabeth is usually identified with Hungary. That connection was emphasized when she was chosen as the patron saint of the St. Louis settlement house, which was located in a heavily Hungarian neighborhood. The reference to Thuringia in this context was probably meant to emphasize her ties to Germany.

21. *Catholic Charities Review* 2, no. 1 (February 1918): 42; CWU, *Official Bulletin*, November 15, 1923.

22. "Ninth Annual Convention of the Catholic Women's Union, 1925," CCCV 9/04, CCV Collection, UNDA. National Catholic Women's Union, "Fifty Years of Catholic Action, 1916–1966," Pamphlet, File: NCWU Golden Jubilee, Central Verein Records, CVA.

23. Sachße, "Social Mothers."

24. "The Catholic Women's Union of the U.S.A.: What Is It? What [Are] Its Objects? What Does It Accomplish?," n.d. [ca. 1922], PCCV 44/05, CCV Collection. On Faulhaber, see *New Catholic Encyclopedia*, 5:856–57, and *Central-Blatt and Social Justice*, January 1920, 324. On Ketteler, see Grebing, *German Labour Movement*, 192, and *Central-Blatt and Social Justice*, April 1914.

25. CWU, *Official Bulletin*, May 15, 1925.

26. "Clergy and the Catholic Ladies of the Land," CCCV 4/09, CCV Collection.

27. "The Catholic Women's Union: Women's Section of the Central-Verein and Its Immediate Aims," n.d. [ca. 1916], Pamphlet, CCCV 9/04, ibid.

28. *Central-Blatt and Social Justice*, April 1915, 14.

29. Ibid., January 1914, 283; April 1915, 14–15.

30. G.R.C. Women's League of Wisconsin, "Bulletin," no. 4 (1919), PCCV 5, CCV Collection.

31. Ibid.

32. Ibid., no. 3 (1918). An indication of the roles women should emulate is made clear in a poem by Robert Southwell, a Jesuit, published in the "Bulletin," no. 1 (1917), ibid.:

EVA AND AVE

Spell Eva back and Ave you shall find,
The first began and the last reversed our harms;
An Angel's Ave witching words did Eva blind;
An Angel's Ave disenchants the charms;
Death first by women's weakness entered in;
In women's virtue life doth now begin.

33. G.R.C. Women's League of Wisconsin, "Bulletin," no. 1 (1917), ibid.

34. "Constitution of the Missouri Section of the Catholic Women's Union," n.d. [1916?], CCCV 9/04, CCV Collection. *Geschlechtsgenossinnen* literally translates as "gender comrades." The term also had an additional connotation, since by that time it was used by socialists. *Central-Blatt and Social Justice*, October 1915.

35. Spael, *Das katholische Deutschland*, 1–18; Dickinson, *Politics of German Child Welfare*, 36. Reagin, *German Women's Movement*, also discusses the development of women's groups. Spael, Dickinson, and Reagin refer to the group as KDF, but CWU sources refer to it as KFD, or Katholische Frauen Deutschlandes. Dickinson notes that prior to 1921 the organization was known as the Katholischer Frauenverband. It is clear from the leaders' names that the two abbreviations refer to the same organization.

36. Spael, *Das katholische Deutschland*, 1–18. In some ways, German Catholic concerns over participation in labor unions echoed the American Knights of Labor controversy discussed in Chapter 1.

37. Liebschner, *Foundations of Progressive Education*, ix–x; Gutek, *Historical and Philosophical Foundations of Education*, 271. Froebel's methods influenced a young Frank Lloyd Wright.

38. As a result of the harsh reparations policy imposed by the Treaty of Versailles, the Weimer Republic's federal budget shortfall in 1919 equaled the entire federal budget of 1913, and the economy was hit by rampant inflation that would ultimately result in hyperinflation by 1923. In January 1923 the dollar equaled 50,000 marks; by November it was worth 4 trillion marks as German currency plummeted. Herwig, *Hammer or Anvil?*, 235–36.

39. CWU, *Official Bulletin*, January 15 and February 15, 1921.

40. Ibid., January 15, 1921, July 15, 1923, June 15, 1925; Spael, *Das katholische Deutschland*, 23–29, 90, 97.

41. See *Wright's Directory of Milwaukee* (1916). Several officers could not be identified with certainty because the names of wives and daughters did not always appear in the directories.

42. "The Catholic Women's Union," n.d., pamphlet, CCCV 9/04, CCV Collection.

43. Ibid. *Pilot*, March 25, 1905; "Boarding Homes in Belgium," *Catholic Charities Review* 7, no. 9 (November 1923): 343; Marguerite Boylan, "Catholic Women's Leagues in Foreign Countries," *Catholic Charities Review* 4, no. 7 (September 1920): 221. Another article in the same journal mentions a 1910 presentation at the National Conference of Catholic Charities by Reverend Monsignor Mueller-Simonis of Strasbourg on the work of the International Catholic Association for the Protection of Young Girls, which might have been affiliated or otherwise related to the first group. See *Catholic Charities Review* 1, no. 2 (February 1917): 46.

44. On railroad station missions as an important child welfare initiative of reformers in Germany during the 1890s, see Dickinson, *Politics of German Child Welfare*, 39. G.R.C. Women's League of Wisconsin, "Bulletin," no. 3 (1918), no. 4 (1919), PCCV 5, CCV Collection.

45. G.R.C. Women's League of Wisconsin, "Bulletin," no. 3 (1918), no. 4 (1919), no. 7 (1921), no. 8 (1921), and no. 9 (1922), ibid.; National Catholic Women's Union, "Fifty Years of Catholic Action, 1916–1966," Pamphlet, File: NCWU Golden Jubilee, Central Verein Records; CWU, *Official Bulletin*, September 1925.

46. The women were not named. "History of the National Catholic Women's Union, Section Missouri," undated typescript [ca. 1925], File: NCWU Missouri, Central Verein Records.

47. "Twenty-fifth Annual Convention of the Catholic State League of New York, 1922," File: NCWU-1922, Central Verein Records; G.R.C. Women's League of Wisconsin, "Bulletin," no. 4 (1919), PCCV 5, CCV Collection. The Central Verein began referring to itself as the Central Society in this era.

48. CWU, *Official Bulletin*, July 15, 1920.

49. "Ninth Annual Convention of the Catholic Women's Union, 1925," CCCV 9/04, CCV Collection.

50. "Ninth Annual Convention of the Catholic Women's Union Held at Cleveland, Ohio, August 22 to 26 inc. 1925," 10–11, CCCV 8; "An Appeal and a Pledge," January 1, 1922, CCCV 9/04, ibid. In 1928 Cecelia Muehl wrote to F. P. Kenkel expressing her frustration that over the decade she had been unsuccessful in interesting German-speaking priests in the Catholic Women's Union. She noted that the Iowa branch had quit the union, "but I do not want you to blame the laity in this case." Cecelia Muehl to F. P. Kenkel, December 10, 1928, ibid.

51. "An Appeal and a Pledge," January 1, 1922; "Catholic Women's Union," n.d. [ca. 1916], ibid.; G.R.C. Women's League of Wisconsin, "Bulletin," no. 1 (1917), PCCV 5, ibid.; Ladd-Taylor, " 'My Work Came Out of Agony and Grief,' " 322; Lindenmeyer, *"A Right to Childhood."* The *Central-Blatt and Social Justice*, January 1920, published an article supporting mothers' pensions, citing the European model as a good example. It added that the distinction between married and unmarried mothers should "not be overthrown," nor should people be "glorifying" unwed motherhood. It suggested that if motherhood insurance were connected to health insurance, the moral issue could be resolved, adding: "For it goes without saying that unmarried mothers may not be excluded from the benefits of mother-protection (*mutterschutz*). She already bears enough of the misery that burdens her without having material burdens added." That

proponents of Sheppard-Towner generally supported birth control might have contributed to CWU members' objections.

52. Dickinson, *Politics of German Child Welfare*, 20–21, 94–95. On an earlier controversy over the practice of placing out children in New York City, see Fitzgerald, "Charity, Poverty, and Child Welfare."

53. Sophia Wavering to F. P. Kenkel, October 18, 1927, CCCV 4/25, CCV Collection.

54. Sophia Wavering to F. P. Kenkel, November 6, 1927; F. P. Kenkel to Sophia Wavering, November 7, 1927, ibid. National Catholic Women's Union, "Fifty Years of Catholic Action, 1916–1966," Pamphlet, File: NCWU Golden Jubilee, Central Verein Records.

55. Charles Korz to F. P. Kenkel, June 27, 1930, CCCV 4/25, CCV Collection. Italics mine.

56. National Catholic Women's Union, "Fifty Years of Catholic Action, 1916–1966."

57. CWU, *Official Bulletin*, January 15 and May 15, 1921, May 15, 1924, August 15, 1921. National Catholic Women's Union, "Fifty Years of Catholic Action, 1916–1966."

58. CWU, *Official Bulletin*, September 15, 1924.

59. Ibid., September 15, 1923, September 15, 1924, December 15, 1923. National Catholic Women's Union, "Fifty Years of Catholic Action, 1916–1966."

60. Finding Aid, RG VI, 4; "By-Laws and Constitution," Folder 1, Box 1, RG VI, 4, LCW Records, AABo. O'Connell became a cardinal in 1911. Reverend George O'Conor took over Haberlin's duties as spiritual advisor for the league when he succeeded him as director of the Catholic Charitable Bureau in 1922. Michael Scanlan to Richard Haberlin, June 14, 1922, Folder 15, Box 2, RG III D.10, CCB Records, AABo.

61. Cardinal O'Connell was known for his centralized control of the Boston archdiocese and his ultramontanism, or Rome-directed outlook, which many historians attribute in part to his education in Rome. Therefore he stood in contrast to the "Americanist" wing of the hierarchy, which included Archbishop John Ireland and Cardinal James Gibbons. See O'Toole, *Militant and Triumphant*, and Slawson, " 'Boston Tragedy and Comedy.' " On the LCW, see Connolly, "Maternalism in Context."

62. Clipping from the *Montreal Gazette*, January 14, 1920, Folder 9, Box 1; Timothy Callahan to Cardinal O'Connell, May 27, 1918, Folder 3, Box 1; Father Joseph A. Curtin to Cardinal O'Connell, December 3, 1919, Folder 8, Box 1, RG III E.10, LCW Records.

63. *Pilot*, May 14, 1910. Few Italian women were involved in the league through the 1920s, except as the recipients of assistance through its programs in the North and West Ends. One indication of the dearth of Italian participation is a letter written in 1920 in which Richard Haberlin instructed Martha Moore Avery of the league's Committee on Reception to appoint Miss De Ferrari to the committee and to ask her about "any other Italian women whom she might suggest" to serve on the committee for the upcoming bazaar. Richard Haberlin to Mrs. Martha Moore Avery, March 25, 1920, Folder 11, Box 1, RG III E.10, LCW Records.

64. "By-Laws and Constitution," Folder 1, Box 1, RG III E.10, LCW Records. Elizabeth Dwight, an early president of the league, wrote to O'Connell that she would be at her summer house until October, suggesting that she was upper class rather than

middle class. A later president, Lillian Slattery, was the wife of an attorney. Elizabeth Dwight to Cardinal O'Connell, n.d. [1910], Folder 1, Box 1, RG III E.10, LCW Records; "Annual Lecture Course for the Study of Social Service Problems, October 1914–1915." Folder 4, Box 1, RG III D.10, CCB Records.

65. Elizabeth Dwight to Cardinal O'Connell, January 26, 1914; J. P. O'Farrell to Mrs. C. G. Flynn, June 23, 1920, Folder 1, Box 1; note to file [unsigned, probably Richard Haberlin], April 23, 1924, Folder 8, Box 2, RG III E.10, LCW Records.

66. "League of Catholic Women" document, October 1920, Folder 14, Box 1, ibid.

67. The LCW Records reveal the names of the regular lectures but with a few exceptions do not contain transcripts or summaries of them. See "History, [1925]," Folder 9, Box 2, RG VI, 4, ibid.

68. "Report on Probation Work," [1914], Folder 6, Box 1, ibid.

69. "Annual Meeting Reports," April 26, 1914; "Report on Probation Work," [1914]; "Report of Probation Work," May 1, 1915–May 1, 1916, Folder 6, Box 1, ibid. As discussed in the previous chapter, the Society of St. Vincent de Paul barred its members from engaging in charitable work with young women, so this particular program was viewed as a suitable task for women.

70. "Report of the League of Catholic Women, 1910–1912," Folder 3, Box 1, ibid.

71. League of Catholic Women, "Short Essay on the League by Mrs. B. L. Robinson," December 1925, Folder 9, Box 2; Lillian Slattery to Richard Haberlin, September 13, 1923, Folder 7, Box 2; Daniel J. Gillen, Secretary, Office of the Mayor, to Lillian Slattery, September 12, 1923, Folder 7, Box 2; T. B. Lothian to James M. Curley, Mayor, [copy], September 11, 1923, Folder 7, Box 2; Richard Haberlin to Mrs. Francis E. Slattery, October 21, 1922, Folder 5, Box 2, all in RG III E.10, LCW Records.

72. M. J. Splaine to Richard Haberlin, July 21, 1918, Folder 3, Box 1, ibid.

73. Catholic groups such as the Catholic Women's Union often used the term "Traveller's Aid" or "Traveller's Aid Society," as did Catholic groups in Europe. But to make matters confusing, there were also Protestant groups with the same title, including one that was a department of the YWCA and called itself the Traveler's Aid Society. The term seems to have been used both generally and also as a formal title. In Chicago, and probably elsewhere, several groups of various religions created independent traveler's aid societies. It is the latter two to which O'Connell seemed to object, but it is often unclear in discussions of this type of work what specific group is being referred to. "Annual Meeting Reports," [oral], May 1916, Folder 6, Box 1, RG IV, 4, LCW Records. On league activities during the influenza epidemic, see "Report of Director of the Diocesan Charitable Bureau to His Eminence, the Cardinal, on Activities of the Bureau, the Religious Communities, and Charitable Organizations of the Diocese in Conjunction with the Public Health Authorities of the State during the Recent Influenza Epidemic," [October–December 1918], Folder 13, Box 1; and Richard Haberlin to Michael Scanlan, February 12, 1917, Folder 9, Box 1, RG III D.10, CCB Records. On the independent Traveller's Aid Society in Chicago and the YWCA department, see Meyerowitz, *Women Adrift*, 120.

74. R. J. Haberlin to Michael Splaine, November 18, 1916, Folder 3, Box 1, RG III E.10, LCW Records. Correspondence on this controversy is also located in the CCB

Records. In a letter to Scanlan dated November 17, 1916, Haberlin said of the "co-terie" of women that they sought "to have Catholic Charities supply the funds while they supply the prestige; and that a strong microscope is required to find any trace of the virtue of Christian charity in the actions of some." See also Haberlin to Scanlan, November 24, 1916, and Scanlan to Haberlin, December 3, 1918, Folder 8, Box 1, RG III D.10, CCB Records.

75. Michael Scanlan to Cardinal O'Connell, November 22, 1916, Folder 8, Box 1, RG III D.10, CCB Records.

76. It is unclear what the CCB's or Cardinal O'Connell's exact policy was.

77. Dwight no longer served as president of the league at this time, although it is not clear whether the end of her tenure was related to the previous controversy. Martha Moore Avery to Cardinal O'Connell, November 16, 1918; Richard Haberlin to Michael Scanlan, December 3, 1918, Folder 13, Box 1, RG III D.10, CCB Records.

78. R. J. Haberlin to Mrs. Slattery, February 20, 1920, Folder 10, Box 1, RG III E.10, LCW Records. Though often critical of the LCW, O'Connell allowed members to express their elite aspirations by building a rather lavish clubhouse.

79. On Sheehy-Skeffington, see Funchion, *Irish American Voluntary Organizations*, 207. A biography on Sheehy-Skeffington does not mention Margaret Ryan. See also Levenson and Natterstad, *Hanna Sheehy-Skeffington*.

80. Ryan also accused the Knights of Columbus of being "the greatest Anglicizing organization in the world." Margaret Ryan to Cardinal O'Connell, September 25, 1919; Margaret Ryan to Miss Hughes, Irish National Bureau, n.d. [1919], Folder 7, Box 1, RG III E.10, LCW Records. The *Menace* was a rabidly anti-Catholic publication begun in 1911 in the Ozark Mountains. It reached over a million and a half subscribers by 1915 and lost its base soon thereafter. See Higham, *Strangers in the Land*, 180.

81. Slawson, *National Catholic Welfare Council*, 29, 76-77.

82. *Catholic Charities Review* 7, no. 9 (November 1923): 343.

83. Mrs. Francis Slattery to J. H. Hackett, Milwaukee, December 6, 1920, Folder 15, Box 1, RG VI, 4, LCW Records. "Ninth Annual Convention of the Catholic Women's Union," August 1925, 8, CCCV 9/04, CCV Collection.

84. National Council of Catholic Women, "What Women's Organizations Can Do," Service Series, Pamphlet, October 1921, 5, 12-13, 14, Pamphlet Collection, State Historical Society of Wisconsin Library, Madison.

85. Slawson, *National Catholic Welfare Council*, 219; Brown and McKeown, *The Poor Belong to Us*, 70-71; Kennelly, *American Catholic Women*, 119; Mohler, "Agnes Regan as Organizer," 24-25.

86. Richard Haberlin to Mrs. Slattery, December 9, 1924, Folder 9, Box 2, RG III E.10, LCW Records. On avoiding politics, see Cardinal O'Connell to Michael Splaine, October 18, 1932, Folder 11, Box 2, ibid. Lillian Slattery, letter titled "for Circulation," June 5, 1929, Folder 10, Box 2, RG VI, 4, ibid. On O'Connell's angry reaction to Ryan's and Regan's support of the amendment, see Broderick, *Right Reverend New Dealer*, 155-59. See also Slawson, *National Catholic Welfare Council*, 222. Clipping from *Congressional Digest*, February 1923, 141, in Folder 8, Box 2, RG III E.10, LCW

Records. Lillian Slattery to Agnes Regan, October 15, 1924, Folder 9, Box 2, ibid. *Catholic Charities Review* 5, no. 9 (November 1921): 302–3.

87. National Council of Catholic Women, "What Women's Organizations Can Do," 6, 25, 27–28.

88. Ibid., 31.

89. *Catholic Charities Review* 5, no. 9 (November 1921): 303.

CONCLUSION

1. Coles, *Dorothy Day.*

2. Ibid., 81.

Bibliography

MANUSCRIPT COLLECTIONS

Boston, Massachusetts
Archives, Archdiocese of Boston
   Catholic Charitable Bureau Records
   League of Catholic Women Records
   Priests Total Abstinence League Papers
   Sacred Heart Parish Records
     Father Mathew Total Abstinence Society Records
   James Anthony Walsh Papers
Massachusetts Historical Society
   Charitable Irish Society Records

Chicago, Illinois
Joseph Cardinal Bernardin Archives and Record Center, Archdiocese of Chicago
   Chancery Correspondence
   Chancery Records
   Madaj Collection
     Irish Catholic Colonization Association Records
   National Catholic Welfare Council Annual Report
   Society of St. Vincent de Paul Collection

Milwaukee, Wisconsin
Archives, Marquette University
   Madonna Center Records

Notre Dame, Indiana
Archives, University of Notre Dame
   Patrick Callahan Papers
   Catholic Central Verein Collection
   Peter Cooney Papers
   William Onahan Papers

St. Louis, Missouri
Central Bureau, Catholic Central Union of America

Central Verein Archives
   Central Verein Records
   Microfilm Collection
   St. Elizabeth Settlement Records

NEWSPAPERS AND PERIODICALS

The Boston Post
Catholic Charities Review
Catholic Citizen (Milwaukee)
Central-Blatt and Social Justice (St. Louis)
Monatsbote (Boston)
Pall Mall Gazette (London)
The Pilot (Boston)
St. Vincent de Paul Quarterly

PUBLISHED PRIMARY SOURCES

Addams, Jane. *Twenty Years at Hull-House, with Autobiographical Notes*. New York:
   Macmillan, 1911.
Amberg, Mary Agnes. *Madonna Center: Pioneer Catholic Social Settlement*. 1942.
   Chicago: Loyola University Press, 1976.
Bennett, Canon J. *Father Nugent of Liverpool*. Liverpool: Liverpool Catholic
   Children's Protection Society, 1949.
Budenz, Louis F. *This Is My Story*. New York: McGraw-Hill, 1947.
Catholic Colonization Bureau of Minnesota. "Catholic Colonization in Minnesota,
   Colony of Avoca, Murray County, Southwestern Minnesota." Pamphlet. St. Paul:
   Pioneer Press, 1880. Pamphlets in American History Microform Collection.
Crèvecoeur, J. Hector St. John de. *Letters from an American Farmer*. 1783. Reprint,
   New York: Oxford University Press, 1997.
Dinneen, Maurice. *The Catholic Total Abstinence Movement*. Boston: Grimes
   Company, 1908.
Fusco, Rev. Nicola. "The Italian Racial Strain." In *Catholic Builders of the Nation*,
   vol. 2, edited by C. E. McGuire, 111–26. Boston: Continental Press, 1923.
Gallery, Mary Onahan. *Life of William J. Onahan: Stories of Men Who Made Chicago*.
   Chicago: Loyola University Press, 1929.
Gladden, Washington. "The Anti-Catholic Crusade." *Century Magazine* 25 (March
   1894): 789–95.
Guild of St. Elizabeth. "Second Annual Report. 1900." Pamphlet.
Gwynn, Stephen. *Charlotte Grace O'Brien, 1845–1909: Selections from Her Writings
   and Correspondence with a Memoir by Stephen Gwynn*. Dublin: Mausel and
   Company, 1909. New Haven, Conn.: Research Publications Microfilm, History of
   Women Collection, 1977.

Hughes, William H. *Souvenir Volume Illustrated: Three Great Events in the History of the Catholic Church in the United States.* Detroit: W. H. Hughes, 1890.

Kerby, William J. *The Social Mission of Charity: A Study of Point of View in Catholic Charities.* New York: Macmillan, 1921.

Montalembert, Count de. *The Life of St. Elizabeth of Hungary, Duchess of Thuringia.* New York: D. and J. Sadlier and Company, 1879.

National Council of Catholic Women. "What Women's Organizations Can Do." Service Series. Pamphlet. October 1921.

Neill, Charles Patrick. "Training for Social Work." In "Proceedings, National Conference of Charities." Washington, D.C., 1914. Reprinted in *American Catholic Thought on Social Questions,* edited by Aaron Abell, 277–86. Indianapolis: Bobbs-Merrill, 1968.

Palmieri, Rev. Aurelio. "The Contribution of the Italian Clergy to the United States." In *Catholic Builders of the Nation,* vol. 2, edited by C. E. McGuire, 127–49. Boston: Continental Press, 1923.

Powderly, Terence. *The Path I Trod.* New York: Columbia University Press, 1940.

St. Raphael Society of America. "Golden Jubilee of the Leo House St. Raphael Society of New York: For the Protection of Catholic Travelers." Pamphlet. New York; Leo House Corporation, 1939.

Sewall, Mary Wright, ed. *Congress of Representative Women.* New Haven, Conn.: Research Publications Microfilm, History of Women Collection, 1977.

Sharkey, Sister Mary Agnes. *The New Jersey Sisters of Charity: Our Missions, 1859–1933.* New York: Longmans, Green, 1933.

Society of St. Vincent de Paul. "Annual Report of the Upper Council of St. Louis for the Year Ending December 1, 1883." N.p., 1884.

———. *Proceedings of the International Convention of the St. Vincent de Paul Society, St. Louis, Mo. September 1904.* St. Louis: Little and Becker Printing Company, 1904.

———. *Proceedings of the National Conference of the Society of St. Vincent de Paul.* Boston: Office of the Central Council, 1911.

———. *Report of Proceedings at the Fourth General Assembly of the Society of St. Vincent de Paul in the United States and Canada.* New York: M. A. Grogan, 1886.

———. *Report of the Superior Council of New York to the Council General in Paris for the Year 1909.* New York: The Society/Press of the Immaculate Virgin, 1909.

———. *Rules of the Society of St. Vincent de Paul.* American ed. N.p., 1924.

———. "Sixth Annual Report of the Society of St. Vincent de Paul by the Particular Council of Milwaukee, Wis., for the Year Ending September 30, 1919." Pamphlet.

Souvay, Charles L., C.M., D.D. "The Society of St. Vincent de Paul." *Catholic Historical Review,* n.s., 1 (1921–22): 441–57.

Spalding, John Lancaster. *The Religious Mission of the Irish People and Catholic Colonization.* New York: Catholic Publication Society, 1880; reprint, New York: Arno Press, 1978.

Toomey, Mary. "The Queen's Daughters' Society." *Catholic Charities Review* 1, no. 2 (February 1917): 43–46.

Workman, Mary J. "Brownson House." *Catholic Charities Review* 2, no. 7 (September 1918): 212–13.

World's Columbian Catholic Congresses and Educational Exhibit. Vols. 1 and 3. Chicago: J. S. Hyland Company, 1893; reprint (2 vols. in 1), New York: Arno Press, 1978.

SECONDARY SOURCES

Abell, Aaron I. *American Catholicism and Social Action: A Search for Social Justice, 1865–1950.* Garden City, N.Y.: Hanover House, 1960.

Alexander, Ruth. *The "Girl Problem": Female Sexual Delinquency in New York, 1900–1930.* Ithaca, N.Y.: Cornell University Press, 1995.

Allitt, Patrick. *Catholic Converts: British and American Intellectuals Turn to Rome.* Ithaca, N.Y.: Cornell University Press, 1997.

———. *Catholic Intellectuals and Conservative Politics in America, 1950–1985.* Ithaca, N.Y.: Cornell University Press, 1993.

Archdeacon, Thomas. *Becoming American: An Ethnic History.* New York: Free Press, 1983.

Audyaitis, Sister M. Timothy. "Catholic Action of the Lithuanians in the United States: A History of the American Lithuanian Roman Catholic Federation, 1906–1956." Master's thesis, Loyola University, 1958.

Badger, Rodney Reid. *The Great Fair: The World's 1893 Columbian Exhibition and American Culture.* Chicago: Nelson Hall, 1979.

Barry, Colman. *The Catholic Church and German Americans.* Milwaukee: Bruce Publishing Company, 1953.

Beck, Bishop George A., ed. *The English Catholics, 1850–1950.* London: Burns Oates and Washburn, 1960.

Bernstein, Iver. *The New York City Draft Riots.* New York: Oxford University Press, 1990.

Billington, Ray. *The Protestant Crusade, 1800–1860.* New York: Macmillan, 1938; reprint, Gloucester, Mass.: Peter Smith, 1963.

Blackbourn, David. *The Long Nineteenth Century: A History of Germany, 1780–1918.* New York: Oxford University, 1998.

Bland, Joan. *The Hibernian Crusade: The Story of the Catholic Total Abstinence Union of America.* Washington, D.C.: Catholic University of America Press, 1951.

Blumin, Stuart. *The Emergence of the Middle Class: Social Experience in the American City, 1760–1900.* New York: Cambridge University Press, 1989.

Bodnar, John. *Remaking America: Public Memory, Commemoration, and Patriotism in The Twentieth Century.* Princeton: Princeton University Press, 1992.

———. *The Transplanted: A History of Immigrants in Urban America.* Bloomington: Indiana University Press, 1985.

Bordin, Ruth. *Woman and Temperance: The Quest for Power and Liberty, 1873–1900.* New Brunswick, N.J.: Rutgers University Press, 1990.

Boyer, Paul. *Urban Masses and Moral Order in America, 1820–1920*. Cambridge: Harvard University Press, 1978.

Braunagel-Brown, Mary Anne. "The Pineapple of Philanthropy: Aspects of Philanthropy and Charity in Early Nineteenth-Century Paris." Ph.D. diss., University of Texas–Austin, 1983.

Broderick, Francis. *The Right Reverend New Dealer, John A. Ryan*. New York: Macmillan, 1963.

Brophy, Sister Mary Liguori. "The Social Thought of the German Roman Catholic Central Verein." Ph.D. diss., Catholic University, 1941.

Brown, Dorothy, and Elizabeth McKeown. *The Poor Belong to Us: Catholic Charities and American Welfare*. Cambridge: Harvard University Press, 1997.

Brown, Thomas N. *Irish-American Nationalism, 1870–1890*. Philadelphia: Lippincott, 1966.

Browne, Henry J. "Archbishop Hughes and Western Colonization." *Catholic Historical Review* 36, no. 3 (October 1950): 257–85.

Buczek, Daniel B. "Polish-Americans and the Roman Catholic Church." In *Other Catholics*, edited by Keith P. Dyrud, Michael Novak, and Rudolph J. Vecoli, pt. 5, 39–61. New York: Arno Press, 1978.

Byrne, Patricia, C.S.J. "Sisters of St. Joseph: The Americanization of a French Tradition." *U.S. Catholic Historian* 5, nos. 3 and 4 (1986): 241–72.

Cada, Joseph. "The Pioneers, Czech-Catholics after 1850." In *Other Catholics*, edited by Keith P. Dyrud, Michael Novak, and Rudolph J. Vecoli, pt. 1, 1–46. New York: Arno Press, 1978.

Campbell, Deborah. "Reformers and Activists." In *American Catholic Women: A Historical Exploration*, edited by Karen Kennelly, 152–81. New York: Macmillan, 1989.

Carson, Mina. *Settlement Folk: Social Thought and the American Settlement Movement*. Chicago: University of Chicago Press, 1990.

Chan, Sucheng. *Asian America: An Interpretive History*. Boston: Twayne Publishers, 1991.

Clark, Norman. *Deliver Us from Evil: An Interpretation of American Prohibition*. New York: W. W. Norton, 1976.

Cleary, James F. "Catholic Participation in the World's Parliament of Religions, Chicago, 1893." *Catholic Historical Review* 55, no. 4 (January 1970): 585–609.

Cochran, Alice Lida. "The Saga of an Irish Immigrant Family: The Descendants of John Mullanphy." Ph.D. diss., Saint Louis University, 1958.

Cohen, Lizabeth. *Making a New Deal: Industrial Workers in Chicago, 1919–1939*. New York: Cambridge University Press, 1990.

Coles, Robert. *Dorothy Day: A Radical Devotion*. Reading, Mass.: Addison-Wesley, 1987.

Connolly, James J. "Maternalism in Context: Protestant and Catholic Women's Activism in Progressive-Era Boston." *Mid-America* 81, no. 2 (Summer 1999): 91–123.

———. *The Triumph of Ethnic Progressivism: Urban Political Culture in Boston, 1900–1925*. Cambridge, Mass.: Harvard University Press, 1998.

Conzen, Kathleen Neils. *Immigrant Milwaukee, 1836–1860*. Cambridge: Harvard University Press, 1976.

Cote, Jane. *Fanny and Anna Parnell: Ireland's Patriot Sisters*. Dublin: Gill and Macmillan, 1991.

Cross, Robert D. *The Emergence of Liberal Catholicism in America*. Cambridge: Harvard University Press, 1958.

Culberson, Diana.,ed. *Rose Hawthorne Lathrop: Selected Writings*. Mahwah, N.J.: Paulist Press, 1993.

Curran, Robert Emmett, S.J. "The McGlynn Affair and the Shaping of the New Conservatism in American Catholicism, 1886–1894." *Catholic Historical Review* 66, no. 2 (1980): 184–204.

———. *Michael Augustine Corrigan and the Shaping of Conservative Catholicism in America, 1878–1902*. New York: Arno Press, 1978.

———. "Prelude to 'Americanism': The New York Accademia and Clerical Radicalism in the Late Nineteenth Century." *Church History* 47, no. 1 (1978): 48–65.

Curtis, L. Perry. *Apes and Angels: The Irishman in Victorian Caricature*. Rev. ed. Washington D.C.: Smithsonian Institution Press, 1997.

Dannenbaum, Jed. *Drink and Disorder: Temperance Reform in Cincinnati from the Washington Revival to WCTU*. Urbana: University of Illinois Press, 1984.

Davis, Allen F. *Spearheads for Reform: The Social Settlements and the Progressive Movement, 1890–1914*. New York: Oxford University Press, 1967.

Davis, Cyprian, O.S.B. *The History of Black Catholics in the United States*. New York: Crossroad Press, 1990.

Davis, Richard. *The Young Ireland Movement*. Dublin: Gill and Macmillan, 1987; New York: Barnes and Noble, 1988.

Davis, Susan G. *Parades and Power: Street Theatre in Nineteenth-Century Philadelphia*. Berkeley: University of California Press, 1986.

Dickinson, Edward Ross. *The Politics of German Child Welfare from the Empire to the Federal Republic*. Cambridge: Harvard University Press, 1996.

Diner, Hasia R. *Erin's Daughters in America: Irish Immigrant Women in the Nineteenth Century*. Baltimore: Johns Hopkins University Press, 1983.

Doenecke, Justus D. "Myths, Machines, and Markets: The Columbian Exposition of 1893." *Journal of Popular Culture* 6, no. 3 (1972): 535–44.

Dolan, Jay P. *American Catholics*. New York: Oxford University Press, 1981.

———. *The Immigrant Church: New York's Irish and German Catholics, 1815–1865*. Notre Dame, Ind.: University of Notre Dame Press, 1975.

Downey, Dennis B. "Tradition and Acceptance: American Catholics and the Columbia Exposition." *Mid-America* 63, no. 2 (1981): 79–92.

Dublin, Thomas. *Women at Work: The Transformation of Work and Community in Lowell, Massachusetts, 1826–1860*. New York: Columbia University Press, 1979.

Faler, Paul. "Cultural Aspects of the Industrial Revolution: Lynn, Massachusetts, Shoemakers and Industrial Morality, 1926–1860." *Labor History* 15, no. 3 (Summer 1974): 367–94.

Finley, Joseph. *The Corrupt Kingdom*. New York: Simon and Schuster, 1972.

Fitzgerald, Maureen. "Charity, Poverty, and Child Welfare." *Harvard Divinity Bulletin* 25, no. 4 (1996): 12–17.

———. "Irish-Catholic Nuns and the Development of New York City's Welfare System, 1840–1900." Ph.D. diss., University of Wisconsin–Madison, 1992.

———. "The Perils of 'Passion and Poverty': Women Religious and the Care of Single Women in New York City, 1845–1890." *U.S. Catholic Historian* 10, nos. 1–2 (1991): 45–58.

Fogarty, Gerald, S.J. "The Catholic Hierarchy in the United States between the Third Plenary Council and the Condemnation of Americanism." *U.S. Catholic Historian* 11, no. 3 (Summer 1993): 19–35.

Foner, Eric. "Class, Ethnicity, and Radicalism in the Gilded Age: The Land League and Irish America." *Marxist Perspectives* 1, no. 2 (Summer 1978): 6–55.

———. *Free Soil, Free Labor, Free Men: The Ideology of the Republican Party before the Civil War*. New York: Oxford University Press, 1970.

Franchot, Jenny. *Roads to Rome: The Antebellum Protestant Encounter with Catholicism*. Berkeley: University of California Press, 1984.

Funchion, Michael F., ed. *Irish American Voluntary Organizations*. Westport, Conn.: Greenwood Press, 1983.

Gabaccia, Donna. *From the Other Side: Women, Gender, and Immigrant Life in the U.S., 1820–1990*. Bloomington: Indiana University Press, 1994.

Gallagher, Mary B. "The Americanist Hierarchy: Their Attempts to Integrate American and Catholic Culture." Ed.D. diss, Columbia University Teachers College, 1986.

Gillis, John. "Servants, Sexual Relations, and the Risks of Illegitimacy in London, 1801–1900." *Feminist Studies* 5, no. 1 (Spring 1979): 142–73.

Ginzberg, Lori. *Women and the Work of Benevolence: Morality, Politics, and Class in the Nineteenth-Century United States*. New Haven: Yale University Press, 1990.

Glassberg, David. *American Historical Pageantry: The Uses of Tradition in the Early Twentieth Century*. Chapel Hill: University of North Carolina Press, 1990.

Gleason, Philip. *The Conservative Reformers: German-American Catholics and the Social Order*. Notre Dame, Ind.: University of Notre Dame Press, 1968.

———. *Keeping the Faith: American Catholicism Past and Present*. Notre Dame, Ind.: University of Notre Dame Press, 1987.

———. "The New Americanism in Catholic Historiography." *U.S. Catholic Historian* 11, no. 3 (Summer 1993): 1–18.

Gluck, Elsie. *John Mitchell—Miner—Labor's Bargain with the Gilded Age*. New York: John Day Company, 1929.

Gordon, Linda. *Heroes of Their Own Lives: The Politics and History of Family Violence*. New York: Viking Press, 1988.

[Gorman], Sister M. Adele Francis. "Lay Activity of the Catholic Congresses of 1889 and 1893." *Records of the American Catholic Historical Society of Philadelphia* 74 (March–December 1963): 3–23.

Grebing, Helga. *The History of the German Labour Movement*. Rev. ed.
  Warwickshire: Berg Publishers, 1985.
Greene, Victor. "For God and Country: The Origins of Slavic Catholic Self-
  Consciousness in America." *Church History* 35 (1966): 446–60.
Gusfield, Joseph. *Symbolic Crusade: Status, Politics, and the American Temperance
  Movement*. Urbana: University of Illinois Press, 1966.
Gutek, Gerald L. *Historical and Philosophical Foundations of Education: A
  Biographical Introduction*. 2d ed. New York: Prentice-Hall, 1997.
Halsey, William. *The Survival of American Innocence: Catholicism in an Era of
  Disillusionment, 1920–1940*. Notre Dame, Ind.: University of Notre Dame Press,
  1980.
Hearn, Mona. *Below Stairs: Domestic Service Remembered in Dublin and Beyond,
  1880–1922*. Dublin: Lilliput Press, 1993.
Hellerstein, Erna Olafson, Leslie Parker Hume, and Karen Offen, eds. *Victorian
  Women: A Documentary Account of Women's Lives in Nineteenth-Century
  England, France, and the United States*. Stanford, Calif.: Stanford University
  Press, 1981.
Helmes, Rev. J. W. "Thomas Mulry: A Volunteer's Contribution to Social Work."
  Ph.D. diss., Catholic University, 1938.
Hennesey, James. *American Catholics*. New York: Oxford University Press, 1981.
Henthorne, Mary Evangela, B.V.M. "The Career of the Right Reverend John
  Lancaster Spalding, Bishop of Peoria, as President of the Irish Catholic
  Colonization Association of the United States, 1879–1892." Ph.D. diss.,
  University of Illinois, 1930.
Herwig, Holger H. *Hammer or Anvil?: Modern Germany, 1648–Present*. Lexington,
  Mass.: D. C. Heath, 1994.
Higham, John. *Strangers in the Land: Patterns of American Nativism, 1860–1925*. 2d
  ed. New Brunswick, N.J.: Rutgers University Press, 1988.
Hoy, Suellen. "Caring for Chicago's Women and Girls: The Sisters of the Good
  Shepherd, 1859–1911." *Journal of Urban History* 23, no. 3 (1997): 260–94.
Huggins, Nathan. *Protestants against Poverty: Boston's Charities, 1870–1900*.
  Westport, Conn.: Greenwood Publishing, 1971.
Hutchinson, Ruth Crocker. *Social Work and Social Order: The Settlement Movement
  in Two Industrial Cities, 1889–1930*. Urbana: University of Illinois Press, 1992.
Ignatiev, Noel. *How the Irish Became White*. New York: Routledge, 1995.
Jacobson, Matthew F. *Special Sorrows: The Diasporic Imagination of Irish, Polish,
  and Jewish Immigrants in the United States*. Cambridge: Harvard University Press,
  1995.
———. *Whiteness of a Different Color: European Immigrants and the Alchemy of Race*.
  Cambridge: Harvard University Press, 1998.
Janus, Glen. "Bishop Bernard McQuaid: On 'True' and 'False' Americanism." *U.S.
  Catholic Historian* 11, no. 3 (Summer 1993): 53–76.
Johnson, Paul E. *Shopkeeper's Millennium: Society and Revivals in Rochester, New
  York*. New York: Hill and Wang, 1978.

Juliani, Richard N. "The Parish as an Urban Institution." *Records of the American Catholic Historical Society of Philadelphia* 96, nos. 1–4 (1986): 49–66.

Kane, Paula M. "The Pulpit and the Hearthstone: Katherine Conway and Boston Catholic Women, 1900–1920." *U.S. Catholic Historian* 5, nos. 3 and 4 (Summer/Fall 1986): 355–70.

———. *Separation and Subculture: Boston Catholicism, 1900–1920.* Chapel Hill: University of North Carolina Press, 1994.

Kauffman, Christopher. *Faith and Fraternalism: The History of the Knights of Columbus, 1882–1992.* New York: Harper and Row, 1982.

Kearney, H. F. "Fr. Mathew: Apostle of Modernisation." In *Studies in Irish History Presented to R. Dudley Edwards*, edited by Art Cosgrove and Donal McCartney, 164–75. Dublin: University College Dublin, 1979.

Kee, Robert. *The Laurel and the Ivy: The Story of Charles Stewart Parnell and Irish Nationalism.* London: Hamish Hamilton, 1993.

Kelly, Mary Gilbert, O.P. *Catholic Immigration Colonization Projects in the United States, 1815–1860.* New York: United States Catholic Historical Society, 1939; reprint, New York: Jerome Ozer, 1971.

Kenneally, James J. *The History of American Catholic Women.* New York: Crossroad Press, 1990.

———. "A Question of Equality." In *American Catholic Women: A Historical Exploration*, edited by Karen Kennelly, 152–81. New York: Macmillan, 1989.

———. "Reflections on Historical Catholic Women." *U.S. Catholic Historian* 5, nos. 3 and 4 (Summer/Fall 1986): 411–18.

———. "Sexism, the Church, Irish Women." *Éire* 21, no. 3 (1986): 3–16.

Kennelly, Karen, ed. *American Catholic Women: A Historical Exploration.* New York: Macmillan, 1989.

Kerrigan, Colm. "Father Mathew and Teetotalism in London, 1843." *London Journal* 2, no. 2 (1985): 107–14.

———. "The Social Impact of the Irish Temperance Movement, 1839–1835." *Irish Economic and Social History* 14 (1987): 20–38.

Kinzer, Donald L. *An Episode in Anti-Catholicism: The American Protective Association.* Seattle: University of Washington Press, 1964.

Kissane, Noel, ed. *The Irish Famine: A Documentary History.* Dublin: National Library of Ireland, 1995.

Koven, Seth, and Sonya Michel, eds. "Introduction: 'Mother Worlds.'" In *Mothers of a New World: Maternalist Politics and the Origins of Welfare States*, 1–42. New York: Routledge, 1992.

Ladd-Taylor, Molly. "'My Work Came Out of Agony and Grief': Mothers and the Making of the Sheppard-Towner Act." In *Mothers of a New World: Maternalist Politics and the Origins of Welfare States*, edited by Seth Koven and Sonya Michel, 321–42. New York: Routledge, 1992.

Lane, Roger. "James Jeffrey Roche and the Boston *Pilot*." *New England Quarterly* 33, no. 3 (1960): 341–63.

Larkin, Emmet. "The Devotional Revolution in Ireland, 1850–75." *American Historical Review* 77, no. 3 (June 1972): 625–52.

Lavey, Patrick. "William J. Kerby, John A. Ryan, and the Awakening of the Twentieth-Century American Catholic Conscience, 1899–1919." Ph.D. diss., University of Illinois, 1986.

Leckie, Robert. *American and Catholic.* Garden City, N.Y.: Doubleday, 1970.

Lee, W. R., and Eve Rosenhaft, eds. *The State and Social Change in Germany, 1880–1980.* New York: Berg Publishers, 1990.

Leonard, John W., ed. *Who's Who in America, 1899–1900.* Chicago: A. N. Marquist Company, 1899.

Lescher, Bruce H. "William J. Kerby: A Lost Voice in American Spirituality." *Records of the American Catholic Historical Society of Philadelphia* 102, nos. 1–2 (1991): 1–16.

Levenson, Leah, and Jerry Natterstad. *Hanna Sheehy-Skeffington: Irish Feminist.* Syracuse, N.Y.: Syracuse University Press, 1986.

Levine, Susan B. "Labor's True Woman: Domesticity and Equal Rights in the Knights of Labor." *Journal of American History* 70, no. 2 (September 1983): 323–39.

Liebschner, Joachim. *Foundations of Progressive Education: The History of the National Froebel Society.* Cambridge: Lutterworth Press, 1991.

Lindenmeyer, Kriste. *"A Right to Childhood": The U.S. Children's Bureau and Child Welfare, 1912–46.* Urbana: University of Illinois Press, 1997.

Liptak, Dolores. *Immigrants and Their Church.* New York: Macmillan, 1989.

Lissak, Rivka. "Myth and Reality: The Pattern of Relationship between the Hull House Circle and the 'New Immigrants' on Chicago's West Side, 1890–1919." *Journal of American Ethnic History* 2, no. 2 (1983): 21–50.

——. *Pluralism and Progressives: Hull House and the New Immigrants, 1890–1919.* Chicago: University of Chicago Press, 1989.

Lubove, Roy. *The Professional Altruist: The Emergence of Social Work as a Career, 1880–1930.* Cambridge: Harvard University Press, 1965.

Luddy, Maria. "Women and Charitable Organizations in Nineteenth-Century Ireland." *Women's Studies International Forum* 11, no. 4 (1988): 301–5.

——. *Women and Philanthropy in Nineteenth-Century Ireland.* London: Cambridge University Press, 1995.

Lyons, F. S. L. *Ireland since the Famine.* New York: Scribner's, 1971.

McCarthy, Kathleen D. *Noblesse Oblige: Charity and Cultural Philanthropy in Chicago, 1849–1929.* Chicago: University of Chicago Press, 1982.

McColgan, Daniel. *A Century of Charity: The First One Hundred Years of the Society of St. Vincent de Paul in the United States.* Vol. 1. Milwaukee: Bruce Publishing Company, 1951.

McDannell, Colleen. "Catholic Domesticity." In *American Catholic Women: A Historical Exploration,* edited by Karen Kennelly, 48–80. New York: Macmillan, 1989.

——. *The Christian Home in Victorian America.* Bloomington: Indiana University Press, 1986.

McDermott, Edith Swain. *The Pioneer History of Greeley County, Nebraska.* Greeley, Nebr.: Citizen Printing, 1939.

McGuinness, Margaret M. "Body and Soul: Catholic Social Settlements and Immigration." *U.S. Catholic Historian* 13, nos. 3 and 4 (Summer 1995): 63–75.

———. "A Puzzle with Missing Pieces: Catholic Women and the Social Settlement Movement, 1897–1915." Working Paper Series. Cushwa Center for the Study of Catholicism, University of Notre Dame, 1990.

———. "Response to Reform: An Historical Interpretation of the Catholic Settlement Movement, 1897–1915." Ph.D. diss., Union Theological Seminary, 1985.

McLellan, Daniel. "A History of the Catholic Charitable Bureau of the Archdiocese of Boston." Ph.D. diss., University of Notre Dame, 1984.

McNamara, Jo Ann. *Sisters in Arms: Catholic Nuns through Two Millennia.* Cambridge: Harvard University Press, 1996.

Maguire, John Francis. *Father Mathew: A Biography.* Edited by Rosa Mullholland. London: Longman, Green, Longman, 1863; reprint, Dublin: Eason and Son, [1890?].

Malcolm, Elizabeth. "The Catholic Church and the Irish Temperance Movement, 1838–1901." *Irish Historical Studies* 23, no. 89 (1982): 1–16.

———. *"Ireland Sober, Ireland Free": Drink and Temperance in Nineteenth-Century Ireland.* Syracuse, N.Y.: Syracuse University Press, 1986.

Meagher, Timothy J. " 'The Lord Is Not Dead': Cultural and Social Change among the Irish in Worcester, Massachusetts." Ph.D. diss., Brown University, 1982.

———. " 'Sweet Good Mothers and Young Women Out in the World': The Roles of Irish American Women in Late Nineteenth and Early Twentieth Century Worcester, Massachusetts." *U.S. Catholic Historian* 5, nos. 3 and 4 (Summer/Fall 1986): 325–44.

Meehan, Thomas. *Thomas Maurice Mulry.* New York: Encyclopedia Press, 1917.

Merwick, Donna. *Boston Priests, 1848–1910: A Study of Social and Intellectual Change.* Cambridge: Harvard University Press, 1973.

Meyerowitz, Joanne. *Women Adrift: Independent Wage Earners in Chicago, 1880–1930.* Chicago: University of Chicago Press, 1988.

Miller, Kerby A. *Emigrants and Exiles: Ireland and the Irish Exodus to North America.* New York: Oxford University Press, 1985.

Mohler, Dorothy A. "Agnes Regan as Organizer of the National Council of Catholic Women and the National Catholic School of Social Service." In *Pioneering Women at the Catholic University of America: Papers Presented at a Centennial Symposium,* edited by E. Catherine Dunn and Dorothy A. Mohler, 21–35. Hyattsville, Md.: International Graphics, 1990.

Moran, Gerard. " 'In Search of the Promised Land': The Connemara Colonization Scheme to Minnesota, 1880." *Éire-Ireland* 31, nos. 3 and 4 (1996): 130–49.

Morgan, Edmund S. *American Slavery, American Freedom: The Ordeal of Colonial Virginia.* New York: Norton, 1975.

———. *Inventing the People: The Rise of Popular Sovereignty in England and America.* New York: Norton, 1988.

Murphy, Maureen. "Charlotte Grace O'Brien and the Mission of Our Lady of the Rosary for the Protection of Irish Immigrant Girls." *Mid-America* 74, no. 3 (October 1992): 353–70.

———. "A Mission Remembered." *American Irish Historical Society Recorder* 43 (1982): 104–9.

New Catholic Encyclopedia. Washington, D.C.: Catholic University Press, 1967.

Oates, Mary J. *The Catholic Philanthropic Tradition in America.* Bloomington: Indiana University Press, 1995.

———. "Catholic Women in the Labor Force." In *American Catholic Women: A Historical Exploration,* edited by Karen Kennelly, 81–124. New York: MacMillan, 1989.

O'Brien, David J. *American Catholics and Social Reform: The New Deal Years.* New York: Oxford University Press, 1968.

———. *Isaac Hecker: An American Catholic.* New York: Paulist Press, 1994.

Ochs, Stephen J. *Desegregating the Altar: The Josephites and the Struggle for Black Priests, 1871–1960.* Baton Rouge: Louisiana State University Press, 1990.

O'Connell, Marvin. *John Ireland and the American Catholic Church.* St. Paul: Minnesota Historical Society Press, 1988.

Odem, Mary. *Delinquent Daughters: Protecting and Policing Adolescent Female Sexuality in the United States, 1885–1920.* Chapel Hill: University of North Carolina Press, 1995.

Orsi, Robert A. *The Madonna of 115th Street: Faith and Community in Italian Harlem, 1880–1950.* New Haven: Yale University Press, 1985.

———. *Thank You, St. Jude: Women's Devotion to the Patron Saint of Hopeless Causes.* New Haven: Yale University Press, 1996.

O'Toole, James M. *From Generation to Generation: Stories in Catholic History from the Archives of the Archdiocese of Boston.* Boston: St. Paul Editions, 1983.

———. *Militant and Triumphant: William Henry O'Connell and the Catholic Church in Boston.* Notre Dame, Ind.: University of Notre Dame Press, 1992.

Pahorezki, M. Sevina, O.S.F. "The Social and Political Activities of William James Onahan." Ph.D. diss., Catholic University, 1942.

Parot, Joseph. *Polish Catholics in Chicago, 1850–1920.* Dekalb: Northern Illinois University Press, 1981.

Phelan, Craig. *Divided Loyalties: The Public and Private Life of Labor Leader John Mitchell.* Albany: State University of New York Press, 1994.

Quinn, John F. "The Vagabond Friar: Father Mathew's Difficulties with the Irish Bishops, 1840–1856." *Catholic Historical Review* 78, no. 4 (1992): 542–56.

Reagin, Nancy. *A German Women's Movement: Class and Gender in Hanover, 1880–1933.* Chapel Hill: University of North Carolina Press, 1995.

Rodgers, Daniel T. *Atlantic Crossings: Social Politics in a Progressive Age.* Cambridge, Mass.: Belknap Press, 1998.

Roediger, David R. *The Wages of Whiteness: Race and the Making of the American Working Class.* New York: Verso Press, 1991.

Rose, Elizabeth. "From Sponge Cake to *Hamentashen*: Jewish Identity in a Jewish

Settlement House, 1885–1952." *Journal of American Ethnic History* 13, no. 3 (Spring 1994): 3–23.

Rosen, Ruth. *The Lost Sisterhood: Prostitution in America, 1900–1918.* Baltimore: Johns Hopkins University Press, 1982.

Rosenzweig, Roy. *Eight Hours for What We Will: Workers and Leisure in an Industrial City, 1870–1920.* New York: Cambridge University Press, 1983.

Ross, Ronald J. *The Failure of Bismarck's Kulturkampf: Catholicism and State Power in Imperial Germany, 1871–1887.* Washington D.C.: Catholic University of America Press, 1998.

Ryan, Mary. *Cradle of the Middle Class: The Family in Oneida County, New York: 1790–1865.* New York: Cambridge University Press, 1981.

Rydell, Robert W. *All the World's a Fair: Visions of Empire at the American International Expositions, 1876–1916.* Chicago: University of Chicago Press, 1984.

Sachße, Christof. "Social Mothers: The Bourgeois Women's Movement and German Welfare-State Formation." In *Mothers of a New World: Maternalist Politics and the Origins of Welfare States,* edited by Seth Koven and Sonya Michel, 136–58. New York: Routledge, 1992.

Schimberg, Albert Paul. *Humble Harvest: The Society of St. Vincent de Paul in the Milwaukee Diocese, 1849–1949.* Milwaukee: Bruce Publishing Company, 1951.

Schlereth, Thomas J. "Columbia, Columbus, and Columbianism." *Journal of American History* 79, no. 3 (December 1992): 937–68.

Schrecker, Ellen. *Many Are the Crimes: McCarthyism in America.* Boston: Little, Brown, 1998.

Schrembs, Rt. Rev. Joseph. "The Catholic German Immigrant's Contribution." *Catholic Builders of the Nation,* vol. 2, edited by C. E. McGuire, 63–83. Boston: Continental Press, 1923.

Schultz, April. " 'The Pride of the Race Had Been Touched': The 1925 Norse-American Immigration Centennial and Ethnic Identity." *Journal of American History* 77, no. 4 (March 1991): 1265–95.

Seager, Richard Hughes, ed. *The Dawn of Religious Pluralism: Voices from the World's Parliament of Religions, 1893.* La Salle, Ill.: Open Court Press, 1993.

Shannon, James. *Catholic Colonization on the Western Frontier.* New Haven: Yale University Press, 1957; reprint, New York: Arno Press, 1976.

Shenton, James P. "Ethnicity and Immigration." In *The New American History,* edited by Eric Foner, 251–79. Philadelphia: Temple University Press, 1990.

Slawson, Douglas. " 'The Boston Tragedy and Comedy': The Near-Repudiation of Cardinal O'Connell." *Catholic Historical Review* 77, no. 4 (1991): 616–43.

———. *The Foundation and First Decade of the National Catholic Welfare Council.* Washington, D.C.: Catholic University Press, 1982.

Smith, Helmut S. *German Nationalism and Religious Conflict: Culture, Ideology, Politics, 1870–1914.* Princeton: Princeton University Press, 1995.

Soyer, Daniel. *Jewish Immigrant Associations and American Identity in New York, 1880–1939.* Cambridge: Harvard University Press, 1997.

Spael, Wilhelm. *Das katholische Deutschland im 20. Jahrhundert: Seine Pionier-und Krisenzeiten, 1890–1945*. Würzburg: Echter-Verlag, 1964.

Spalding, David, C.F.X. "The Negro Catholic Congresses, 1889–1894." *Catholic Historical Review* 55, no. 3 (October 1969): 337–57.

Stibili, Edward C. "The Italian St. Raphael Society." *U.S. Catholic Historian* 6, no. 4 (1987): 301–14.

Stivers, Richard. *A Hair of the Dog: Irish Drinking and American Stereotype*. University Park: Pennsylvania State University Press, 1976.

Tentler, Leslie Woodcock. "On the Margins: The State of American Catholic History." *American Quarterly* 45, no. 1 (March 1993): 104–27.

———. *Seasons of Grace: A History of the Catholic Archdiocese of Detroit*. Detroit: Wayne State University Press, 1990.

Thompson, Margaret Susan. "Sisterhood and Power: Class, Culture, and Ethnicity in the American Convent." *Colby Library Quarterly* 25, no. 3 (1989): 149–75.

Tomasi, Silvano. *Piety and Power: The Role of Italian Parishes in the New York Metropolitan Area, 1880–1930*. New York: Center for Migration Studies, 1975.

Touhill, Blanche M. *William Smith O'Brien and His Revolutionary Companions in Penal Exile*. Columbia: University of Missouri Press, 1981.

Towey, Martin, and Margaret Sullivan. "The Knights of Father Mathew: Parallel Ethnic Reform." *Missouri Historical Review* 75, no. 2 (1981): 168–83.

Trattner, William. *From Poor Law to Welfare State: A History of Social Welfare in America*. New York: Free Press, 1974.

Traverso, Susan. "The Politics of Welfare: Boston, 1910–1940." Ph.D. diss., University of Wisconsin–Madison, 1995.

Trolanger, Judith. *Professionalism and Social Change: From the Settlement House Movement to Neighborhood Centers, 1886 to the Present*. New York: Columbia University Press, 1987.

Vecoli, Rudolph. "Contadini in Chicago: A Critique of the Uprooted." *Journal of American History* 51, no. 3 (1964): 404–17.

———. "Prelates and Peasants: Italian Immigrants and the Catholic Church." *Journal of Social History* 2, no. 3 (Spring 1969): 228–33.

Walch, Timothy. "New Tools for American Historical Research: A Review Essay." *U.S. Catholic Historian* 3, no. 3 (1983): 191–201.

Walsh, Francis R. "Who Speaks for Boston's Irish? The Boston *Pilot* in the Nineteenth Century." *Journal of Ethnic Studies* 10, no. 3 (1982): 21–36.

Walsh, Sister Marie de Lourdes. *The Sisters of Charity of New York, 1809–1959*. New York: Fordham University Press, 1960.

Walton, Susan. *To Preserve the Faith: Catholic Charities in Boston, 1870–1930*. New York: Garland Publishing, 1993.

Wangler, Thomas. "Americanist Beliefs and Papal Orthodoxy: 1884–1889." *U.S. Catholic Historian* 11, no. 3 (Summer 1993): 37–51.

Weir, Robert E. *Beyond Labor's Veil: The Culture of the Knights of Labor*. University Park: Pennsylvania State Press, 1996.

Wiebe, Richard. *The Search for Order, 1877–1920*. New York: Hill and Wang, 1967.

Wilson, Grace. *The Religious and Educational Philosophy of the Young Women's Christian Association*. New York: Columbia University Teachers College, 1933.

Wolkovich-Valkavičius, William. "Lithuanian Immigrants and Their Irish Bishops in the Catholic Church of Connecticut." In *Other Catholics*, edited by Keith P. Dyrud, Michael Novak, and Rudolph J. Vecoli, pt. 4, 1–59. New York: Arno Press, 1978.

——, ed. *Lithuanian Religious Life in America*. Norwood, Mass.: Lithuanian Religious Life in America Publishers, 1991.

Woodward, C. Vann. *The Strange Career of Jim Crow*. 2d rev. ed. New York: Oxford University Press, 1966.

Worland, Carr Elizabeth. "American Catholic Women and the Church to 1920." Ph.D. diss., Saint Louis University, 1982.

Wyman, Mark. *Round-Trip to America: The Immigrants Return to Europe, 1880– 1930*. Ithaca, N.Y.: Cornell University Press, 1993.

Index